David Wilson

TO RIDE A RED ENGINE

GW00455039

AUSTIN MACAULEY PUBLISHERS™

LONDON • CAMBRIDGE • NEW YORK • SHARJAH

A CIP catalogue record for this title is available from the British Library.

ISBN 9781398431003 (Paperback)
ISBN 9781398431010 (ePub e-book)

www.austinmacauley.com

First Published 2022
Austin Macauley Publishers Ltd®
1 Canada Square
Canary Wharf
London
E14 5AA

Preface

One of the reasons I decided to write this book is that nowhere, to my knowledge, is there to be found a book that deals with the life of an operationally long serving fireman. Not even in the comprehensive library at the Fire Services College, Morton in Marsh, could I find an autobiography by a fireman, or even fire officer of this type. Even if this book were never to be published, the story of a hairy arsed fireman's life and career, during the period 1961 to 1971, (1971 to 1987 is written and awaits publication) would at least be down on paper, for either my family, or some future historian to read.

I felt that I was fully qualified to write such a book. I was in the fire brigade for nearly 27 years, and in all that time was an operational fireman at an operational fire station and riding the red fire engines. I like to think that I was a fireman's fireman, I was always looking for busier fire stations to work from, and bigger fires to go to. Consequently over the years, I have gathered a lot of tales to tell.

My schooldays were not very productive; I left school at 15 years of age with no certificates or qualifications. To my everlasting thanks, they taught me at school to touch-type. For many years, I did not use this skill, until I then joined the brigade and needed it for paperwork in various station offices. Then, rather like riding a bicycle, the skill came back, and of course without it, I would not have written this book.

My writing style is my own and cannot be altered. It is no doubt affected by many years of writing official reports. On the other hand, I find my love of humour is irrepressible in my writing. As in life, I seem to see humour in the bleakest of situations.

I began writing about three years after I left the brigade, which was good, because I now found that I did not need to worry about what my fire service peers would think. Some of the stories I tell, if I had told them whilst still in the brigade, I would then have found it necessary to have toned them down, for fear of being

3

accused of blowing my own trumpet, i.e., boasting of my own exploits. Now I can tell them as I really saw them, without this fear.

Swearing! In case my mother-in-law, (or for that matter, anyone else's mother-in-law) should read this book, I feel I must explain my use of swear words in the stories. Most firemen do swear, quite proficiently, not in front of the general public or ladies. Mainly in the privacy of the fire station, and of course on the fireground when under stress. When in a fire or other situation, when the danger is such that his only course of action is retreat. He could hardly be expected to say, "excuse me old chap but I think I will depart." He would of course say, "Fuck this for a game of soldiers, I'm off," and if that is what he would say, then that is what I write.

I once had to interview a lady for the position of cook at the fire station. She was a delightful lady by the name of Pearl, and a lady of mature years. She seemed suitable in every way for the job, but I was worried that the habitual swearing of the firemen in the mess might worry her, so I asked would she be able to cope with this. "Don't worry, Mr Wilson," she replied, "that will not bother me at all." She was quite right – it did not bother her at all, Pearl could and did swear as well as any fireman. I do not normally like to hear ladies swear, but Pearl was gifted. None of the swear words that came from Pearl's mouth caused offence, unless of course she intended them to do so, then they really hurt. Pearl could compliment someone with a sentence containing three 'F' words, two 'bloodies' and one 'C' word. But in such a manner that the recipient of the compliment would still feel ten feet tall. Pearl was the much-loved cook at Hammersmith fire station for around three years, when she died sadly of cancer. Pearl wasn't just a Pearl, she was a diamond, not too well polished, but nevertheless a diamond.

Published in the London Fire Brigade Magazine at one time, was a debate between two senior fire officers of the brigade. One of whom was a church going gentleman and hated swearing, the other a quite genteel but basic fire officer. The second quoted in defence of swearing, the words of a lady victim of the Moorgate tube train disaster, who said that when she was trapped, injured, in the debris of the crushed tube train, in the inky black of the underground tunnel, the sweetest words she ever heard in her whole life was the swearing and cursing of the firemen as they struggled to reach and free her.

Blasphemy is to be found in the mind of the hearer, not in the words of the sayer.

Good firemen are born that way not made, is an old brigade saying. There is a large amount of truth in it. Some recruit firemen within a year of being posted to a station, will be excellent firemen, others will take ten years just to reach a mediocre standard. I do not know what it is in a man's character that makes a good operational fireman, for they come in all shapes, sizes and colours. I have noticed that firemen who would often be described as incorrigible rogues, never out of mischief or trouble, would often be very good firemen. Other firemen when discussing such a man's latest escapade would invariably gloss over the offense with the remark, "Oh yes he is a rogue, but nevertheless he is a damned good fireman."

The busier stations within brigades will invariably have at least half of the firemen who have been at that station ten years or more. The two main reasons for leaving such a station are promotion. When a man will be promoted to a higher rank and posted away, or what I call a ten-to-twelve-year depression. After serving is period of time at a busy station, with all its pressures, the man will start to think, 'why should I be up all night every night, when three quarters of a brigade are lying in their beds?'. The same man will no doubt be under pressure from his wife. "Why do you have to stay at that fire station, coming home shattered after every duty? Why can't you find a nice, quiet fire station, like Bertha's husband, he's always doing little jobs around a house?"

After a busy night of rubbish fires, releasing people from lifts, or washing down roads following traffic accidents, even the stalwarts on the station will be saying, "I'll give it another five years, then I'm definitely transferring to a quieter station." But then, just one good four pump fire with people rescued, and all thoughts of transferring leave their minds.

There will occasionally be firemen who have served their entire career at very busy stations, having been posted to the as recruits. My own opinion, anyone who spends more than twenty years at this type of station should get special recognition, for he is truly extraordinary. a will by en invariably be in his mid-forties, but his firefighting skills coupled with experience will be at a peak.

5

The Author newly promoted to Station Officer at Chiswick 1971

In my later years, I once carried a breathing apparatus set up nineteen floors of a high-rise building, along with younger firemen. When eventually arrived at a nineteen floor, was e only one not gasping for breath. I had realised at an outset that when we arrived at a nineteenth floor, we might possibly be involved in hard physical firefighting work. I had paced myself to arrive in a condition to do this, unlike the younger firemen who had hurried on ahead. Although they had arrived at the scene thirty seconds or so before me, they were still panting and out of breath when I arrived.

The mysterious ingredient that makes a good fireman is always present even off duty. I could never go past a bad traffic accident, or person collapsed in the street, without having to stop. No matter how urgent a business I was on, I was compelled to stop. If the incident was in competent or capable hands, I could cheerfully go on my way. But I had to stop and check.

Some years after I had retired from the brigade, I was with my family in a local public house one Sunday lunchtime. I was quite smartly dressed and sitting with my family with my back to the bar. Out of the corner of one eye, I saw a lady remove something from off the wall. I did not see what the object was, but I subconsciously knew that it was a fire extinguisher. I turned to look over my shoulder, and saw the lady was the barmaid, and that smoke was drifting into the bar area. I stood up, went over to the barmaid, told her that I was a retired fireman and could I help. It was a totally reflex action, I gave it no thought, I had no control over it, I just did it. If I had given it some thought, I might have considered I was wearing good clothes, I was with my family and we were in the middle of a long country walk. Perhaps then, I might have decided it would not be convenient to leave them and go firefighting.

The fire was on an upper floor of the pub, and was a bedding fire, very smoky and very dirty. I discharged two large extinguishers on it. It made my clothes dirty and reeked of smoke. I burnt a hole in my good trousers. My nose was running with soot black mucus. I coughed up black phlegm. I possibly prevented a serious fire developing. But I had done everything on automatic pilot, after a break of five years from firefighting. I still remembered to remove the safety catches from the extinguishers (done in the dark and by touch), and check that they worked before entering the room.

All the skills gained over twenty-seven years had not been lost but were of no practical use to me in my present life. Unless I should decide to write a book and tell of them.

Chapter 1

A21 Paddington

I am going to start my story, not where all good stories should start, at the beginning, but instead in the middle. Yet for me, it was a new beginning, at a point in my career, indeed in my own life, where things began to change. It is the story of a fire that completed my life's pupation from caterpillar to butterfly, from boyhood to adult mature male. It was not the most dangerous, or even frightening fire in my career, just the one that I felt altered it. It was not just this single fire that transformed me, for I had quite recently been involved in one of the largest rescues at a single fire in the United Kingdom, which to say the least I found quite exciting, the story of which I tell later.

Somewhere in this period of service at A21 Paddington fire station in the late 1960s, I decided that as a fireman, and indeed as a man, I was better than some and at least as good as most. I had nine years' service under my belt and done a lot of dodgy and dangerous things along the way and had not been found wanting.

This fire that I tell of, and perhaps one or two other incidents combined, resulted in my receiving (if there were such a thing) a battlefield/fire ground promotion from the rank of fireman to that of station officer, in the space of only thirteen months. I hasten to add there is not, nor ever has been to my knowledge, such a formal procedure for such promotions, nevertheless it happened. It was a typical example of being in the right place at the right time and doing the right thing.

A21 Paddington was a divisional headquarters station. I happened to be on duty and riding the right fire engine at the right time, the municipal dustmen were on strike creating stress conditions in the Brigade. Lastly and most importantly, somebody up above liked me and allowed me an inordinate amount of luck.

Here I want to insert a little anecdote which may help explain some of the story later. It allegedly occurred at Southwark Training School, where a very bucolic and venerable sub officer instructor had detailed a recruit training squad crew to carry out a virtually physically impossible task, whilst he and the remainder of the squad looked on. This would most likely have been bridging an extended 50ft escape ladder, which meant in effect bringing the top of the extended ladder down towards the ground. This drill needed all available manpower at the base of the ladder to counterbalance the heavy weight. The crew leader, obviously a very astute man, probably with some previous military experience, called upon the assistance of the remainder of the watching squad. The sub officer, in the way that training instructors do, countered this, shouting loudly, "You can't do that, you are on the fire ground, you are the only firemen there." Then with a sweep of his arm indicating the rest of the squad said, "These are not firemen, they are all members of the public." Then with a big smirk on his face, he stood and watched.

The crew leader was perplexed for a brief moment, but was obviously of good practical fireman potential, for he in turn uttered the following commands. "Members of the public TEN-SHUN, members of the public FALL-IN and get your bloody weight on the back of this ladder." Since that day, in fire service parlance, members of the public refers to odds and sods, firemen in particular, who are standing around doing nothing but gawking.

*

A21 Paddington was at that time a brand new multi appliance bay station, the station's fire appliances were a pump escape, pump, turntable ladders, emergency tender, breathing apparatus control vehicle, plus divisional staff cars and general-purpose vehicles, giving watch strengths of around forty personnel. The fire occurred after I had been stationed at Paddington for around six months and was by then very much one of the lads on the watch. It occurred on a night duty in I think the month of February.

On this particular night duty, I was an acting leading fireman, riding in charge of the pump escape. Another fireman, Pete Mynors, who had four years' service, was driving the appliance. Seated in the back were two relatively junior firemen, one with four month's service, Ken Palen, and one with just two weeks operational service, Chris Reynolds.

The pump with the station officer in charge of it had been out of the station for several hours dealing with a long list of rubbish fires. We were currently in the middle of a dustman's strike, which created a vastly increased workload.

At around 11.30 pm, a fire call was received to Kilburn High Road, A21 Paddington's pump escape to attend. Kilburn High Road was on neighbouring Belsize fire station's ground, just over the station boundary between Paddington and Belsize. It was also the border between two mobilising controls, one at Wembley, the other at Lambeth. The fire call had gone into Lambeth fire control, and so they would mobilise the nearest pump escape (A21 Paddington) and then pass the call over to Wembley fire control to mobilise the rest of the initial attendance. This would be two appliances from Belsize fire station and would normally mean that the pump escape from Paddington would arrive at the incident well in front of the Belsize appliances.

The pump escape turned left out of Paddington fire station into the Harrow Road, and then headed for Edgware Road. It turned left again into the Edgware Road; from there it was a simple journey. Edgware Road was a main, wide through traffic route, and after a short distance, it was still the same road, but changed its name to Maida Vale. Maida Vale continued straight for a mile or so, and again changed its name to Kilburn High Road. So having turned left into Edgware Road the run was a straight one, down a big broad highway for about two miles.

Surprisingly, there was very little traffic about for this time of night. By sheer chance, for they were not speed or time controlled, we were catching the numerous traffic lights at green. The driver was getting quite exhilarated, because the fire engine was thundering along at its top speed of around sixty-five miles per hour, which was something you didn't get to experience very often in central London. The appliance had its blue beacons flashing, two-tone horns blasting, and the driver adding to the noise with the sonorous deep road horn whenever we came up to overtake occasional traffic. Occasionally, we would catch a traffic light at red or amber, then with the deep sounding road horn blasting continuously, sounding very much like a mega tonnage tanker on the wide ocean, we would sail gracefully through them.

We didn't know it at the time, but I think the gods were with us, we must have cut two minutes off our usual journey time to Kilburn High Road that night. Those two minutes made a great deal of difference to the lives of seven people, eleven if you count the crew of four firemen involved.

From about a quarter of a mile away from the address, we could see smoke billowing across the road. We also saw a blue flashing light, so that we assumed that Belsize had beaten us there, despite our speedy arrival. Then as we drew closer, we saw that a large crowd of people had gathered outside the building and were waving to us as we approached. Then in the last 100 yards of our approach, I saw that the blue flashing light was coming from a police vehicle. It then dawned upon me, whatever it was, and it was looking decidedly dodgy, Temporary Acting Leading Fireman Wilson was in charge of it. I had never had the opportunity to make pumps four in my own name before; it looked like I was going to get the opportunity tonight.

As we drew up to the building, I saw that it was four-storeys high, with a shop on the ground floor, and dwellings or flats above. There was a dull, deep red glow behind the plate glass window of the shop. Angry flames were issuing from a broken glass panel above the shop door. From every window on the upper floors, thick grey smoke was issuing. From two of these windows, people were waving and shouting for help.

A searchlight from the police vehicle was playing upon the upper floors of the building, creating a kaleidoscope effect with the swirling smoke. One moment the people calling for help could be seen brightly lit at the windows, the next moment they would disappear into the thick clouds of smoke.

As the appliance came to a juddering halt in front of the building, I turned to the driver intending to tell him to send a priority assistance message, "Make pumps four, persons reported." Radio messages from fires were normally sent by the appliance driver. Before I could stop him to get him to send the message, he was out of his seat and gone. It crossed my angry mind at the time that this man (Pete Mynors) was most definitely not temporary acting leading fireman material, I best send the radio message myself. Now the London Fire Brigade was a most peculiar institution. It would judge its officers, especially junior officers, not by their bravery or skill at extinguishing fires – although these matters did count somewhat – but by the attention to detail and sequence of the messages that they sent from the fire ground. At this stage in my career, I sometimes considered that a great number of geriatric senior officers were employed to sit around their VHF listening sets, then mark points out of ten as to the clarity, grammar and correct procedure of messages transmitted from the fire ground. If so, I would not have received many points for my messages that night.

The driver having disappeared, it was left to me to send the message, which on the face of it was not too difficult to do. "M2FN" (controls call sign) "from Alpha two one" (A21 Paddington's pump escapes call sign) "PRIORITY from Acting Leading Fireman Wilson at Kilburn High Road, make pumps four, persons reported." Which I duly sent, then awaited acknowledgement of receipt from fire control, I heard nothing! I repeated the same message over again, and in the middle of sending, it felt the appliance lurch, indicating to me that the rest of the crew had removed the big fifty-foot ladder from the back of the appliance. Yet again, I received no reply from Lambeth Fire Control, so I abandoned the attempt to send the message in order to attend to what I considered more immediate matters to hand. It subsequently turned out that the volume switch on the appliance radio had been turned down. That both transmissions were received loud and clear, and that I merely could not hear Control's acknowledgement of them.

I jumped down from the appliance and dashed to the rear, where I found the fifty-foot escape ladder had been slipped from the back of the appliance. It had then been turned in its axis in the road, and its large wheels bounced up the high kerbside onto the pavement, having been assisted in this heavy task, apparently by co-opted members of the public. There was much for my eyes and brain to take in quickly.

The ladder was already being extended upwards. Surprisingly, it was being extended by a member of the public who had been seconded into the crew, and was vigorously working the winch handle, extending the ladder up towards the second floor of the building. A crew of four was normally considered the minimum to work a fifty-foot escape ladder. Thus, the crew had shown great initiative in co-opting members of the public to assist them, both in bouncing the ladder up onto the pavement, and then delegating some of the harder jobs. Winching up the escape ladder itself was very hard work, and the firemen were saving their energies for what was to come.

The top or head of the escape ladder approached the second-floor window. There we could now see between the billows of smoke that a man, a lady and two children were trapped. At this stage, the member of the public on the winch handle was relieved of his duties and stood down with a brief "Well done, mate. Thanks," he having done most of the hard work. Before climbing up the ladder, it would need to be seated on its ladder pawls, which required a fireman with knowledge of the ladder. Then the ladder was pushed hard into the building and wedged into place with wheel chocks under the large wooden wheels.

At this stage, I leapt up onto the foot of the ladder, pausing to turn and instruct the most junior fireman, Chris Reynolds, to lay out a large hose and jet, and then direct it through the opening above the top of the shop door from where the angry flames where still issuing. This was to attempt to cool down somewhat the fire that was raging there. If the main plate glass window of the shop should shatter and release the pent-up fire and gases whilst we were up the ladder and above it…this was a thought I preferred not to dwell upon at the time. After the event, the thought did cross my mind of a kebab, ie roast meat skewered on a wooden stick, but a Fire Brigade ladder would serve equally as well as a wooden stick!

I climbed up the ladder and into the smoke, where I found the man, the woman and the two children all suffering badly from the effects of the heat and smoke. At the very top, I took a leg lock on the ladder – that is I put one leg through the rounds of the ladder and hooked it onto the rounds. This would secure me onto the ladder and leave both hands free to work with.

Below me on the ladder were two other firemen, Pete Mynors the driver, and below him Ken Palen, the fireman with four month's service. The first of the children was passed out of the window to me by the mother. This is an extremely traumatic moment in two people's lives. The mother has the baby grasped firmly by two hands around its waist; she now has to pass her precious bundle to a complete stranger, perched precariously on the top of a rickety stick, fifty foot up in the air. I certainly realised the implications even if the lady did not. Although I had both hands free to work with, because the window opening was to the extreme right of the ladder, I could only grasp the child with one hand. I grasped it tightly around the wrist with one hand only – never was a babe held more tightly, then quietly saying to the mother, "Right let go now," which after a reluctant pause, she bravely did. If that child had no other injuries whatsoever from its night's adventures, so tight was my grip it would still have had a very bruised wrist. I passed the child very carefully back down to Pete Mynors, who again passed it on down to Ken Palen, who carried it in one arm down to the ground.

The second child was again passed out of the window to me, and thence in a like ultra-careful manner down to Pete Mynors, who himself carried this one down to safety. The lady was then helped out of the window and onto the ladder. This was done only with great difficulty by myself and her husband, who was behaving remarkably well and bravely under the circumstances. Then very slowly, the lady was assisted by myself and partly carried down the ladder. The husband thankfully made his own way down the ladder unassisted behind us. This seemed to take an interminable amount of time, and all the while, I was trying to hurry things up, for the fire was still raging below and we still had yet another rescue to affect.

Back down on the ground, again the crew were keyed up, waiting for the lady's husband to finally get clear of the ladder. Even before the man got fully clear of the base of the ladder, it was pulled slightly away from the building with him still on it, then quickly extended up to the third floor. This time, I firmly delegated the hard donkeywork of winding the handle to the second junior of the crew, Ken Palen.

As the head of the ladder inched its way upwards from the second to the third floor, its direction of travel was being guided by Pete Mynors and myself. Our objective, the third-floor window, could only occasionally be seen through the swirling, billowing smoke. The top of the ladder was waving from side to side as Ken Palen vigorously worked the winch handle. I then made a decision which in retrospect proved to be dangerously wrong.

As the ladder inched through the smoke and neared the window, Pete queried with the simple words, "Under the window?"

In reply, I answered tersely, "No, to the left." These four simple words could have been my undoing.

What I believe Pete had noticed through the gaps in the smoke swirls and I had not, was that the window was an outward opening window and opened to the right, or our left as we faced the building. I had just given the order to rest the head of the ladder against the open metal framed window, which was to cause one or two problems very shortly. This speaks mightily for the training of London firemen, at least. I had given a wrong order, albeit in the heat of battle, it was obeyed instantly and without query.

The ladder was once again rammed back into the building and secured with chocks. In the background, I was aware that young Chris Reynolds was almost ready to get the covering jet to work, and thankfully, that another fire engine had arrived on the scene. Hopefully, our ascent aloft this time would be covered by a jet of water, as per the manuals of firemanship, if not the rules of self-preservation.

This time, I was beaten to first position on the ladder by the driver, Pete Mynors, who was on the ladder and going aloft before I could blink. Good firemen hate to be beaten into first place on the ladder, so I was somewhat miffed, but hard on his heels up behind him.

Again, the head of the ladder was wreathed in smoke and fumes, and again the people trapped – a man, a woman, and a small baby – were in distress from the smoke and gases.

The small baby was passed out to Pete Mynors, who in turn passed it to me. I turned and there was nobody behind me on the ladder, so I carried the baby down and handed it to somebody, I know not who, down there. Then I sped back up the ladder again. This time, Pete Mynors was having great difficulty in getting the lady from the window opening and onto the head of the ladder, caused in the main by my decision to site the ladder to the left of the window instead of underneath it. I could not assist him, other than to help steady him on the ladder, for there wasn't room for two people at the head of the ladder. Finally, after what seemed an age, she was out and onto the ladder and with a lot of assistance from Pete Mynors was making her way slowly down.

I now managed to do something quite difficult, and that was for two people to pass on the upper extensions of an escape ladder. For the man still wreathed in smoke was also finding it difficult to negotiate the gap between the head of the escape and the window opening. With our so far unblemished performance, I did not want him to fall, so I climbed to the top of the ladder and helped the man across the gap, and once he was on the ladder, he required no further assistance and made his own way down to the ground. We were for a time delayed on the ladder, for the lady was still being assisted by fireman Mynors and was taking a long time to make her way down.

Fortunately, time was now on our side, for the Belsize crew had made an entry through the front door of the shop with a jet, and the danger of the fire breaking out and coming up to meet us had now in the main passed.

At last, back on the pavement again, with the difficult part of the proceedings over, I could relax slightly and take stock of the situation. The Belsize crews were getting stuck into the fire and would be no doubt quite happy to deal with what in effect was their fire – the address being just on their own station's ground, without assistance from the rival 'A' division men, who had already pinched most of the glory anyway. Also, I should seek out the station officer in charge of Belsize station and inform him of events before his arrival.

This was all passing through my mind when Pete Mynors dashed up and said, "Come on Dave, get a breathing apparatus set on."

There are times when I use strong language; this was one of them. "Piss off Pete! Don't you think we've done enough? Let some other bugger fight the fire."

He said urgently, "No, not to fight the fire, there's an old lady who lives in a back room above the shop, and she's still in the building." He had got the information I think, from one of the people we had just rescued.

We dashed over to the appliance to get the breathing sets, there were still only three fire engines in attendance, and all the firemen were at full stretch. On Paddington's crew, only Pete Mynors and myself were qualified to wear breathing apparatus, so it would have to be just a two-man effort, him and myself.

We rigged in the breathing sets, put the mouthpieces in and started up the flow of oxygen. Then we made our way back to the ground floor shop. There was a door to the right of the shop, which was open and smoke was billowing out. This was the entrance to the accommodation above the shops. Most of the fire had died down in the shop itself, where the Belsize crew were working with a jet. Unless the fire had spread to the floors above, it should be a fairly routine search and rescue, with no nagging doubts as to whether the fire would be chasing us up the stairs.

We made our entrance through the door at the side of the shop. Immediately, we entered the building; the smoke obscured all vision. We made our way up the stairs by keeping up against the wall on our right-hand side, checking that each stair tread was in place as we went. It had been a pretty fierce fire, and they could have quite easily burnt away. When we reached the first-floor level, the heat became intense, seeming to tighten the skin on our cheekbones and exposed ears. Once again, it was a great relief to know the crew down below were extinguishing the fire.

At the top of the staircase, we turned blindly left, up another short flight of stairs. We were now directly above the fire in the shop below. Moving forward in the smoke, still keeping in touch with the right-hand wall for direction, we came across a door set in the right-hand wall. Our general sense of location in the building told us that this should be the door to the first floor back room. The room situated directly over the shop, and where the old lady was thought to be.

With the proto breathing apparatus, the mouthpiece must never be removed when in a fire, but this was not always practical. So I slipped my mouthpiece aside and said to Pete Mynors, "Pete, we will do this room first, I will search from the right-hand wall, you search from the left-hand wall." Which basically meant with two men searching independently, the room would be searched in half the time.

Very carefully, we opened the door to the room, for we could not be sure that the fire had not spread upwards, and still be burning in this room. This being the case, if the door was opened without due caution, the fire could explode outwards into our faces.

As the door was opened, other than a slight increase in the heat level as the pent-up fire gases escaped, nothing happened. What we had been carefully watching for was through the black-grey murk of the smoke, a dull-orange glow. That when the door was opened, and the oxygen rushed in, would turn into the bright red, then white tinged flames of a fire that had been starved of oxygen. Then being fed with the oxygen it needed by the opening of the door, would roar out to meet us.

I moved into the room and went around the back of the door to try to pick up the right-hand wall to begin my search. My way forward was obstructed by unseen furniture. I moved another two or three steps forward, still with my right hand outstretched, seeking the wall to gain my bearings. I bumped into yet another obstruction. Reaching down with my left hand, I found that it was a bed. I leaned forward over the bed, searching with both hands to see if it was occupied. My hands touched bare flesh, and my body gave a slight shudder. This is a most peculiar reaction, and I think it affects most firemen. Deprived of all other senses but the sense of touch, you are using your bare hands to seek the unknown. The unknown in some fires can be quite horrendous.

I clapped my hands together, the universal fireman's signal that he has found that which he is seeking – usually a body or unconscious person – slipped my mouthpiece aside to tell Pete Mynors that I had found the old lady, and that she was on the bed. He then crashed directly across the room towards the sound of my voice, and handclaps, and joined me at the side of the unseen bed.

I had already managed to pull the old lady around, so that her head and shoulders were pointing towards the side of the bed. She was wearing only a nightdress of a light synthetic material, and her skin was moist and clammy from the heat of the fire so that it was very difficult to find any way to get a firm grip on her slippery body.

When Pete joined me, I managed to get a grip with the lady in a face-up position, and my arms underneath hers, and my fingers intertwined across her chest. Then with Pete carrying her by the legs, we made our first attempt to carry her out of the building.

Because she was unconscious and limp, and with the damp slippery skin, we could make no more than two or three steps before she would slip through my arms again.

A normal breathing apparatus rescue crew would consist of three firemen, and how we missed that third fireman. With one fireman each taking an arm, and the third fireman taking both legs, the lady would have gone straight out of the building, with little effort. We tried to get the lady up and onto my shoulders, but she weighed around eleven stone. Every time Pete tried to lift her up so that I could grasp her in the standard fireman's carry over my shoulders, she would slip down through his hands again. I made a mental note – it was never like this with the canvas dummies we used to train with in Southwark Training School smoke chamber. So rather unceremoniously, we half carried and half dragged her from the room and down the stairs.

We were halfway down the main flight of stairs, when a fireman not wearing breathing apparatus, on hearing our struggles, came up the stairs to assist us. Together, we carried her out into the open air and deposited her roughly but gently onto the flagstones of the pavement for the waiting ambulance crews to deal with. With all this activity in such a short space of time, I was feeling quite shattered. Both Pete and myself made our way wearily back to the appliance to remove our now leaden breathing sets. I then spent the next ten minutes carefully rolling and then quietly smoking a cigarette in the back cab of the appliance.

Smoking is allegedly a filthy, vile habit, but at times like this, when you were shattered physically, your lungs were already chock full of dark filthy carcinogenic hydrocyanic fumes, by comparison a dose of nicotine seemed quite innocuous. When you were pleased merely to be alive, in one piece and relatively unscorched, rolling and then quietly smoking a ciggy was positive ecstasy!

After this short break, my temporary acting leading fireman's hormones surged back through my blood. Fortunately/unfortunately, only time would tell – I had been in sole command of this fire (on paper at least) for a considerable period of time. On the principal that in municipal or corporate heaps, falling bricks always fall to the lowest level before actually causing damage, you don't come much lower than a temporary acting unpaid leading fireman. If anything at all had gone wrong with this fire, it would be my head that they would be after.

18

My newly awarded, albeit temporarily, but proudly worn, chromium plated leading fireman's shoulder bars could be snatched from me forever.

I jumped down from the back cab of the fire engine. I was now suddenly aware of all the paraphernalia of a four-pump fire cluttering up the street. Fire engines, turntable ladders, control units, senior officer's cars, ambulances, police cars, where had they all come from? I hadn't seen them all arrive. I made my way to the entrance door to the fire blackened shop, and walked in. The fire damage to the shop was extensive, it was a burnt-out shell in fact.

I now felt happier for two reasons; firstly, I was looking at what by anyone's standards was a decent four-pump fire, thus upholding my honour in initially declaring it so! Secondly, I was more than ever bloody damned pleased that a fire of this severity had stayed inside the shop, and not broken out to chase me up my ladder.

My name was being called out loud through the still grey murk of the shop. "Leading Fireman Wilson," the voice was repeating. Ever aware of the subtleties and nuances of the London Fire Brigade's etiquette I noted that the words temporary or acting, instead of being emphasised, had in fact been omitted from in front of the words 'Leading Fireman Wilson', always a favourable sign this.

I answered back, "Over here," then in the grey murk met up with a station officer, to learn that I had been summoned to the divisional officer's presence.

The divisional officer was standing grimly beside the control unit, and alongside him another station officer, (if possible looking even grimmer) whom I believed was the station officer from Belsize fire station, on whose fire ground this little episode had occurred. The divisional officer simply said, "Right, tell me what happened, right from the beginning." So I told him! As the story went on, the divisional officer was becoming visibly more pleased. Belsize's station officer was becoming visibly gloomier, through no fault of his own he had missed all the glory, had seen a decent fire stolen from him by the disreputable 'A' division. Even worse, adding insult to injury, it was A21 Hollywood that had stolen it from him (A21 Paddington's derogatory nickname, bestowed upon it by reason of all the high-profile fires and resulting press attention it was receiving at that time). All he was left with was a mountain of paperwork and clearing up after the fire to do.

I was dismissed from the exalted divisional officer's presence, with quietly spoken words, "It looks a bit like the old lady you pulled out is not going to make it, so you had better go and make some notes for a coroner's report." Then turning to the station officer that had found me in the shop added, "Go and help him." As he uttered these last words, I knew that I was home and dry, safe and sound, bombproof. He had just instructed an apparently very senior station officer to go and assist a very junior, spotty, temporary acting and all the rest of it, leading fireman! Whereas normally this level of life is left to stew in their own juices. In fact, it was not quite like that, the senior station officer himself acknowledged a job well done. He was more than happy to advise and assist me to make notes for compiling what turned out to be the very first of very many coroner's reports I would subsequently write over the years.

Finally, after a long time, we were ready to leave the fire. The big escape ladder had been retrieved and placed back on the top of the appliance. The hose and other gear that we had used had been recovered and re-stowed, I had collected our nominal roll board from the divisional control unit. We finally set off back for the fire station, a very tired but very pleased crew. We had done well and we knew it. Pete Mynors and I would know that this had been an exceptional fire. That we had had a great deal of luck in that nothing had gone wrong with the rescues. Ken Palen, the fireman with four month's service, would certainly not have seen anything like this before in his short career. Chris Reynolds, with his two-week's service, would probably think that this kind of thing happened every Saturday night.

Arriving back at the fire station, we drove in through the rear gates into the darkened drill yard, then out of the dark into the brightly lit appliance room. Here most of the station and divisional headquarters personnel were waiting. Then something happened which I have never seen before, nor since. They clapped us back into the station. It probably happened because a large number of the firemen there were relatively junior, but nevertheless it happened. They clapped us back into the station! I personally found it all a little bit embarrassing, but still it was nice.

The firemen back at the fire station would have followed the course of the fire over the appliance radios. When the message came back detailing all the rescues, it would have been impressive. "One woman, two children, carried down escape from second floor, one man assisted down escape from second floor. One woman, one child, carried down escape from third floor, one man assisted down escape from third floor. One woman found unconscious in back room on first floor, rescued by breathing apparatus wearers." Soon after we drove into the appliance room, one of the first questions I was asked by one of the younger firemen was, "How many did our lads rescue?" (Meaning, the pump-escapes crew.)

And I was very proud to be able to reply, "All of them." In my opinion, it was a very lucky fire and all went well. The first crew to arrive (Paddington's escape) was relatively inexperienced and was on its own at the fire for five or six minutes or more. A single rescue down an escape ladder can take that long itself, although it may only seem to take seconds. We managed to carry out two entirely separate such escape rescues.

I am convinced the gods were with us, especially on the drive to the fire. For if, we had not made such remarkably good time it would have been quite likely that the fire would have shattered the plate glass windows and broken out of the shop before our arrival – with disastrous results for the people trapped above. Even worse, done so whilst we were up the ladders above the fire, affecting the rescues.

In the national newspapers, the next day was a large picture taken at the fire, showing Ivor Rice, Paddington's sub officer at that time, who had attended the fire later. It showed him attempting to revive a dead cat that had been found in the building, with mouth to muzzle resuscitation. The article again said something about firemen being heroes. Well, I personally agreed. Ivor was a hero in my opinion as well. I for one certainly didn't much fancy kissing a dead cat.

A few days after this fire occurred, I was summoned in to see the 'A' divisional commander in his office on the ground floor at Paddington divisional headquarters. He asked me all about the fire, and the rescues, and then told me to submit all the details to him in writing. The outcome of this was that some months later, the whole of Paddington's pump escape crew at the fire that night were awarded chief officer's commendations for brave conduct at that fire. As one cynic was heard to comment upon hearing this, "Seems an inordinately large number of commendations for one fire, must have had some left over unallocated from last year." Then as a cutting last remark adding, "Could only ever happen at A21 Hollywood!"

This all happened a long time ago, and if asked for my comments now would simply like to add, "The members of the public crew in particular, performed magnificently."

Chapter 2

Southwark Training School – October 1961

The following is to be found in the preface of the manuals of firemanship, in the volume on practical firemanship, the fireman's bible.

A fireman, to be successful, must enter buildings, he must get in below, above, on every side, from opposite houses, over back walls, over side walls, through panels of doors, through windows, through loopholes, through skylights, through holes cut by himself in the gates, the walls, the roof, he must know how to reach the attic from the basement by ladders placed on half burned stairs, and basement from the attic by rope made fast on a chimney. His whole success depends on his getting in and remaining there and he must always carry his appliances with him, as without them, he is of no use.

The above was written by Sir Eyre Massey Shaw, one of the London Fire Brigade's most famous Chief Officers over 100 years ago, most of it is as true of the fireman's job today, as the day it was written.

I remember it so well, for in conjunction with part of the following it comprised the dictation test when I first applied to join the London Fire Brigade in 1961. It is only in reflection that I see, although I did not realise it for twenty-one years, my vocation in life was to be a fireman and ride the red engines.

The dictation test included the following: The fireman must be physically fit for work as a fire will almost always in involve great physical exertion. He must be courageous and yet be calm. He must be patient. He must have initiative and possess the will to keep going for long periods under adverse conditions.

*

I was born in 1940 in the London borough of Fulham, then considered very much a working-class district of London. Of my father, I have no memories, he went away to war in 1939. He did the grand tour, North Africa, Sicily, then a leisurely trip up through Northern Italy (successfully dodging 'D' Day on the way). On 17 April 1945, the tour ended abruptly for him. Having been away for six long years, he no doubt forgot the way home. He is now to be found at Plot 15, Row G, Grave 8, Coriano Ridge, British War Graves cemetery, in Northern Italy.

I am not sure, but I think I was a slum kid, underprivileged and all that stuff. Since all my relations and friends lived the same life, I did not at the time realise it, thus it did not unduly bother me. It did bother a certain gentleman though. Adolf Hitler, ahead of his times by years for slum clearance programs, because he demolished five of my mother's houses. I personally can only remember two of them. I was intrigued to note that a V 1 rocket could remove an entire front wall of a four-storey house without unduly damaging the remainder. Also, that it could remove my bed from the front bedroom on the top floor of the house, then deposit it neatly on top of the mound of rubble in the basement, fortunately I was not in it at the time.

The idea to join the Fire Brigade did not come until early 1961, but I was gaining some of the skills required long before that.

I was learning the theories of building construction from the early age of five years, when my playground was the bombed houses and derelict sites that abounded in Fulham in the early post war years.

When floorboards were removed from a bombed-out building to build a bonfire, underneath were the joists, when lathes were required with which to make our bows and arrows. These were to be found in the partition, or stud walls, of lathe and plaster construction. Not internal brick walls, which were invariably load bearing walls.

As I grew older, I learned the monetary values of copper and lead, and where to find them in the bombed houses. The sash window counterweights were of cast iron and could also be sold for cash. In retrieving them, a knowledge of sash window construction was acquired. I gained my head for heights on the roofs of these very same houses. As Sir Eyre Massey Shaw said, I knew my way from the chimney stacks to the basements when I was seven years old.

One of our favourite Saturday morning games was to climb up on the roofs of the bombed terraced houses on the main route to and from the North End Road street market. When the housewives appeared laden with their shopping bags in both hands, we would then leap and dance about on the front parapets of the houses some 50ft up in the air, in an attempt to frighten the ladies by our perilous exploits and make them drop their bags of shopping.

Then the basements of the dark, derelict, bombed out houses, only the boldest of kids went down into them. That's where the dirty, old men that your mother warned you about lived. Full of debris and junk, with only a lighted match to see with. Only the foolhardy would go down those dark basements alone. I was either brave or foolhardy or both, certainly not claustrophobic, because down them I went. Future fire service smoke chambers would hold no fears for me.

I would see our local firemen quite often, as the bigger kids tired of stripping the bombed houses for wood. Then seeking bigger and bigger fires and more excitement would set fire to the actual bombed houses themselves. Thus, I learned a little about the spread of fire. To have a really big fire, it needed to be started on the ground floor of the building, so the fire would spread up to the upper floors.

I joined the scouts at eleven years of age. Amongst the many badges I received was the fireman's badge, which entailed a visit to the local fire station. This alone still did not give me any ideas about a future career as a fireman. In retrospect though, being in the scouts must have shown a certain degree of the required strength of character and courage allegedly required. For to walk through the council flats where I lived, wearing the large Baden Powell hat and short trousers certainly took courage, and you had to be able to fight, or you wouldn't still be wearing your big hat when you came out at the other end of the estate.

After the scouts came the army cadets, where at 13 years of age, I learned how to produce razor sharp creases in the uniform and to press my own shirts, which my mother duly noted and delegated my civilian clothes to my care. I learned to shoot and maintain both the Lee Enfield rifle, and the Bren light machine gun. Pretty heady stuff for a kid of fourteen.

It was not until I attended one of the cadet's annual summer camps that I was able to display another quality the Fire Brigade seemed to require – 'Tenacity' – although in a somewhat perverse form.

On a Saturday afternoon, it had been decreed that the whole of the camp would go for a five-mile cross-country race. I enquired how far that was, as being a city lad distance was gauged not in miles but in money. It will cost you one shilling and sixpence on a number 11 bus to go that far I was informed. I was aghast, horrified! That far, include me out, I am definitely not going. I'm here on my holidays, that would knacker me for the rest of the week.

The regimental sergeant major was an old campaigner; he got to hear of the impending mutiny. He simply decreed that any cadet not taking part in the cross-country run would do guard duty that night instead. He was a clever, devious man, that was about the only thing that could have persuaded me to take part in the run, having to do guard duty on a Saturday night.

The cross-country run started. I was about one of the last of the two hundred and fifty participants to cross the line. With a cigarette dangling from my mouth which the sergeant major duly noted, I was there under protest. I was jogging along and in conversation with the other lads, who seemed intent on taking the mickey out of me. "Thought you wasn't taking part in this run then, old Wilson" and the like.

So to get away from them I moved up the field a bit, and met with the same problem, more mickey takers. Thus, it came about through a combination of mickey takers, and people that were too puffed to talk, that I arrived at the part of the race where the runners were taking it seriously, more by accident than design. Now once again these lads also began to take the mickey, but with a different theme. "Think you're going to beat us then, old Wilson, do you? How many cigarettes do you smoke a day now then, is it ten, fifteen?" So yet again, I pressed forward, trying to meet a nicer kind of person. When I finally met him, he was right at the front of the race. He was a very nice chap and as he wasn't puffing too much, we had a conversation. "Who do you run for?" he enquired.

I thought he had said what did I run for. So I told him about the nasty sergeant major that had threatened to put me on guard duty if I didn't participate. No, he meant what club did I run for, he ran for the something harriers, did this sort of thing every week apparently. So I informed him I did not normally run. That I was now merely engaged in practising escaping from policemen.

Then giving him a practical demonstration of my prowess, I showed him a clean pair of heels.

This chap was obviously a good club runner, for we were both some hundred yards in front of the rest of the field. He stayed about three yards behind me all the way. Then at the last 200 yards of the race, he went past me like a rocket, which rather upset me. He had seemed far too nice a chap to do a sneaky thing like that, giving me no chance to catch him up again. This only served to change my opinion of the man, he was almost certainly an accomplished villain, and if he wasn't then he ought to be. For with a turn of speed like that, no policeman could ever hope to catch him.

There was some consolation in all this though, for the sergeant major was now positively beaming at me. The camp was a mixed camp, with cadets from different units, and the sergeant major and I were from the same company. His good humour stemmed from the fact that no one from our company had apparently ever been in the first ten in the cross-country run before today. I tried to explain to him how it really was all a bit of a mistake, that I had not really intended to run quite so fast. How the other cadets kept taking the mickey out of me, and I was merely trying to get away from them, then had perhaps got a little bit carried away with it all. The sergeant major then said something about the second prize being two pounds ten shillings. I was astonished; I had known nothing of prizes! So I said no more, I swallowed my pride and humbly accepted the unexpected bounty. That bloke from the something harriers, I had got him sussed, all that waffle about competitive spirit and the like. The first prize had been five pounds, then a small fortune to a fifteen-year-old boy. He definitely was a villain!

*

Like most boys of that era, I was resigned to the fact that at the age of eighteen years, I would be dragged off to do two-year's national service. So from the age of fifteen when I left school, till I reached the age of eighteen, I entered three years of limbo. I had already decided that when my call-up papers came, I would sign on for three years as a regular soldier and join the parachute regiment. Some months before I was due to receive my call-up papers, national service was abolished.

Now it was a strange thing, but the army cadet service was supposed to prepare and encourage young boys for future service in the army. Nevertheless, at grass roots level, there was still the same old serviceman's outlook on life – don't volunteer for anything. So I didn't, and I never did get to jump out of an aeroplane.

*

I remember very clearly the day that I decided that I really did want to join the Fire Brigade, it was the day that they told me that I couldn't. I had seen a recruitment advert in a national newspaper for the London Fire Brigade and duly applied. After a wait of some months, I was invited to attend Fire Brigade Headquarters to sit the entrance examination, and interview.

The entrance exam had not proven too difficult. I found myself in a long line with the others who had been successful in the examination, waiting to have our chest measurements and height checked. The home office had laid down minimum physical requirements for firemen. A minimum chest measurement of 36 inches with a two-inch expansion, and a minimum height of five feet seven inches. Now these two measurements had been checked over and over again by my family at home and I just conformed.

Standing in line, I was beginning to worry, for the man at the head of the queue, a magnificent specimen of a man, was having his problems. The initial chest measurement was forty inches, but he just could not get the two inches expansion. I did notice that the officer conducting the tests was quite red in the face, and grimly hanging on to the tape measure, which was sinking into the man's flesh as he inhaled, and he called out to the clerk who was recording the results, "Forty inches, no expansion." This man when he arrived had been wearing a leather jacket, in those days perhaps a little casual for a job interview, he had obviously had his card marked. What must he have thought as he was getting dressed again, and a little runt by comparison, myself, went through at chest measurements thirty-six normal and thirty-eight expanded?

I was to get my comeuppance when it came to measuring the height. Shoes off and in stockinged feet, underneath a measuring stick with a bar that lowered to the head. The officer kept saying higher; stretch higher and then finally said to the clerk, "Five feet six-and-three-quarter inches."

I vehemently denied it. "I am five feet seven inches," I insisted, but it made no difference, I had just failed to join the London Fire Brigade.

Three others and myself who had failed for various reasons had been told by the clerk to stand to one side and wait. After the proceedings were over, he came across to us and said, "Take my advice, lads, give it two or three months and then apply again." I protested to him that I was unlikely to grow a quarter of an inch in two months. He replied that it costs a great deal of money to train a fireman for four months, so they like to make sure that if they accept a man for training, he really wants to be a fireman and will stay the course. Adding that if we applied again, we would almost certainly be accepted. He also went on to say to those that had failed the written part of the examination, that if they went to the public library and looked at part one of the manual of firemanship kept at most public libraries, they would find the dictation test printed there, a quotation by Eyre Massey Shaw, one of London's past famed fire officers (the quotation at the beginning of the chapter).

So it came about that three months later, I again attended Fire Brigade Headquarters. This time, I was only required to have my height checked before qualifying for interview. I was now found to measure five foot seven and a quarter inches, amazing! The interview itself was quite searching, after which I was told to wait in a nearby room, in which four other men were already waiting. I again felt depressed – the other four men to my mind's eye did not look at all like prospective firemen. No doubt they felt the same about me. Tall ones, short ones, thin ones, fat ones; it did not look promising. Then at last, the friendly clerk entered and told us that subject to us passing the medical, we had been accepted for training as firemen.

We were all taken in a Fire Brigade vehicle, the short distance to County Hall, the Headquarters of the London County Council, where we were all examined by the council's doctors. The doctor was quite friendly and told us that although he was not allowed to give us the results of the examination, as far as he was concerned, we had passed.

So I went home and waited. After around a month's delay, I received a letter, posted in London SEl, the London postal district of the Fire Brigade's headquarters. I slowly opened the letter and read the contents. I had been accepted for training as a fireman, and was to report to Southwark Training School, Southwark Bridge Road, on Monday, 23 October 1961.

*

On that Monday morning, I walked through the entrance archway to Southwark Training School. I was not impressed, drab Victorian buildings, parts of which looked derelict. A large 'L' shaped drill yard, in one corner of which stood a seven-storey iron drill tower. Scruffy corrugated iron sheds, in which the training school fire engines were kept.

I was directed to the training school office, were I joined a group of men wearing civilian clothes. Some of the group I recognised from the interviews and medicals two months previously. We stood and watched as the morning parade took place. Twelve squads of immaculately uniformed firemen lined up as on a military parade, and then saw two late comers getting a stern dressing down.

After a lengthy talk by a senior Brigade officer, we then set off for the Fire Brigade stores, then situated at Shepherds Bush in west London, to be issued with our first uniform. Much to my surprise, and unlike military storemen, the Brigade storeman was concerned that our uniforms should actually fit. If there were any doubt, he would actually take our measurements to ensure a good fit. Then the rest of the day was spent marking our new uniforms in the prescribed Brigade manner.

The next day, our training started in earnest. Our squad was a mixed squad, some of the members had previous military training, others none. So our first instruction was in military foot drill, in the Fire Brigade manner. Marching and counter marching, learning to salute navy style, with the palm of the hand held down, and other such evolutions.

After a month at training school, it seemed as if there had been no other life. We had been instructed in, and were training with most of the ladders and equipment at the school, carrying out daily hose and ladder drills. Every day, almost without fail, we would pitch the big fifty-foot wheeled escape ladder up to the third floor of the drill tower, then carry each other down it. Here I found out what a popular body (as opposed to person) I was. Each fireman was supposed to carry down a man of approximately his own weight. I was quite light in weight, but what was more important, I bent neatly in the middle, so that I would drape easily around the shoulders of the man carrying me, then slip easily through the wires supporting the ladder. The training was quite intensive, involving much instruction in the lecture rooms. Also, a searching written examination at the end of each week, of which a set minimum mark was essential.

The Brigade had recently reduced its working week from sixty hours to fifty-six. This required a large influx of new firemen into the Brigade. As a result of this, the training school was bursting at the seams.

At eleven o'clock, tea break, or stand-easy in Brigade parlance, the canteen would have the appearance of a canteen in a forced labour camp in Siberia. One hundred and forty-four trainee firemen, in various combinations of uniform, all dishevelled, sweating, dripping wet and steaming from their recent exertions on the drill ground. All crammed in the small messroom together, to eat their cheese and onion rolls, and drink their cocoa or tea. There the semblance to Siberia would end, for these were all fit, healthy, cheerful, laughing men, happy in their work and their present company.

Two other trainee firemen and myself lived in the borough of Fulham. We would meet each morning at Fulham Broadway, to cycle to the training school, a journey of around 45 minutes.

On one particular morning, there had been a heavy fall of snow, and it lay around nine inches deep on the ground. We set off on our cycles to training school, anticipating a nice warm day spent in the lecture rooms, as a result of the heavy snowfall. After the morning parade and roll call, the order was "All personnel rig in tunics and boots."

I thought they surely cannot make us drill in this deep snow; they didn't, first we cleared away the snow, then we drilled. The whole training school spent the best part of the morning clearing the large drill yard of snow, using jets of water, brooms and shovels, sweeping the whole lot into the sewers, via a large manhole in one corner of the drill yard.

It is of course impossible to have one hundred plus firemen together, with nine inches of snow on the ground, without a snowball being thrown. It is also impossible for a man who is wielding a large jet of water to clear snow, upon being struck by a snowball, not to retaliate with his large jet of water. So on the coldest day of the winter so far, one hundred and forty-four firemen got themselves totally, but happily, soaking wet. So much so, that the very limited clothes drying facilities at the training school were totally swamped. We all suffered damp or wet gear for the rest of the week. In retrospect, I remember this period as being one of the coldest, dampest, most uncomfortable, busiest and yet happiest and proudest of my life.

*

Around week eight at the training school, we were reaching the zenith of our hook ladder prowess, in single- and two-man hook ladder drills. Each day, we would scale the iron drill tower to the fifth-floor level. On this tower, it was as high as was permitted; the tower was apparently unsafe above this level.

We were now using the parapet mount on the hook ladder, which meant in effect that to enter the building we had to keep climbing up the ladder to the very top, only then stepping directly from the ladder onto the windowsill. In reverse, this entailed standing upright on the fifth-floor windowsill, bending down and forward out from the building into free space, to grasp hold of the top of the ladder, twisting around, and at the same time, stepping down onto the top round of the ladder. Not for the faint hearted was this drill.

One morning, I was performing single man hook ladder drill to the fifth floor of the tower. Which in effect meant that only one man could work on the face of the tower at a time. Whilst this was happening, the sub officer instructor would keep one eye on the hook ladders, at the same time giving the remainder of the squad questions and answers on the forthcoming examination.

It had been raining this day and the face of the tower was wet. As I climbed the hook ladder up to the fifth floor, and then leant outwards and back on the ladder to swing my leg over the windowsill, the ladder swung violently away to the left, skidding on the wet surface of the tower. I abandoned the hook ladder and desperately grasped hold of the fifth-floor windowsill with both hands, hanging suspended five floors up. The hook ladder completed its violent swing to the left, then pendulum like it swung back in the opposite direction to crash against my body clinging to the windowsill, five floors up, like the swatting of a fly.

I climbed gingerly back onto the ladder; my heart was pounding. I had survived a near miss. I was not yet completely out of danger; danger to my career, not my pride that is. For I was waiting for the cry, "You dozey little man, Wilson," from the instructor down below. He didn't normally miss a thing, but to my relief, the stentorian shout never came. I hurriedly scrambled back into the relative safety of the fifth floor of the drill tower, I had got away with it!

When I rejoined the squad on the ground floor, a fireman whispered to me, "Christ you was lucky up there."

"Yes," I replied, "it was a near thing."

He then said, "Not the near miss with the hook ladder, I meant the sub officer, he was so busy talking that he never saw it happen."

"Yes," I said grimly. "That's what I meant as well."

*

We were now the senior squad in the training school, we had lost one man on the way, he had resigned for personal reasons, our instructor was quite pleased with us. At the end of ten weeks, there were still twelve in the squad. One man having been back squaded to our squad from a preceding squad, through sickness and injury. The silly man had fallen off a ladder and broken his leg at drill. It was not unknown for squads at the end of training to be as low in numbers as seven or eight. So for us to finish with twelve in the squad, our sub officer felt was a reflection on his ability as an instructor.

Our daily drill sessions were now being carried out at Fire Brigade Headquarters, Lambeth, in preparation for our pass out drills and parade, which would also be held in Lambeth's big drill yard. On the day of the pass out drills, we performed with huge, chalked numbers on our backs, so that the senior officers judging us could tell us apart, for marking. But in practice, apart from any major cockups on the day, we knew that we had made the grade.

On the Wednesday of the last week at training school, we had all been told that we had passed both the written examinations and the practical drill tests, and in theory were now London firemen. The last of the days at training school were spent in going back to the Brigade stores and collecting the last of our uniform and gear.

There was of course the official passing out pissup to be arranged. It was unanimously decided that ours would be a night up west, clubbing. That is to say a night out in the west end of London, going around the clubs and strip joints. Surprisingly, enough one of the other sub officer instructors at the training school arranged the whole evening's itinerary, and even volunteered to accompany us. This sub officer, who subsequently rose to quite an elevated in rank in the Brigade, and whose name I diplomatically seem to have forgotten, really impressed me. He seemed to know just about every club, club manager and stripper in Soho. He was held in such high esteem by these people that he never paid an entrance fee or bought a single drink all night long.

Thursday was the day we had been waiting for, Thursday was the day we were given our postings. The whole morning was taken up with discussions as to the relative merits of the stations as they were allocated to us. Mine was to be A3 Camden Town in the 'A' Division. The division was okay as I lived in the 'A' Division. Camden Town was almost as far away from my home as one could get, yet still remain in the division. None of the instructors seemed to know whether it rated as a busy station or not, which didn't bode well. Still never mind, tonight was the night of the big piss-up. The next day, Friday, was a happy yet sad day. Most of us were nursing sore heads. Two of the squad didn't make it home the previous night and had already spent their very first night in a fire station. They begged a night's lodging from the adjacent Southwark fire station.

We spent the morning playing cards and marking our newly issued gear. Then from around two o'clock in the afternoon, the respective divisional vans began arriving to take us and our gear to our new fire stations. Then, in ones and twos, we began to split up, part of our lives was over. Some of them never to be seen again, some to be joyfully met at some future big fire. Invariably so it always seemed, cup of tea in hand whilst gathered around the canteen van. Thus, the fireman's parting salutation to old friends, "See you at the next big one."

Southwark Training School 1961

Taylor Lawler Foxwel Dixon Anon Gascon Mills Luke Clarkson St O Nelson Beardwell Me! Heyho

Chapter 3

Camden Town Fire Station – 1962

The divisional lorry pulled up outside Camden Town fire station, in Pratt Street, northwest London. I was not impressed immediately with the station; it was 1914 style, five-storeys high and had Fire Brigade residential accommodation above. It was a two-appliance bay fire station, in a not very imposing setting, surrounded by industrial buildings.

The driver helped us to unload our gear, and led us into the fire station, announcing brusquely to the dutyman in the watchroom. "Two new boys for you." Then departed back to his divisional lorry.

The dutyman picked up a telephone and said, "The two new boys are here guvnor," put down the telephone and proceeded to ignore us.

After a short wait, a leading fireman came into the watchroom saying, "Pick up your gear and I will show you your lockers." We went back out through the appliance room, through a pair of double swing doors and into a locker room filled with metal lockers. He allocated us each a locker, telling us to stow our gear in them. When we had done so, we were to report to the station office and to see him again.

Now began our first operational problem, for we had two full kitbags of gear plus a large bedding roll to stow into this relatively small locker. Whilst we were attempting this operation, strange firemen were wandering back and forth through the locker room. No doubt coming to see what sort of rubbish the training school was turning out these days. Unfortunately, for us, we were bound for duties on the blue watch, and we had been deposited at the fire station on a white watch duty day. Since we were not to be future watch mates of the firemen currently on duty, they could afford to be standoffish.

Luckily, someone took pity on us; it was the junior fireman on the watch, only one month out of training school himself. He explained that our bedding did not go into the locker, but into a special bedding rack in the basement. Then led us down to show us where it was. Our helmets and fire gear also did not go into the locker but was hung up on pegs in a fire gear room also down in the basement.

With our gear finally all stowed away, we reported back to the leading fireman. He told us to report for duty at 9.00 am on the coming Monday morning, when our own watch, the blue watch, would be on day duties. He advised us, as it was our first day to be at the fire station at least an hour before that time, in order to be ready for roll call at nine o'clock. He made us write down the telephone number of the fire station and told us that if for any reason we could not report for duty and remarked it had not better be anything less than a broken leg, to contact the fire station on that number.

We were now free to wander around the fire station and found our way to the messroom where the firemen were at stand-easy and drinking tea. As a group, they found it easier to talk to us, and after initially questioning us about what was new in training school, began to give us information about our new watch, the fire station and fire ground.

I left the fire station for the journey home. One of the reasons that I had not been too pleased with this posting was the long distance between home and station. It was around a quarter of a mile walk from the fire station to Camden Town underground station, then on the tube train, changing at Earls Court, and alighting at Fulham Broadway, then a further quarter of a mile walk to my home. I would need to allow at least an hour for this journey on Monday morning.

Although I was an adult and twenty-one years of age, for the whole of that weekend, I was like a five-year-old on the day before his birthday. Monday just could not come quickly enough. Until such time as I had been to at least two or three fires, I would still consider myself a recruit fireman.

Monday morning, I arose at six o'clock, left the house at seven o'clock to arrive at the fire station by eight. Again, I found the firemen standoffish, and remote, for I did not realise that these firemen were the night duty watch (the red watch) and due to go off duty at nine o'clock.

During the course of the hour, other firemen would come into the locker room, dressed in part uniform and part civilian clothes. These firemen would say, "You the new boy?" and then introduce themselves and tell me their names, for these were the blue watch firemen reporting for duty, and my future watch mates.

Down in the gear room as we rigged in our fire gear for the change of watch parade, the difference between me and them was startling. My fire gear was in gleaming pristine condition, having been last worn at the passing out parade at training school, theirs was chipped, battered and a dull, matt-black colour. I was told by a smiling older fireman called Buck Ryan to put my leg and boot up upon the gear table, where he proceeded to smear it liberally with boot polish, and then did likewise to the second boot, saying, "Now leave them like that, don't polish them off, because if the guvnor sees shiny boots like they just were on parade, it will give him ideas, and we will all have to have shiny boots."

On roll call, the off-going watch were dismissed, and the riders and appliances for the day read out. My name was called out as riding the pump escape – from that point on, I was officially riding to fires.

After roll call, all the firemen disappeared off to the messroom for a cup of tea. Officially, this was the time to check appliances and equipment, but the oncoming firemen had been arriving for duty from eight o'clock onwards, and the checking of appliances had been done in their own time, prior to duty, to enable them to have their cup of tea.

Immediately after tea, it was escape ladder in the drill yard for a carry-down drill. At that time, this drill was carried out every day duty at this and most other fire stations in the Brigade. I think this was the cause of some of my later life back/spine problems.

The ladder was pitched into the third floor of the tower and secured, then the order all men aloft given, on which order all the firemen would proceed up the ladder to the third floor. From there, we took turns to carry each other down the ladder.

A rule at this fire station was that junior firemen were only allowed to carry down other junior firemen, and not the senior hands, whereas normally a fireman would carry down another fireman of similar build and weight to himself. It was my misfortune that a fireman, Terry O'Neill, had been posted to Camden Town two weeks prior to me. Fireman Terry O'Neill, after four months in training school, was fighting fit, fifteen and a half stone in weight, and about five feet eight inches tall. He was built, as firemen like to say, "like a brick shithouse" (which meant that he didn't bend in the middle very easily), and I had to carry him down in practice, draped around my shoulders, from the third floor of the drill tower each day only with his physique he would no more drape than would a barrel of beer! At the time, I was a very fit, tough young man, and managed this relatively easily, but by the time I was twenty-four years old, I was experiencing my first back problems.

The carry-down and other drills took until eleven o'clock, which was stand-easy time. A lot of naval terms were used in the Fire Brigade, and stand-easy meant tea break. Stand-easy was invariably the same, a cup of tea and a cheese or cheese and onion sandwich, it never varied. It was a time when the whole watch sat down together, and the conversation could be quite humorous.

I remember at the first one, two senior hands discussing us, the new boys, and how we had performed at the drills that morning and saying loudly so that we could plainly hear. "They weren't too bad, the little thin one," (me) "carried the big fat one," (Terry O'Neill) "safely down from the third floor okay, much to our surprise."

After stand-easy came station work and appliance routines, which lasted until lunchtime – 1300 hours. The drivers worked on the appliances, and the remaining firemen cleaned the fire station, junior firemen invariably getting the unpopular jobs. My first job was scrubbing down the station steps from top to bottom. I was given a bucket, a cloth, a scrubbing brush and soap, shown the stairs and told to get on with it, and so pleased was I to be a real fireman at last, that I actually enjoyed doing it.

Later on, at Camden, the leading fireman detailed me for window cleaning duties, and enquired had I ever cleaned windows before. "No," I replied, "right I will show you how to do it then, come with me." He proceeded to show me how to clean windows; he was obviously a window cleaner in his spare time. He would demonstrate cleaning a whole window, then ask me to have a go. Nothing I could do would satisfy him. "No, no, no," he would say, then take the chamois leather out of my hand and proceed to clean that window as well. He would then move onto the next window and clean the whole of that window, again as yet another demonstration. It wasn't too long before I had it figured out that this man actually enjoyed cleaning windows, and all I had to do was provide cheerful, amicable company and he would do the lion's share of the work, which is what duly happened. I did learn from him though, for he was most anxious to demonstrate the technique, and in later years when I took up window cleaning as a part time job, I had not forgotten the lessons he had taught me, and very quickly became an efficient and profitable window cleaner.

At 1300 hours, six short bells rang out, the signal for lunch time, and still no fire calls had been received at the station. The meal would be plain, but well cooked. For half an hour or so, the men would eat the meal, accompanied by much banter, and then the remaining half an hour until 1400 hours would be taken up with more individual pursuits, such as reading, snooker, and the like.

At 1400 hours, six bells rang and station routines would begin again. I was informed that the pump escape and crew were to go out on hydrant inspection duties. The appliance was to drive to the part of the fire ground where we were to inspect the street fire hydrants. Then, with the exception of the driver, the crew would dismount and walk from hydrant to hydrant, with the pump escape following at a reasonable distance in case a fire call was received via the appliance radio.

We inspected the first hydrant, lifted the lid, shipped the standpipe, turned the water on, turned the water off, un-shipped the standpipe, replaced the lid and walked away. I was amazed. According to the training school, there were at least fifty points to be checked on each hydrant, which would take at least fifteen minutes. On this station's ground, there were around 1,250 hydrants, each about 150 yards apart, each hydrant to be tested four times a year, and at the end of this one-and-a-half-hour session of testing, we would have only tested around twenty hydrants, so there was apparently enough time allowed merely to check that water came out of the hydrant when turned on.

After half an hour of walking around the streets of Camden Town with him, I was beginning to realise that this Buck Ryan was a bit of a character. He was around thirty years of age, had short, cropped hair and a rugged, lived-in type of face, and he had apparently spent three years serving in the military police in Palestine. We were being followed around by a gang of small kids of around five to seven years of age who wanted to know what we were doing. "Looking for money," replied Buck, explaining to them, "if you lift up these iron covers on the pavements, sometimes you find money down the holes, so far we have found one shilling and three pence." Before we reached the next hydrant, Buck had secreted a coin into the palm of his hand, and when the hydrant cover was raised, he reached down into the hydrant pit and produced the coin in his hand, saying, "Look at this, this is a bit of luck, a half a crown down this one." Now a half a crown to those kids was around five week's pocket money, the kids were amazed at Buck's great fortune. Upon being told by the sub officer in charge of us, that he was a rotten, cruel sod, teasing the kids like that, Buck then asked the kids who was the oldest, then gave him the half a crown, instructing him that it was to be divided equally amongst them all.

I later found another of his tricks was that when the kids followed us asking what we are up to, he would tell them that we were turning off the water in the street. Then he would tell the kids to hurry off home and get their mums to fill up their baths, kettles and pans before we did so, assuring them that we would wait at least five minutes after they had gone until we turned off the tap.

We returned to the fire station at 1530 hours for a tea break. During tea break, the mess manager informed me that the messing bill at this station was twelve shillings and sixpence a week, payable in advance, and that this bought the food for one week's messing, which he, the mess manager, cooked, so could he please have my money now, or tomorrow at the latest.

Six short rings on the fire bells announced that it was 1530 hours and the end of afternoon tea break; this was immediately followed by a cry of, "Get the net up." I was about to be introduced to fitness training, which comprised a crude form of the game volleyball, played Fire Brigade style. The main difference being that in volleyball played on fire stations there were no penalty points for touching the net, and that the size of the court was dictated by the size of the station drill yard, (on some fire stations that had very small yards, they painted the court lines around the walls of the buildings). This was not a game for the squeamish, for the official Fire Brigade issue volleyball, in use at this time, was in fact a heavy leather football. Tactics for the game seemed to be for the server to serve the ball so hard that the players at the other end were afraid to block it for fear of breaking their fingers.

During the first rally, I was at the net, and jumped up to strike the ball. Before I could do so, I received a violent blow to my head, which knocked me to the ground. When I got up, I saw Buck Ryan, who was playing opposite me, grinning at me. I was a bit annoyed with him and accused him of hitting me. With a look of great innocence on his face, he replied smugly, "I may have accidentally done so but I was going for the ball," and all around me the other players were nodding their heads in agreement. Yes, he was definitely going for the ball. Being the new boy at this station was going to be difficult, if not quite painful.

A year or so later when my own volleyball skills had increased, I was on the winning side in a game of volleyball, my own side being some seven points in the lead, and I was in a jubilant mood. Buck Ryan, playing for the opposing team, glaring at me, said, "If you win this game, Wilson, then I personally will buy the ice creams." Being seven points in the lead, I thought this a safe bet. I nodded my acknowledgement of this to him. He then added, "If you lose, you buy the ice cream," to which I naturally agreed, being seven points ahead.

The game resumed. Buck's team seemed from that point on, to get just about every piece of luck going, and I myself played like a demon, and despite all my efforts, Buck's team won. To rub salt into the wound, I was blamed by my own team for bringing bad luck on the game by betting on the result. The following day at lunch, we had ice cream with our sweet, which of course I had paid for. One of the firemen who had been on my team the previous day complimented me, saying, "Dave, you played a blinding game of volleyball yesterday."

"Thanks," I replied.

He then went on to say, "In fact you were so good, we had one hell of a job to lose that game."

"But you were on my team," I protested.

"I know," he replied, "but you don't think we were going to turn down free ice creams, do you?"

"Yes," I insisted, "but Buck would have bought them if his team had lost!"

He studiously and thoughtfully replied, "Yes, but Buck's ice cream just doesn't seem to taste quite as nice as yours." I'd been had yet again!

Volleyball ended with the ringing of six short bursts on the station call bells at 1700 hours and stand down time, also time for another cup of tea. This time was designated as free time, to be used in the cleaning of personal fire gear, washing and brushing up before going off duty, and in recreational activities. It was also the time at which the oncoming watch members would start to arrive at the station, prior to going on duty, and from this time onwards, the mutual exchanges would begin.

An oncoming fireman would relieve his opposite number already on duty, ie the driver of the pump escape would only relieve the driver of the pump escape, and so on, allowing the on-duty firemen to get away perhaps half an hour early and miss part of the evening rush hour. This privilege worked both ways, in the event of a fire call just before the change of watch, the majority of the crews would be oncoming riders, saving the Brigade considerable overtime payments.

Another six short burst clatters over the station call bells, the signal for the change of watches at 1800 hours, the end of my first day on the fire station and not a single fire call.

The next morning, I was at the station bright and early at 8.15 am, and as I walked into the locker room a senior fireman from the other watch actually said

40

good morning to me, which made me feel good, but then he followed this with, "Ride the ladders for me."

"Pardon?" I queried, looking puzzled.

He then explained to me very slowly, "You are down on the roll board to ride the turntable ladders today, will you relieve me on them?" So that was why he had said good morning to the junior fireman, he simply wanted to go home early. Although he had a low opinion of recruits, I was certainly good enough to relieve him on the fire engine. I agreed to ride for him, and he explained to me that first, I must collect my fire gear from the gear room in the basement, and then he would book the mutual exchange with the dutyman in the watchroom, and from then on, I would be riding in his place.

The whole of the drill period this day was taken up with turntable ladder drills. Although we had been introduced to turntable ladders at training school, and been given a ride up on one, we had not carried out drills with them. Now that I was going to ride this set of ladders quite regularly at this station, I needed to practice all the standard drills in order to become a useful crewmember, instead of just a passenger, or so the sub officer said.

The turntable ladders stationed at Camden had been built around 1930 and were a Merryweather mechanically operated set which extended to a maximum of 100 feet in length. They were of an open body design, which meant no crew cab, and the crew faced the elements of the weather. In good weather, they were wonderful to ride on, powered by a huge, quiet petrol engine, the bonnet of which protruded eight feet in front of the driver's position. When driven by a skilled driver, the drive to the fire could often be more exhilarating than the fire itself.

During the course of the day's drill period, the ladder operator played all the usual tricks ladder operators like to play on new boys. Shooting the ladders up to maximum extension, with me at the top 100 feet up in the air, then waving the ladders violently about, calling me up on the intercom, supposedly to reassure me, but in reality, to see if they could detect fear or panic in the new boy's voice, but the many and varied tricks didn't frighten me. It was against Brigade orders to actually kill firemen, no matter how junior, and I was firmly hooked onto the top of the ladder by a huge webbing belt and hook, which I knew was regularly tested by having the weight of four men applied to it.

*

My first tour of duty at Camden Town was very frustrating. Camden Town was considered to be a quiet fire station by 'A' division standards, but at this time was going through a particularly quiet spell. I went through the whole tour of duty, two days and two nights, without attending a fire call. The blue watch (my watch) had received around four fire calls during this period, but they had all been single machine attendances, and I had always been riding the other machine.

My very first fire call, which I attended on the second tour of duty, was a malicious false alarm. The first fire of any substance that I attended was a two-storey derelict house, with the ground floor well alight. To the senior hands, this was pretty boring stuff, but I was suitably impressed.

Upon arrival at the fire and as I jumped down from the appliance, Buck Ryan detailed me to help him set into the street fire hydrant. Having laid out the hose and connected up the hydrant, I was waiting for Buck's signal to turn the water on. When it came, I attempted to turn the hydrant on but it was stuck fast. I gave an almighty wrench on the metal hydrant bar, which violently freed the stuck hydrant valve, and then carried on to strike a parked motor car. Fortunately, the metal hydrant bar caused little damage to the motor car, because I had somehow managed to insert my thumb between it and the car and thus cushioned the blow, but my thumbnail turned black and subsequently fell off. A not very glorious start to my firefighting career, injured at my first fire.

*

It was a Saturday morning and my first weekend tour of duty, and I discovered a very different station routine. Immediately after our morning cup of tea, a cry went up of "scrub out" and everybody left the messroom. The appliance room doors were opened and the two appliances driven out into the street and parked there. All the ancillary equipment stored around the outside of the appliance room was moved out into the station yard, and the appliance room was left bare.

One fireman was busy in the station yard mixing up in two large dustbins a solution of Comprox (heavy duty detergent) and hot water. He always did this particular job, because before detergents were available on the fire stations, it had been his job to cut up bars of soap into cubes, then boil these up in water with household soda, to make the soapy solution for scrub out.

Bass or yard brooms were fetched from the store, and scrub out began. The Comprox man poured neat detergent on badly oiled patches on the floor; these were then worked in with the bass brooms. Then the Comprox man decanted the solution from the dustbins into a two-gallon watering can and proceeded to pour this evenly all over the appliance room floor. Then all available firemen, clad in their fire boots and leggings, and with bass brooms in their hands, proceeded to scrub the appliance room out. This would normally take around half an hour.

One of the senior firemen had meanwhile disappeared, only to reappear minutes later carrying four empty buckets and a bar of soap. Two buckets were placed at each end of the appliance room, spaced apart, to serve as goal posts. The senior fireman then shouted out, "Right, it's the pump escape's crew versus the ladder's crew." The bar of soap was dropped between two facing firemen, and a game of soap hockey began.

Soap hockey was almost as dangerous as ice hockey, for the leather soled fire boots had very little grip on the soapy floor. I quickly found out that ice hockey tactics were also employed. Body checking, slamming a man into the appliance room walls, a sly push with the bass broom at another man's boots would usually upend him, to sit squarely down into the soapy solution. There was also the danger from the flying bass brooms, an almighty swipe at the bar of soap that missed could produce a severe case of crotch ache in another player, for unlike hockey players, we wore no padding.

The end of the hockey game signified the end of scrub out. Now began washout. A length of hose was connected to the hydrant in the station yard, a hand-controlled branch fitted. Then all the soapy water was washed from the appliance room into the street at the front of the station, to run away down the gutters. Although we were allowed to wet and bruise ourselves, it was taboo to harm the members of the public. A senior fireman always stood guard in the street to ensure the big jet of water did not wet or endanger them.

*

From a firefighting view, Camden Town could be dull, but station life was not. Buck Ryan especially was pleased; he had three relatively junior firemen on the watch to practice his japes on. As time went by, we junior firemen began to retaliate, I had just managed to wet Buck with a jet of water from the hose reel in the drill yard, in return for a wetting I had received the day before. Buck was now stalking me around the station with a bucket of dirty water in his hands. He finally caught me in the open in the middle of the drill yard and I made a frantic dash for an outside toilet in the drill yard before he could catch me. I then bolted myself safely inside. Peering through the ventilation holes cut in the door, I could see that Buck had given up the chase, for he was walking nonchalantly away towards the appliance room. In the appliance room, I saw him open up an appliance locker, and withdraw a scaling ladder, a short sturdy ladder around six feet in length. Then he returned equally casually across the drill yard to the door of the toilet, where I was safely ensconced. He then proceeded to wedge the scaling ladder under the handle of the door to the toilet and the drill yard floor, trapping me in the toilet like a rat in a trap. Again, he walked very casually away back into the appliance room, to appear minutes later wearing a huge grin on his face and carrying under his arms a standpipe key and bar, I now knew that I was doomed. The standpipe was fixed to the drill yard hydrant, and Buck was now proceeding very casually once again, to unroll a length of fire hose, to which he then attached a three-quarter-inch hand-controlled branch.

By this time, the word had gone around the station, and the other firemen were gathered in the drill yard and on the balconies to watch the fun. Even the office staff were peering out of their opened windows in anticipation. There was nothing I could do about it, I was locked in the toilet and would just have to take my medicine, but when the medicine came, it was horrible. There were seemingly thousands and thousands of gallons of it, coming underneath the door, then over the top of the door and bouncing off of the ceiling, and all of it freezing cold, and all of it going all over me. When Buck finally let me out, I was like a drowned rat, soaking wet from head to toe and shivering with the cold. Strangely enough though, I was quite popular after it, for everyone agreed, I had livened up what could have been an otherwise boring afternoon.

The other fireman who had been posted to Camden Town the same time as I was called Phillip Mills, he was a nice, gentle man, but underneath had a fiery streak. He was only to remain in the Fire Brigade for around six months before retiring, I think because the wages were so poor. Which I think was probably just as well, because Phil was accident-prone. His accidents tended to come in twos and threes and were such that I am convinced he would never have lasted the full thirty years' service without serious injury and medical discharge, had he not decided to resign himself.

The pump escape had been ordered to a rubbish fire, which on arrival turned out to be an old sofa smouldering away on a derelict site. A hose reel jet was set to work on it, and in order that the jet would penetrate fully, it was decided to break the sofa up. I raised my fire boot and brought it crashing down on the sofa, as I did so, a piece of wood broke away and went cartwheeling slowly up in the air. We all watched it go up, and we all watched it come down, and when it did so it landed fairly and squarely in Phil Mill's eye, causing him considerable pain.

Back at the station, first aid was rendered, and his eye was quite red and sore, but he declined to go to hospital, and he declined to go off duty. Phil carried on with his duties, one of which was to derv-up the pump escape (replenish the fuel tanks with diesel oil).

The diesel oil was kept stored in forty-gallon drums laid on their sides on stands in the fuel store; a brass tap was inserted into the end of the drum and the fuel drawn off into containers, to be poured into the fire engines. Phil was wearing his fire boots and leggings, which is the norm when working in the oily, smelly fuel store. Whilst drawing off a two-gallon container of diesel fuel, he turned to talk to another fireman. Standing upright, with the two-gallon can in his hand, as his body turned his leggings caught the handle of the fuel tap and turned it on again. So whilst he was engaged in conversation, the oil was being funnelled down his leggings and filling his right hand fire boot up with diesel oil. When he realised this, he gave a loud cry and dropped the two-gallon can of diesel all over the floor, then in his haste to get out of the store, slipped on the oil and sat squarely down into it. He was then so concerned about the pint or so of diesel oil in his boot, that he didn't notice he had left the tap still open. The end result was that he had two pints of derv in his right-hand boot, and ten gallons all over the fuel store floor, not to mention the half pint or so soaking into the seat of his trousers.

After all the excitement had died down, Phil still had to clean up all the mess. For oil spills and de-greasing, fire stations are supplied with five-gallon containers of a strong detergent called Comprox. Phil was now in a very bad mood, and he stomped off over to the cleaning store to get a drum of Comprox. Now this particular container of Comprox was almost full and was without a cap on the spout. So that when Phil in his bad temper slammed it down onto the floor outside the oil store, its contents slopped upwards and into his remaining good eye. Comprox in the eye is very, very painful, and so he emitted another loud shriek, as much in frustration as in pain. The medical remedy for this type of injury is to irrigate the eye with copious supplies of clean water, which on a fire station means the hose reel in the drill yard.

Since he could not see to do it himself, I did it for him, washing his eyes with the hose reel full on, and eventually it eased his pain, at least it relieved his physical pain. For not only had he got two bad eyes, a boot full of derv, derv all over his bottom where he had sat down in it, but now he was soaking wet as well. In retrospect, this man was wise to leave the Fire Brigade, before something really major happened to him.

The above story seems so farfetched, that I feel I have to assure you it is entirely true, I have not even disguised the name of the fireman.

*

My fire ground experience was coming on well, I had been to a twenty-pump fire, an eight-pump fire, and numerous four-pump fires, but now looking back, they all seem blurred together. At larger fires, an inexperienced fireman will suffer a form of tunnel vision, he will only see or digest that which is immediately around him, his senses being fully taken up with the newness, excitement and to him danger of his present experiences. Rather akin to not being able to see the trees for the forest is in the way.

At around this time in the London Borough of Camden, huge areas of the borough were being cleared under slum clearance. Whole streets of houses would be empty prior to their actual demolition, and these houses would invariably be set on fire by kids or vagrants. This is where I gained a lot of my skills, for the older, senior firemen would deign not to get involved in these type of fires and get all their gear mucky for nothing, let the youngsters get on with it. Sometimes when it was a three-storey derelict going well, they would join in, but they would invariably join in as helpers, lightening up the hose as we worked our way up the staircase, whilst the younger firemen worked the jet. They would of course be ever alert for hidden dangers or pitfalls that might lie waiting for us, and at the same time be very quick to check us if they saw any, for by now, though inexperienced by their standards we might be, we were now Camden Town firemen.

At any London fire station around this time, the nerve centre of the station was the station watchroom, it was manned twenty-four hours a day by a duty watch keeper, one of the station's firemen. All fire calls to the station were received at this point, and many automatic fire alarms and fire telephones from important buildings on the station fire ground terminated there. All comings and goings to and from the fire station of firemen, officers, workmen and tradesmen were duly recorded and timed in the station logbook. As was anything else of the slightest importance that happened on the station, and the dutyman also manned the fire station mini telephone switchboard.

Although at training school, we had received extensive training in watchroom procedures, we were not allowed to be alone in the watchroom unsupervised until we had received practical experience under the guidance of a senior fireman, and then only when we had taken a written examination at Divisional Headquarters. Here was the catch, the sooner we took the watchroom examination and passed it, the sooner we would be incarcerated in the boring bloody watchroom. Taken out of general station circulation for periods of four hours or more, sitting up for half the night wide-awake, sometimes for two nights in succession, and for the younger firemen, missing exciting fire calls. The senior firemen knew this also, for the more hands there were to do watchroom duties the less irksome it would be. They made it abundantly and plainly clear that any man failing his watchroom examination would have his life made bloody impossible.

So with the above incentives, I passed my watchroom exam first time.

I was on day duties and on duty in the watchroom and had not as yet taken my first unsupervised fire call. At around 10.00 am, the sub officer came into the watchroom, and asked me to book the pump escape off of the run to proceed to the bank and collect the wages monies (at this time, firemen were still paid wages in cash on a Friday). The pump escape was booked off the run for this duty, ie not available for fire calls. The reason for this I was told, was that at some time in the past, an officer with the wages of forty firemen in his pocket had been ordered onto a large fire. Then duly (and allegedly), inconsiderately lost the lot whilst fighting the fire.

About fifteen minutes after the pump escape had left the station, a gentleman in smart civilian clothes came into the watchroom and said to me, "Good morning. I am ACO Cunningham, could I please use the Brigade line?" ACO stands for Assistant Chief Officer, third in command of the whole London Fire Brigade, of course he could use the Brigade line. I keyed into the Brigade line and gave him the handset, and whilst he was talking, I was busily trying to remember if I had been taught how to sit to attention or not. At that point, the sub officer came into the watchroom, returning with the appliance from the bank. I breezily if somewhat nervously informed him, "This gentleman is ACO Cunningham, Sub Officer." A useful piece of information I thought, so did the sub officer, for he appeared even more nervous than me.

At that point, just to make life more interesting, the station call bells began to ring. A loud buzzer sounded in the watch room, and a red flashing light on the watch room consul was announcing "fire flash, fire flash", my very first fire call, how nice!

ACO Cunningham handed me back the handset, and stepped back out of the way, (at least he had been well-trained). Over the handset, a voice was telling me, "Order your pump escape to a fire at 19 Smith Street on your own station's ground." As I was writing this down on the call slip, the sub officer was shaking his head. I in return kept nodding mine, which caused him to shake his head even more vigorously, he was apparently trying to tell me he still had the wages for the whole fire station still in his pocket. Unfortunately, I had not been trained for the NON-receiving of fire calls, especially in front of Assistant Chief Officers. The sub officer was bloody well going to the fire, wages or not, and go he did.

After the pump escape left on the fire call, Mr Cunningham said quietly to me, "Was that by any chance your first fire call?"

"Yes, sir," I replied.

"Well done," he said. "I must have rather complicated matters by being here and on the telephone at the time."

"Not at all, sir," I replied, tongue very much in my cheek.

On the return of the pump escape, the sub officer rushed straight past the watchroom, and up to the station office, to put the wages in the safe, he was taking no more chances. Luckily for me, when he had originally asked me to book the pump escape off of the run, he had been standing beside me whilst I did so. The mistake had been made at Brigade Control, who had omitted or forgotten the appliance was off the run, and thus ordered it onto a fire.

*

There were lots of jolly japes that could be played on newly qualified dutymen, and duly were. Buck Ryan seemed to be involved in an awful lot of them, and they always seemed to take place in the early hours of the morning. The simplest was to get the long or extended billiard cue from the snooker table, lean out of the first-floor window, and press the enquiry button outside the watchroom door. This required the dutyman to stir himself from his seat and go to the front door of the station to answer the 'non-existent enquirer'. If the jape had been squared off with the office first, and they were sympathetic, it was possible to improve on this gag with a bucket of water from aloft when the dutyman opened the door and stepped out to look for possible enquirers. So that any late-night revellers that might have otherwise thought they were hallucinating when a fireman appeared at the front door of Camden Town fire station bearing an open umbrella on a fine summer's night can set their minds at rest, they were not!

On two occasions during the night, usually around 1.30 am and 4.30 am, divisional control would circulate a test message. This was done ostensibly to make sure the telephone line was in good order, but really to ensure the dutyman was awake. The test message took the form of a single sentence, to be written down and then copied in the station logbook. On my first night on duty in the watchroom, at around 1.00 am, a bell rang and the yellow light came on over the divisional line on the watchroom consul. I answered the call A3 Camden Town, a voice then said simply, "Test message," the voice then went on to speak to other stations, "A4 Euston test message…A5 test message…" When the voice had gathered in around half a dozen replies, the voice said, "Test message begins." I started to write the message down on a message pad. Tonight, it seemed they were using the test message to send a general instruction about testing hook ladders around the division, for it went on and on. I had filled up four sheets of message pad, and was in danger of running out of paper, so I interrupted the voice to ask, "How much more of this message is there to come?"

A voice which I was sure I recognised said, "All depends on how much more you're prepared to put up with." The bastards had got me again! I later found out they were in the very next-door room using the coin box telephone. They would phone divisional headquarters, then ask to be put through to Camden Town, thus the call would come through on the divisional line. All the other stations apparently acknowledging the call were the same voice but disguised each time to make the call sound authentic. The voice I thought that I had recognised was of course Buck Ryan's.

It was around 2.30 in the morning and I was again in the watchroom, quietly reading. At this time in the morning, the whole of the fire station, with the exception of the watchroom, would normally be in darkness. Apart from his

49

brightly lit watchroom, all the dutyman would normally see was a large glass-viewing panel, which separated the watchroom from the darkened appliance room. Through this panel and against the reflected glare of the watchroom lights could just be seen the darkened outline of the pump escape. I had been reading for around half an hour or so, when to rest my eyes, I leant back in the watchroom chair and looked up at the ceiling. Then I vacantly let my gaze drop to the glass-viewing panel in front of me. There to my utter horror, in the middle of the glass panel, and apparently floating in mid-air, was a ghostly white face and disembodied head grinning at me. My heart leapt, and my jaw dropped, and for a full fifteen seconds, I stared in utter fright and amazement. Then the grin on the ghostly face changed to a great big smile, a smile that I instantly recognised, it was him again! "You bastard, Ryan, you just frightened the life out of me that time."

He came into the watchroom all smiles, saying, "Took you long enough to see me, I was stuck out there for twenty minutes before you finally looked up." This wasn't a spur of the moment gag on Buck's part, for he had whitened his face with flour from the kitchen. He was wearing his black fire tunic the wrong way around, to get the disembodied head effect, and as he said, had been sat in the back cab of the pump escape for twenty minutes waiting for me to finally look up and be duly frightened.

*

Until now, I have made no mention of a station officer on this fire station, that is because there wasn't one on the blue watch. A sub officer was in charge of the watch, and he held the rank of temporary station officer, and only fully fledged station officers were given the honorary title of guv. Sub Officer Wilson, for that was his name, was to me a quite elderly gentleman, for he was around fifty years of age, and approaching the end of his fire service career. He apparently wanted a quiet life with no hassle, and as long as he got that, he was happy and did not unduly worry others.

He had, so I was told, missed promotion to the station officer rank as a result of an unfortunate incident. In the late 1950s, a major train crash had occurred at Harrow Weald with many injuries and much loss of life. As a result of lessons learned at this train crash, a new procedure was instigated in the London area to deal with major disasters, called 'major accident procedure'. It was meant for any major incident where live casualties were expected to exceed fifty and was intended to mobilise all emergency services such as police, hospitals, ambulances and the like.

Now Sub Officer Wilson was one of the very first officers to initiate this procedure after it was introduced. Unfortunately, for him, he got it wrong, he had been called to a train crash at Camden High Road on Camden Town's fire ground. When he arrived at the incident, he found that a goods train had been derailed, and that two of the empty goods wagons had crashed through the parapet on the bridge down onto the Camden High Road below, injuring one or two people in doing so. In his mind, he associated train crashes with major accident procedure, and so sent the fatal message. 'Initiate major accident procedure', and then ambulances, doctors, policemen and hospitals, not to mention the Fire Brigade, all over London began to mobilise. All this for two crappy old railway wagons derailed! From that point on, his career was blighted.

An inordinate importance is or was placed on messages from fires in the London Fire Brigade. To send a message from a fire, such as 'false alarm', and then to amend it to 'small fire', implies that the fire officer has not carried out correct procedures in the first place, and is therefore lacking in officer qualities.

A fire call was received ordering the pump escape and turntable ladder to a fire in a garage, in a Mews property in the Regents Park area of Camden Town's fire ground, Sub Officer Wilson in charge of the attendance.

On arrival at the address which was one of a row of Mews properties, all with garages underneath, the property to which we had been called was obviously being used as a small commercial car repairer, for there was a car in it over an open repair pit, and all around were the general tools of a car repairer. But of the occupier, there was no sign, the doors were wide open and it looked as if the occupier had suddenly decided to go off on an urgent errand. There was no sign of burning, or of fire in the premises. The sub officer had, I think, subconsciously made up his mind that the call was a false alarm and was ready to send the false alarm message. Then just as an afterthought said casually, "Have a quick look around and see if you can see anything."

I made my way into the next garage; nothing, just another car repairers, out again and into the next garage. This one was empty but for a large, galvanised iron tank over in the far corner. The interior of the garage was dark, and I walked into the garage over towards the iron tank at the rear.

When I got near enough to be able to see into the tank, to my utter amazement sitting in it up to his chest in cold water was a fully clothed man. My first thought was another nutter, but his answer to my question, "Why are you sitting in that tank of cold water?" Had me dashing away to fetch the sub officer before he sent the fatal false alarm message.

The man it transpired had been working on the car in the first garage; he had been down the inspection pit draining off a small amount of petrol from the car's petrol tank. The petrol vapour had ignited, causing him to spill all the petrol in the container over his clothes, which of course also ignited. Knowing about the tank of water two garages along, he had dashed there with his clothes alight and jumped in, where he remained until I found him. Although his burns did not appear that severe to me, the man later died. Now if the sub officer had not merely as an afterthought uttered the words, "Have a quick look around, lads," the Brigade's reputation, and his career, would once again have been in tatters. For senior fire officers and indeed Her Majesty's Coroners, don't much like the idea of dead bodies lurking around undiscovered for too long! It's not so much the smell, it just complicates the paperwork.

Chapter 4
Camden Town Fire Station – 1962/3

I had been at Camden Town for around eight months, when a Brigade memorandum was circulated asking for volunteers for Brigade driving courses – the Brigade at that time being very short of fire appliance drivers. Applicants were to be at least 21 years of age and hold a full driving licence.

I held the qualifications necessary to apply and decided to do so, despite all the advice from the wise heads not to do so. In retrospect, the wise heads were absolutely correct, I had not really even begun to master the art of being a fireman, I had not even done the eighteen month's operational service required to enable me to train in proto breathing apparatus wearing at that time. When you are 22 years of age, and the chance to actually drive the big red engines comes along, you don't always listen to wise advice. So I completed and sent off the application form for the driving course.

After around a two-month wait, I received instructions to report to Southwark training school for motor driving training. The course was of two week's duration, which on the face of it seemed long enough to familiarise one selves to driving the large heavy goods type vehicles that fire engines are.

I reported to Southwark Training School at the due time and date, where I met the three other trainee drivers that would make up the squad. Then we met the instructor in charge of the squad. Thus, one instructor, one fire engine, four trainees and two weeks in which to become appliance drivers. I worked it out, that allowing for the numerous tea breaks, meal breaks, washing down the fire engine at the end of each day, then the carrying out of general station cleaning routines at the driving school on Friday afternoons.

In total, over the two-week period, I received about eight hour's actual driving instruction, on three makes of fire engine, one petrol, two diesel. Ten hours of cleaning routines, fifty hours of being totally bored out of my skull, looking out of the fire engine window, whilst the other firemen drove, and I still passed their driving test.

In the 1960s, all that was required in law to drive a heavy goods vehicle was to have a full driving licence and attain the age of twenty-one years. Having attained this, you were not then expected to screech around central London in a ten-ton vehicle, at forty miles per hour. Which apparently was expected of me now by the Fire Brigade. I was not very impressed!

On return to the station, for around a week, I drove the appliances back from fires, then out on hydrant inspections, which was to familiarise me with our own particular fire engines. Which was just as well, for on these particular Dennis fire engines, the gearbox layout was the complete reverse to any other vehicle I had ever driven.

The great day came and I was down on the roll board to drive the pump escape. Not until 11.30 am did the bells go down. "Order your pump escape to standby for fire cover at Islington fire station." This would normally mean that the Islington firemen had picked up a make-up fire, and that the fire station would be empty for a considerable period of time. Thus, we were being sent in to cover the gap in fire cover. I had been to Islington fire station a number of times before as a passenger, and knew the route well, so had no need to look it up on the station map.

In the 1960s, appliances ordered to stand by at other fire stations went on the bell, that is to say with the blue fights on and fire bells ringing. The station doors opened and off we went, turn right out of the station, and right into St Pancras Way. Carry on down to Kings Cross, turn left at Kings Cross then through the busy traffic and road junctions, onto the City Road. A long fast run down the City Road, to the Angel Islington. Turn left and negotiate the red traffic lights at the Angel, continue on through heavy traffic, the Angel ran into Cross Street and the fire station was in Cross Street.

Having done all this relatively successfully, and at a reasonable speed, the fire station was now but only fifty yards away and we had had a superb run. A big flatbed lorry in front of me pulled in, then slowed down to let me pass. As he pulled in and slowed down, a lady on a zebra crossing just in front of him thought that he was slowing down to enable her to use the crossing. She walked out in front of him, he then slammed on his brakes and I crashed into the back of him, "just like that". My very first drive on the bell, fifty yards away from a home run, and my very first crash, (or Biff in Brigade parlance).

As a result of the accident damage the appliance was not now available for fire calls, so we made our way back to Camden Town. As we were passing through Kings Cross, I pulled up alongside a number 14 bus at the traffic lights and was aware of the driver of the bus waving to me. Prior to joining the Fire Brigade, I had spent fourteen months as a bus conductor on the number 14 bus route, and who should be driving this particular bus, but my ex-bus driver friend. He was gleefully pointing at the nearside accident damage to the fire engine – so far, this was not one of my happiest days.

Upon our return to Camden Town, it was apparent from the black looks that I was getting that I was not exactly flavour of the month. This accident would mean that a spare appliance would have to be fetched. Spare appliances always seemed to be located at some far distant fire station, in some remote corner of the Brigade. When the spare appliance was collected and brought back, every single item of equipment on the damaged machine would have to be transferred to the spare machine, careless drivers are not popular people in the Fire Brigade.

I had my own cross to bear though, for I was now confined to the station office completing my very first accident report. The London Fire Brigade had its own special way of doing just about everything, and this included accident reports. They had to be completed in a special ink, on special paper, and just about every conceivable detail of the accident recorded. The weather, the wind, the road surface, colour of the driver's eyes, what he had for breakfast, and whether he enjoyed it or not, (the breakfast of course), seemed to be required.

I was approximately one third of the way through the accident report, for the second time of trying, when the fire bells rang. I dashed out of the office and down the short flight of stairs, and as I passed through the double swing doors into the appliance room and discovered that somebody had left a rolled-up mat just inside the door. As my right foot went down onto the soft mat, instead of the expected firm appliance room floor, my ankle twisted under me and I crashed to the floor, in pain. The fire call had been for the turntable ladders, the pump escape being off the run for the very sound reason that I had recently broken it, and it now appeared that I had broken my ankle as well.

After much prodding and poking and jiggling of the injured foot, listening for the crackling and crunching sound of broken bones grating together – a very certain, but painful method of determining whether or not the foot was broken – the consensus of opinion by the gathered first aiders was that I was perfectly all right, that I had merely sprained my ankle. Although when put to vote, they did agree that it was quite a bad sprain. I had been lying on the floor pale faced and listening to their deliberations and was most pleased when it was voted a bad sprain. I didn't want to be the cause of all this fuss and trouble for nothing.

The sub officer then decided that seeing as I had sprained my ankle, I may as well go home and he would have to finish the accident report himself. He stared at me fiercely saying, "And then the report that will have to be filled in because you fell down the bloody stairs and hurt yourself."

Because the pump escape was off of the run due to the accident, we had plenty of spare riders. Roy Walker agreed to take me home in the sidecar of his motorcycle combination. Now, because my ankle had swollen up grotesquely, we would stop off at my local hospital on the way and get it X-rayed. Roy was being far too solicitous for his normal nature, serving to convince me it was he who had left the rolled-up mat at the entrance to the appliance room in the first instance, and thus caused all this grief.

On the way home, we spent an hour at St Stephen's Hospital, Chelsea, where the verdict was no broken bones, just a bad sprain. After this terribly bad day, I finally made it to the safety of my own home. Roy helped me up the stairs and I invited him in for a cup of tea, which he accepted. Whilst I was in the kitchen making the tea, Roy called out from the living room. "Dave, is your budgerigar all right?"

"Why what is the matter with it?" I called back.

"I was just wondering," he said, "only it's lying on its back in the middle of the cage floor."

"It has probably sprained its ankle just like me," I replied jokingly, but of course when I looked at it, there was no doubt this was a wrong diagnosis, for budgies don't die of sprained ankles, and this one was definitely dead.

They do say accidents tend to happen in threes, assuming the budgie's death was indeed an accident, they were quite correct on this occasion. To me though, it was a day of firsts. My very first drive to a fire, my first road traffic accident, my first personal accident of significant magnitude at work, and for sure it was the very first time this particular budgerigar had ever died.

Now that I was a driver, my firefighting was very strictly curtailed, for when I was driving the appliance, I was now expected to operate the fire pump, look after water supplies, set the pump into street hydrants when necessary and send the radio messages.

I think the older drivers liked my keenness. Perhaps it reminded them of themselves as younger firemen. For upon arrival at any kind of working job, I would scurry around doing all the heavy jobs, such as setting the pump into the street hydrant, and then ask the other driver's permission to go and do some firefighting, which they invariably gave.

It had been a bad mistake to take on appliance driving so early in my career, but on the plus side, I was learning that there was more to fighting fires other than just grabbing the jet and rushing into the fire. With just a year's operational service, I was now seeing fires from the driver's point of view, which were water supplies and water pressures. I was even beginning to gain an insight into the officer in charge's view of fires, which is messages to be sent and safety of personnel, fire spread etc., and on the whole, I think I gained more than I lost. I think at the time I was perhaps inordinately proud of not only being a London fireman, but also of being a fire engine driver, but pride came before a fall, somebody found the chink in my armour and pierced it.

Shortly after I had passed out as a driver, I was attending what would be described as a difficult chimney fire. I was driving the pump, and Buck Ryan was driving the pump escape. The incident was a six-storey block of flats, with a chimney fire going like the clappers of hell, blotting out the entire neighbourhood with black putrid smoke issuing from the roof. The chimney fire was being fought from the flat roof of the block of flats with a hose reel jet. As the driver of the pumping appliance, I was the fire pump operator. Thus, newly out of driving school, and the driver and pump operator of a great big scarlet London fire engine, I felt myself a person of great importance.

So it came about that I was standing at the rear of the pump, operating the fire pump from the controls, when a small boy of around six or seven years of age came up to me and asked, "Excuse me, mister, are you a fireman?"

I looked down at him, and proudly replied, "Of course I am a fireman, young man." The young boy said nothing, and casually walked away, out of sight. Some minutes later, the young man approached me again.

This time, he asked seriously, "Here! Mister, are you sure you are a fireman?" I went to some pains to explain that not only was I a fireman, but I was the driver and the operator of this pumping appliance. It was in fact me that was supplying the water to put out the fire. The young lad once again made no reply and once again casually walked away.

Yet a third time the young lad approached me, this time saying in a totally disbelieving manner, "You're not really a fireman, are you? Tell the truth." This last statement badly hurt my pride; a six-year-old kid couldn't bring himself to believe I really was a fireman. I spent some minutes giving every reason I could think of to convince the young boy that I really was a London fireman. Then it suddenly occurred to me to ask him why he thought that I could not be a fireman. The answer was short and simple. "That man over there said you're too small to possibly be a real fireman." That man over there, wearing a huge grin across his face, was of course none other than Buck Ryan.

*

Over the Christmas period of 1963, around six inches of snow had fallen and settled over London. The blue watch at Camden Town were on duty on Boxing night, and after a fairly quiet, sociable evening went to bed fairly early at around 1.30 am. At approximately 3.30 am, the bells went down for a fire call. The pump escape and pump were ordered to a fire call on Camden Town's fire ground. The turntable ladders had been transferred back to Euston fire station, and a pump was now stationed at Camden Town.

That night, I was driving the pump escape, and I jumped up into the cab, turned the master switch, which switches on the vehicle ignition and pre-set road lights, blue flashing lights etc., and then started up the vehicle's road engine. Both appliances and crew were now only waiting for the dutyman to arrive with the call slips. As the dutyman came into the appliance room, he would call out loudly, so that all the crews would hear. "Fire number 19 Smith St Camden Town's ground," then hand the call slips to the respective officers in charge of the machines. As he handed over the call slips, he would pull down on a braided cord suspended from the appliance room ceiling, which would open the appliance room doors.

The appliance room doors opened and folded inwards. As they did so, I engaged first gear and made ready to move off, but then hesitated, something wasn't quite right. There in front of me where the doors had folded away, was a three-foot high brilliant white wall. Instead of being able to see the building opposite across the road, all I could see was an opaque, swirling, white cloud. I leaned forward across the steering wheel, the better to see through the windscreen. My brain finally registered, it was snowing like crazy, snowflakes as big as half crowns, coming down sideways in blizzard conditions. The three-foot white wall was in fact a snowdrift that had built up against the appliance doors, before they had opened inwards.

I drove out into the blizzard; it was a most unusual experience. London would normally be quiet at 3.30 am in the morning, but other than the noise of the road engine inside the cab, there was total silence. The thick twelve inches of snow on the ground, and the huge volume of snow drifting around in the air, completely muffled all sound. So in eerie silence, we made our way through the blinding, swirling snow, at a speed of around 20 miles an hour, to the address on the call slip.

The visibility was such that when I arrived at what I thought was the road we had been called to, a fireman had to jump down from the fire engine to read the road nameplate high upon a wall, and only with great difficulty could he do so.

Having found the correct road, we now had to find the house to which we had been called. It was only with great difficulty that we could see the actual houses from the fire engine, and it was totally impossible to see the house numbers. Scouting parties of firemen on foot had to lead the way forward. If these men went forwards more than five yards, they disappeared from view completely in the swirling snow.

Finally, out of the murk, a fireman appeared running back towards me, waving his arms to attract my attention, and beckoning me forward. I could tell by his actions that he had found something exciting. He then disappeared back into the murk again, and I increased the speed of the fire engine to catch up with him. Finally, I found him again standing squarely in the road, pointing down at the ground, shouting, "Stop here, this is the house."

I dropped down the driver's window and shouted back to him, "No, I am going to pull past, and leave room for the escape ladder to be used if we need it." Then giving me the thumbs up sign, he jumped back out of my way.

It was Brigade practice for the pump escape always to pull up forward of a building on fire, and the second machine, usually the pump, to stop short. This was to leave enough room free in front of the building for the escape ladder to be released from the appliance, then turned and used on the building without obstruction in the event of a ladder rescue being required. Also, when both machines arrived together, the hose lines would be taken out from the pump, again in order to leave the pump escape free for rescues.

I stopped the pump escape and applied the hand brake. Then I jumped down into the deep snow and walked back in the direction of the pump. As I approached, I could see the hose reel was already snaking out in the direction of an adjacent house. The hose reel pump was screaming, and Buck Ryan was adjusting his pump controls. "What have we got, Buck, do you know?" I asked him.

"Back room on first floor going well," was what I was told. "You had better start looking for a hydrant."

I opened the door to the water locker on the appliance and took down a standpipe key and bar. Then carrying them with me as was the custom, set off back down the street in the direction of the pump escape.

I had not gone far before I realised, I had made a tactical error. Before I could use the standpipe, I would first need to find a hydrant, and in looking for a hydrant beneath 12 inches of snow, a spade would be a far more useful tool. I deposited the standpipe on a low wall and went back to the appliance for a spade.

On the back of each appliance was carried a hydrant location book, which gave the location of hydrants in every street on the station's ground. These books tended not to be used too much in central London stations, because street hydrants were so abundant it was quicker just to look for the nearest one. Tonight, the hydrant location book could prove invaluable.

The house on fire was number sixty, and according to the book, the nearest hydrant was outside of number eighty, so armed with my spade, I set off. There was more urgency to my task now, for I had seen that a second hose reel was now leading off into the burning house. The blizzard was still raging, and at 15 yards down the road, I had lost sight of the fire engines, even though all their lights were blazing. At 20 yards, I could just hear the high-pitched whine of the hose reel pump, and at 30 yards, I could hear nothing, absolute silence. With the snow coming down horizontally, blown furiously by the wind, I could equally as well have been at the North Pole.

To find the house numbers, I had to open the garden gates, walk up the paths and then shine my torch onto the house doors from only feet away. Finally, after trying many houses, I found house number eighty. I then looked for the yellow and black hydrant tablet, which would not only tell me the size of the water main, but more importantly, how far from the tablet the hydrant was located. But the tablet was either missing, or I just couldn't see it in the blizzard conditions. I made my way to the pavement outside the house and started searching for the hydrant. It was impossible to shovel the snow in these conditions. So I crashed my spade down onto the pavement, listening for the hollow or metallic ring of the metal hydrant cover, but all to no avail.

Whilst I was doing this, a figure approached me from the opposite direction of the fire, appearing dramatically from nowhere out of the swirling blizzard. Then very casually said to me, "You haven't by chance seen a fire anywhere down this street, have you, mate?" The figure was a fireman from Kentish Town fire station, riding the third appliance on the call. Our meeting under these conditions was so bizarre, that I would not have been at all surprised if he had removed his helmet, shaken me by the hand, and said, "Scott of the Antarctic I presume." The Kentish Town firemen like ourselves had sent scouts forward to look for the fire.

"This is your lucky day," I replied, "there just happens to be a fire not 30 yards down the road, and if you hurry, you might be in time to get warm before they put it out."

After much searching, I had been unable to locate the hydrant, and had made my way back to the appliances, firstly to tell Buck the pump operator of the problem and then re-consult the hydrant book. When I got back, I saw that Buck having used up the 100 gallons of water carried on his machine, had run a length of hose from the pump escape to the pump and was now using the water from that machine to pump onto the fire. I told him of my hydrant problems, and he replied, "Hold on for now. The lads seem to think they have stopped the fire, and with the water I have still got left and the 100 gallons from Kentish Town's machine, we should be able to manage."

Very shortly, the breathing apparatus wearers came out of the building, their bodies steaming in the cold air, and announced that the fire was all out, just a little damping down and cutting away to be done. We transferred the 100 gallons of water off Kentish Town's fire engine and let them get back to their station. I then started to make up the large diameter hose that had been used to transfer the water between the fire engines. Under these conditions as I rolled up the length of hose, it began to gather up snow along its length. Rather like a snowball does when rolled in the snow, so that when I came to put it back onto the fire engine, it was about four feet in diameter, and I had to get Buck to give me a hand to lift it up into the rear cab, for it would not fit back into its own locker.

As we drove back to the fire station, the blizzard was still howling and we were once again driving through virgin snow. Our original wheel tracks having been completely obliterated by the swirling, drifting snow. We reversed back into the nice warm fire station, and for the first time ever, I was envious of the dutyman, who had remained behind snug and warm.

The big appliance room doors swung closed, and the firemen began to disperse. The mess manager went to the kitchen to get a nice hot brew of tea going. The three breathing apparatus wearers with their sets draped over their arms, disappeared down to the basement to service and re-charge their sets. The officers, clutching their little pieces of paper, went off up to the office to complete the fire reports. Buck and I went once more out into the blizzard through the rear door of the appliance room. Here we had to dig out the fire hydrant in the station yard, connect up a large length of hose, and replenish the 100-gallon tanks on the two fire engines before they could be put back on the run for further fire calls. Then at last to sit in the messroom drinking scalding hot cups of tea.

Over the hot cups of tea, I told the other firemen that that night, one of life's little mysteries had been explained to me. In the past when I had seen pictures of American firemen in action, and seen their street pillar hydrants, I had thought to myself, why do they have hydrants like that, in such exposed positions above the ground? So that motor vehicles could crash into them, vandals have access to abuse them. Why don't they do as we do in Great Britain, dig holes and put them in little boxes under the ground? After that night's little escapade, I now knew why.

*

Buck still never ceased to amuse me. Over the past six weeks whilst we had been playing volleyball, a small boy of around two years of age had appeared on a third-floor balcony overlooking the drill yard. He was the small son of one of the tenants living in the accommodation above the fire station. These tenants were serving London firemen, but stationed at different fire stations throughout the Brigade. It seemed that every time we played volleyball, the small boy appeared on the balcony, and shouted down to the firemen, "Hello." When we called back hello to him, he repeated the call hello back to us, and all through the games of volleyball, there was this cry of "hello" ringing from the heavens. It was obvious that this was the only word he knew.

During the course of a volleyball game, Buck said, "Listen to him, just like a bloody parrot," whereupon, a huge grin came across his face. "I'll teach him some new words," he said. From that moment on, whenever the young boy called out "hello", Buck would repeat back to him, "Pieces of eight," the famous cry of Long John Silver's parrot from Treasure Island. This went on for weeks, the little voice from above calling down, "Hello," followed by Buck's voice from below in a parrot-like screech, "Pieces of eight, pieces of eight." Buck was now waiting in eager anticipation of the day when the boy would repeat the words "pieces of eight" back to him. For the joke as Buck saw it, would be on the day his father returned home from duty, to be told by the mother, "Little Tommy has learnt some new words today." Then his father, no doubt expecting to hear that the new words were something like mummy or daddy, only to be told, no it's 'pieces of eight'. Such was Buck's sense of humour that he had spent something like six weeks patiently tutoring this little boy to say "pieces of eight", for a joke, the punch line of which when delivered he could never hope to see but could only imagine.

*

The harsh weather of the winter of 1962/63 lingered on with sub-zero temperatures, and the snow staying on the ground. The Brigade received a huge increase in calls to chimney fires as people burned their coal fires night and day to keep warm. The resulting smoke from the chimneys caused one of the last really bad, heavy fogs, or smog as they were then called, that London was to experience, lasting for many days.

We would proceed to emergency calls at a speed barely above walking pace, visibility was so bad. On one or two occasions, a fireman had to walk in front of the appliance with a lighted flare to disperse the fog, in able to proceed.

The chimney fires seemed endless, our hands and fingernails were black and ingrained with soot. On one Sunday day duty of nine hour's duration, we extinguished thirteen chimney fires, with just a crew of three on the pump, the officer in charge, the driver and one fireman.

Chimney fires were not popular with firemen; they involved a lot of hard, dirty work. They would be extinguished by one of two methods. Firstly, by pushing up the chimney on fire cane chimney rods with a hose attached, which then sprayed water onto the inside of the burning chimney flue to extinguish the fire.

This method was only really practicable for a chimney flue not exceeding two floors in height, because the combined weight of the hose and rods became too great. Also, the chimney rods seemed to have a mind of their own and would want to go anywhere but up the chimney. In the event of the chimney rods passing all the way up the flue to the chimney pot, there was always the danger that if the chimney pot was not firmly attached to the stack, the rods would dislodge it, and a hundred-and-fifty-pound weight of clay pot would come crashing to the ground, or worse still through the roof of the building.

With only a three-man crew, the preference was, wherever possible, to extinguish chimney fires from the stack down. On flat roofs, this was relatively easy, the two short six-foot length scaling ladders would be taken up to the roof in order to reach the top of the chimney stack. Then water from the main fire pump via the hose reel tubing poured down the chimney. On pitched roofs, the 35-foot extension ladder would be extended to the eaves of the roof, then a hook ladder used to gain access to the ridge of the roof. Then depending on the height of the chimney-stack, a scaling ladder perched precariously on the ridge of the roof and leant against the stack to reach the chimney pot, in order to pour the water down – not for the faint hearted this.

The fighting of chimney fires from the top down had its own inherent dangers, other than the fireman falling off of the combination of ladders in use. If great care was not taken, the water could go down the wrong chimney flue, and cause great damage as black, sooty water flooded out in a room or flat other than where the fire was. If the chimney were not obviously on fire, ie belching out flames and smoke, the fireman on the roof would first try shouting down the chimney flue to the firemen in the room below. If at all possible, contact between the two firemen would be established this way. Then a stone would be dropped down the chimney, to make absolutely sure it was the correct stack. Only then would water be directed down the chimney from the hose reel, in short ten or twenty second bursts. Again, with these short bursts, precautions were being taken. If the fireman on the roof was simply to keep pouring the water down the stack, and if despite precautions, it was the wrong flue, or as is found in older houses, many flues leading off of a common flue, it is not unknown for some room of the house remote from the fire to be inundated with black, sooty water.

On more than one occasion, despite the above precautions, I had found myself trying to hold back a flood of black sludge. Sludge that has emerged from down the correct chimney, but in such quantity as to be almost uncontainable with only chimney cloths and my bare arms.

The Brigade had had a busy month or so, snow, ice, fog, chimney fires, a big increase in building fires, all resulting from the extreme cold weather. Now to cap it all off multiple calls to floodings. As the general thaw set in, all those frozen and burst pipes began to thaw out. The whole Brigade was inundated with calls to flooded premises. The pumps and crews would be given a list of addresses up to ten on one call slip, and all flooded premises. On most of them, we could render little assistance, other than to turn off the water supply into the house, for there was insufficient depth of water for pumping. With the elderly or infirm, or mothers alone with young children, we would assist as much as we could with the mopping and clearing up. But the numbers of calls were such that we seldom spent more than half an hour or so at one address.

I remember it as a very cold, wet two weeks of my life. After just a couple of days, our leather fire boots became sodden with the wet. Nothing we could do would waterproof them, being continually in the water. All sorts of oil preparations were applied to them in order to make them waterproof, all to no avail. In the end, we took to wearing plastic bags over our socks inside the fire boots, which helped to some extent.

The calls would all be to flooded premises, but in fact, it was usually a burst pipe, very often in the roof space, that allowed water to flood and drain down through the whole house. There was little we could do to help people, other than to prevent further damage. If a ceiling were in danger of collapsing under the weight of water, we would pierce the ceiling with a ceiling hook to allow the water to run out, then catch the water in bowls. Whilst doing this on two occasions, I had a very unpleasant shock, quite literally. I was catching the water in a metal bowl; I had not noticed that the electric light bulb nearby was glowing very dimly. This, had I been more alert, should have been a warning sign. Suddenly, and totally unexpectedly, a powerful electric shock travelled down the column of trickling water and gave me one hell of a belt.

It was quite common for members of the public calling the Brigade in order to gain priority treatment, to exaggerate the amount of water involved. Saying at times, they had two or three feet of water in their premises. Always when we arrived, they would say we did have two or three feet of water when we called you, but that was an hour ago.

On one occasion when we were working on A5 Soho's fire ground assisting them with large numbers of flooded premises, we arrived at an address in Bloomsbury, which was a large, old, traditional type building converted into offices. We were met by the caretaker, who informed us that the basement boiler room had six feet of water in it. This chap was obviously going for the record, for nobody so far had claimed to have had more than three feet of water in their premises. He led us to the door to the basement, and said, "It's down there" and "There are no lights, because all the electric power to the building is off."

Roy Walker went through the door first, paused at the top of a short flight of steps and shone his torch down into the darkened room. He then said, "I can't see any water at all down here."

The caretaker said, "Surprise, surprise. Well, there was six feet of water when I called you."

I had followed Roy into the doorway, and looking down past a short flight of stairs, I could not see any water either. Although I was somewhat puzzled, as there was definitely something different about this room that I could not quite determine.

From the foot of the short flight of stairs, Roy started to make his way forward across the room. As he stepped forward, and around his third or fourth step from the foot of the stairs, he suddenly disappeared from sight with a loud splash. When I saw him once again, all I could see were his head and shoulders in the light of my torch. He was coughing and spluttering, and he seemed to be saying it is six foot deep. I helped him back onto the stairs, and once again, there was no sign of water. Once Roy had been safely rescued, we solved the mystery. The boiler was a coke-fuelled boiler, and the coke supplies were kept in the boiler room alongside the boiler. Coke being lighter than water will float upon the surface. Thus, when the water entered the basement, all the coke floated on the top, and formed a layer of around nine inches deep hiding the water from sight. In the dim light of a torch, it gave the appearance of being a solid floor, which Roy had duly stepped upon. Good church going Catholic, and ex matelot though he was, even Roy couldn't walk upon water, albeit topped with a layer of coke.

The caretaker was quite jubilant at Roy's misfortune, had he not told us, us the disbelievers, that there was six feet of water in the basement? He would nevertheless have to wait a while for it to be pumped out. First, we had to go back to the fire station to get Roy a complete change of clothes.

*

The Sunday cook at Camden Town was a tiny little lady called Bertha, she appeared on the station only on Sundays to cook the meals. She was quite a fiery little lady, and held her own, and stood no nonsense from the firemen.

One Sunday, when we returned from a fire call at around 12.30, or half an hour before dinner, I happened to venture into the kitchen. At first, I thought the kitchen was empty, but as I walked around the serving hatch, what I saw amazed me. Bertha was kneeling down on the kitchen floor, surrounded by plates, and in the centre of the plates was a big roasting dish filled with a large joint of meat and roast potatoes. Bertha was serving out the Sunday dinner on the floor of the kitchen! I quietly went back out of the kitchen and sought out the mess manager, Fred Viner. I said to him, "Fred, is Bertha all right, only she is dishing out the Sunday dinner on the kitchen floor?"

Fred never turned a hair, saying, "She always does that if I am out on a fire call. The roasting dish is too heavy for her to lift up onto the table; I always have to do that for her. So if I am not here to do it, she simply dishes out the dinner on the kitchen floor, then all she has to lift up is the individual dinner plates."

Breakfast on the fire stations was served at eight o'clock. They could be very quiet and subdued meals, or very lively, depending on the events of the previous night duty, or which firemen were on duty. They were invariably a full English breakfast. Fried egg, bacon or sausage, fried potatoes, fried bread, black sausage, baked beans, toast any combination of the former, all depending on the state of the mess funds.

I collected my breakfast from the mess manager and sat down at the mess table opposite Buck Ryan. The mood at the table this morning was quiet and subdued. I had been eating my breakfast for around five minutes, and I turned around briefly to speak to Fred Viner, the mess manager, behind me. I turned back to resume eating, but something puzzled me. I thought I still had a sausage on my plate, but now I hadn't. I searched my brain but I couldn't remember eating it. I looked around the faces at the table but they were all intent on quietly eating, I was damn sure I had a sausage left on my plate, but where was it now?

It was not so much that I was hungry, just that it was rather worrying when sausages disappeared off one's plate, never to be seen again.

I decided to confront them. I cleared my throat and said, "Did somebody just take a sausage off of my plate?"

The effect of my quietly spoken words was startling, almost as if I had been having breakfast at the Ritz, and then enquired, "Has somebody farted?" All conversation ceased, all eyes were upon me, movement was frozen, knives and forks paused in mid movement. Who was this young whippersnapper, accusing them, the senior firemen, of stealing his breakfast?

I lost my nerve and began to stammer out an excuse, "I'm sorry but I thought I had a sausage on my plate, and it suddenly disappeared."

"What, like this?" said Buck, as he speared a sausage from his plate with his fork, placing the whole sausage into his mouth, he slowly and methodically chewed it.

All the firemen now watched Buck, as he slowly munched and then swallowed the sausage. Buck leaned over the table towards me and said, "Let that be a lesson to you, young Wilson."

I was puzzled. "Let what be a lesson?" I repeated.

Buck quietly and slowly said, "When you eat with pigs, never ever take your nose out of the trough." I was not quite sure what the moral of Buck's story was, but I now felt totally convinced that that was my sausage I had just watched Buck eat.

Buck had his very own sense of humour and would bring it into play at the most unexpected moments. His humour was such that if you did not know the man, you would think he was deadly serious. His face would always remain deadpan, and sometimes even if you did know the man, you could not be entirely sure if he was joking or not.

Again, it was at breakfast one morning, whilst there was a lull in the conversation, Buck said in a loud, clear, stern voice. "Mess manager, why has this man got two eggs on his plate, and I only have one? Does the man pay more mess money than me?" Whilst he was saying this, he was pointing his knife, indicating his best mate Roy Walker sitting opposite him at the mess table.

Once again, this stopped all conversation at the table, and all eyes were now fixed first on Buck, then Roy Walker. The mess manager called out from the kitchen, "It's Friday, Buck, that's why Roy has two eggs."

"I know it's Friday, mess manager, it's Friday for me too, and I have only got one egg." The mess manager now appeared at the kitchen opening and said, "Buck, you know that Roy is a Roman Catholic and can't eat bacon on a Friday, so I give him two eggs instead of bacon."

Buck was now getting into his stride. "So if I want two eggs on a Friday, I've got to become a Roman Catholic, have I?" He then queried to Roy Walker, "What do I have to do to become a Catholic then Roy, fill in an application form and post it off to the Pope? Dear Pope, I would like to become a Catholic, so that I can have two eggs with my breakfast on Friday." Buck was now in full flow, "What about the poor old Jews, they can't eat bacon any day of the week, do they get two eggs every day for their breakfast? I would be quite prepared to convert to Judaism, if it meant two eggs every day for my breakfast." Then adding as an afterthought, "On the other hand, I don't think I could stand the pain of having my foreskin cut off."

Roy Walker was becoming frustrated and embarrassed, he had not asked for two eggs instead of bacon, that was just the mess manager's sense of fair play. He picked up his one remaining fried egg with his knife and fork, and placed it on Buck's plate, as he did so, saying to Buck, "Right, now you have got two fried eggs, now shut up."

For a while, there was silence at the mess table, as Buck ate Roy's egg. Soon Buck's voice was heard again, "You know what, Roy, your mate the Pope carries a lot of weight, doesn't he? Even the guvnors don't get two fried eggs with his breakfast."

*

My becoming a Brigade driver was now to be my undoing, for there were now five appliance drivers on the watch. Over at the other side of London, at Brompton fire station, there were only two drivers for two appliances, which was deemed an unacceptably low level. I was to be transferred to Brompton, partly because I was the junior driver, and partly because I lived at Fulham, a few miles down the road from Brompton.

When I had first been posted to Camden, I was not too pleased; it was a quiet station, miles from my home. But over the past two years, I had become a reasonably proficient fireman, qualified as a Brigade driver, and was now qualified to wear proto breathing apparatus. Also, my whole social life was now very much involved with the Camden firemen. Buck had found me a part time job, shifting stage scenery at the Palace theatre, Cambridge Circus. I badly needed the money to join Buck and the others in our main hobby, drinking beer.

The transfer would mean that I would lose my friends, for the posting was on the red watch at Brompton, so that when I was off duty, the blue watch would be working. So it was with a very sad heart that I bade A3 Camden Town goodbye.

Chapter 5

A8 Brompton Fire Station – 1963

Brompton fire station in 1963 was probably confusingly named, for Brompton was a small district in the then London borough of Chelsea. Whilst the station's fire ground covered basically the whole area of the borough of Chelsea, the station was situated in a leafy square, in a very affluent area between the Old Brompton Road and the Kings Road area of Chelsea.

The station was a very small and pretty fire station, obviously designed to blend in with its very salubrious surroundings. The station had two appliance bays and residential accommodation above for the firemen. The two appliance bays were such that only the smallest fire engines then in service with the London Fire Brigade would fit into the appliance bays, mainly because of the headroom in the appliance door openings. So the two fire engines stationed there were the immediate post war machines, the Dennis F11 petrol machines.

You had to get used to the gearbox of these fire engines, they were of the old-fashioned crash gearbox type. They needed careful selection of engine revs, and double declutching to operate them and change gear. The powerful Rolls-Royce petrol engines powered them around the fire ground like racing cars.

Brompton had what also must have been the smallest drill yard in the London Fire Brigade, about four metres by five metres square, there was only room for one car in it on night duties (the station officer's of course). Only Cannon Street fire station in the city of London could challenge this, because they had no drill yard at all, but their huge appliance room more than compensated for this.

Brompton was not a popular choice of postings for firemen, because of the restrictions of the station accommodation. Also, the fact that the station's fire call numbers were considered to be fairly low. Nevertheless, there were a number of high and interesting fire risks on the ground. The Natural History and Victoria and Albert museums, the Duke of York's barracks and the Royal Hospital, (where the Chelsea Pensioners lived). Three large hospitals, and a very large power station at Lots Road, Chelsea, being some.

The red watch to which I was posted comprised a split watch, junior firemen with less than two years' service, and senior firemen with a least ten years' service, with the senior firemen tending to bully or at least dominate the younger firemen. My two and a half years' service with time spent at a different (and happier) fire station, and being a motor driver to boot, placed me midway in the pecking order of the watch and I feel in retrospect this helped to blend the two factions together.

Within the first week at the station, I had taken over the vacant position of nuttyboat, or canteen manager, an unpaid and largely unthanked job. At Brompton, the nuttyboat or canteen consisted of a cupboard under the stairs which sold such items as bars of chocolate, crisps, razor blades and packets of three (condoms). Purely as a matter of convenience to the firemen who could not leave the fire station if they needed these items. This of course did not apply to the condoms, they were stocked because in the days of retail price maintenance, they could be sold at half the shop price, and a small profit still be made. The other quite important item that the canteen sold was beer, and the stock was confined to about a dozen crates of strong light ale, called John Courage, normally referred to by the firemen as JCs.

I took the canteen manager's job quite seriously, and over the next few weeks, I increased the number and variety of items for sale. I was subsequently quite pleased with myself when overall sales began to gradually increase.

Then came the first Sunday day duty with the watch. In 1963, only essential work and of course fire calls were carried out on the fire stations on Sundays. So barring any of the preceding, the day was spent in relaxation, playing volleyball, etc.

In most stations that had a wet canteen, ie sold beer, the firemen so inclined would adjourn to the canteen and partake of a few bottles of beer, and so at Brompton, it was my duty to serve them. The bar (the cupboard under the stairs where the beer was kept) was situated in the basement, so the firemen would purchase their bottles of beer and usually adjourn to the nearby table tennis room to drink them.

Trade before lunch was quite brisk, I had sold about two crates of beer, when, according to the canteen records, normally about one dozen half pint bottles of beer would have been sold. I was feeling quite pleased with myself.

Lunch proved a very jolly affair – most of the firemen had brought a bottle or two to wash down their lunch. One particular senior fireman, normally of a taciturn nature, was on great form, keeping the watch in constant laughter with his humorous remarks and funny stories. On this particular day, I also had to carry out the duties of mess assistant, which basically meant that I had to do the washing up and tidy the mess following the meal. This entailed about 45 minutes work after the meal had finished, and surprisingly firemen kept popping into the messroom to see how the work was progressing. Eventually, when the work was finished, a senior fireman informed me that my presence was once again required at the nuttyboat to serve.

I went back down to the basement where now only the senior firemen were gathered, opened the cupboard under the stairs and sold more beer. It just proved that a willing and helpful canteen manager really could do wonders for sales. After about another three visits to the basement canteen to sell more beer, I was beginning to smell a rat. Things were getting a bit out of hand down there, one particular fireman, the senior taciturn fireman who had entertained us so much at lunch, was now roaring drunk and was fast entering the belligerent stage of drunkenness. This rather surprised me, because this particular man had visited the canteen only once to purchase two bottles of JC, which had apparently had this violent effect on him.

The sub officer who was in charge of the station that day, (the station officer being on leave) eventually heard the commotion in the basement. The sub officer was around 45 years of age and had served many years in the merchant navy before joining the Fire Brigade. He was thus a man of the world. He took one look at the drunken, belligerent fireman, turned to me and demanded, "What the bloody hell did you sell him all that beer for, you know he's not supposed to have more than two bottles?"

This was news to me, nobody had told me that fireman Slocombe, for that was his name, was allowed to purchase two bottles of beer only, and under no circumstances anymore.

Fireman Slocombe had in fact only purchased two bottles of beer off of me, but it was pretty obvious his mates, the other senior firemen, had been busy purchasing on his behalf. For during the course of the day, we had gone through four cases of JC, and judging by the way Slocombe was now performing, I reckoned he must have drunk at least two of them.

The sub officer as I have said was a man of the world, and fortunately, we had more than enough riders to man the two fire engines. So with the grimmest of threats, he told fireman Slocombe that he was off the run, and that he was to go and get his head down. Adding threateningly that if he saw his face or heard his voice just one more time before six o'clock, that this time it would mean the sack. From that last remark, I deduced that there had obviously been plenty of other times that Slocombe had over imbibed on duty.

The younger firemen were no doubt muttering old Slocombe has got away with it again. For I was later to find out that most of the senior firemen and officers serving with the Brigade at that time had either served through the London blitz with the Brigade or had been in the armed forces for the duration of the war and tended wherever possible to cover one another's backs.

Chester Slocombe, for that was his full name, had joined the Royal Navy just prior to the war. His regulation tot of rum each day was the beginning of his habit. For Chester was a controlled alcoholic, if there is such a thing. He did not drink immediately prior to coming on duty, and did not drink on duty, with the exception of his two half pints of JC with his Sunday lunch. He had a wife and I believe four young children, plus a bad habit to support. The combination of these cost him a lot of money, which he did not have, certainly not working for the Fire Brigade. Which meant that any time that he was not at home or in the pub, he was busy working to pay for them, with many and various part time jobs.

It was about a year later that I found out something else about him. He was off duty that day and had appeared at the fire station in the late afternoon. I don't know what he had been drinking that day for this time he was not drunk, but nevertheless well under the influence, he was all smiles and in a good mood. He had called at the station to collect something from his locker, and another fireman and myself happened to be there in the locker room at the time. He delved in his locker and called me and the other firemen over, saying to us, "What do you think of these then?" Showing us a medal bar with six medals and ribbons on it. "One for each bloody year," he snarled, meaning I thought that he had served six years in the Royal Navy. Then he started giggling and said, "Could have been worse, could have been one for each bloody ship, but then I would have only got four medals."

Thinking to humour him, I said, "What, you served on four ships then, Chester?"

He then laughed out loud and replied, "No, I served on at least six ships. I was talking about the buggers that got torpedoed from underneath me." He then dug deeper into his locker and showed us a pile of newspaper cuttings, some with a picture of a very fit, good-looking sailor on them. Some showing him dressed in boxing shorts and gloves, he had indeed been a useful man in the boxing ring in his day. From that time on, I began to see Chester in a different light, later I confirmed most of the above with the senior firemen who of course had known it all along.

Some months after the above drunkenness incident, and again on a Sunday day duty, Chester had collected and paid for his two bottles of JC at around twelve o'clock. I was up on the first floor messroom at around 12.45 awaiting lunch, and idly looking out of the window which overlooked the tiny drill yard and the mews which gave access to the rear of the fire station.

There standing by the rear gates nonchalantly lounging around was Chester Slocombe. Chester did not normally nonchalantly lounge around out in the cold without good reason, so I decided to observe.

After five minutes or so, a gentleman strolled down the mews. He was dressed in what might be described as city gentleman's attire – black coat, pinstriped trousers, briefcase and rolled umbrella, and a bowler hat upon his head.

Chester waited until the man drew level with him, then raised his hand and touched his forelock, in true peasant style. Then he began to speak to the gentleman and judging by the look on the man's face whatever Chester was saying to him was outside his normal range of experiences, for he now was looking totally bemused and nodding his head. Chester then reached down behind the gate pillar and produced one of the old-fashioned quart size, screw top beer bottles, which he then handed to the gentleman.

The penny dropped; Chester was busy obtaining further supplies of beer. He was sending this magnificently dressed gentleman down to the jug and bottle bar at the pub at the end of the mews. There to get his quart size beer bottle filled with beer from the pumps, an activity not normally associated with immaculately dressed city gentlemen. I could only think that Chester must have told him an extraordinarily good tale, or that the city gent had already had a few bevies himself. For when he returned and handed over the now full beer bottle, he apparently gave Chester back his money as well as the filled bottle.

Chester had one or two other little fiddles, which over a period of time I found out about. He used to purchase an amazing amount of packets of three (condoms) from the canteen. Which suggested an extraordinarily active sex life, until I was told that he used to sell them at a profit to the men at his part time job.

The canteen also used to sell the unlabelled products of the Heinz Company, baked beans, soups etc. Normally seconds or end of production runs, these were very good value for money, being a fraction of the shop price. Although occasionally, a tin of baked beans would be opened and found to contain only tomato sauce and bean husks, but for the price they sold at considered well worth the risk.

It was strongly rumoured that the Slocombe family existed on a diet consisting entirely of Heinz products. Usually on paydays, fireman Slocombe would come down to the canteen with his fire service issue kitbag. He would then purchase enough tins of beans etc., to feed his family for a month, invariably filling up the kitbag with tins. He could have simply purchased the tins in the brown cardboard boxes they were delivered in. Since his method of travel to and from duty was by bicycle, he had discovered that the full kitbag sat easily on the crossbar of his cycle. Thus, he could transport a far greater number of tins by this method. Not even the Slocombe family of six could possibly eat a kit bag full of baked beans in one week. So Chester was obviously buying them in bulk for re-sale at a profit.

There is no doubt though that they did consume a large amount of these products. For a fireman enquiring of Chester as to the merits of a Heinz product called 'Sausages and Beans' was duly informed without hesitation that they were okay, but that the sausages were only this big, indicating the size with his fingers to about one inch long, adding that you only got eight in a tin and that it took four tins to make a meal for all of his family.

Chester had another little wheeze that it took me a while to discover exactly what it was. Chester would arrive for duty carrying perhaps his empty folded up kitbag, but no other baggage. Occasionally, and mainly during the winter months, he would leave the station at the end of the shift with a bulging kitbag perched on the crossbar of his cycle. I knew it was not tins of baked beans because I hadn't sold him any. Also, tins made distinct bulges in the side of his kitbag which were easily recognisable, also a full kitbag of tins was a very heavy load. Whatever it was in his bag was fairly light in weight, uniform in size, for it filled his kitbag without large bumps protruding. There must also be a pretty adequate supply of it somewhere on the station, for at times he would carry away as many as two bags a week.

I was puzzled but knew better that to ask him directly. When I enquired of the other senior firemen did they know what was in Chester's kitbag on these occasions, they professed total ignorance of the matter. I then asked the most junior fireman on the watch, "Tell me, what does Chester take home in his kitbag at the end of the shifts?"

He looked at me in surprise and said, "What? Don't you know? Everybody knows what he's up to, he's nicking the coke from the boiler room down in the basement!"

So all was revealed, he was merely stealing the station boiler fuel. The firemen all apparently knew of this and turned a blind eye to it. If Chester himself wanted to keep warm, he'd take a little less water with his rum. The coke was to provide a fire to keep his kids warm at home, there invariably being no money available to buy such luxuries in the Slocombe household. But I had been almost correct in my guess of the contents of his bag. For coke was light in weight, and uniform in size, and abundant in supply, for the London Fire Brigade had it delivered by the lorry load to feed the station's heating and hot water boilers.

*

One of the first things that I had done on my arrival at Brompton was to road test and familiarise myself with the Dennis F11 petrol fire engines stationed there. I had driven this type of machine during my driving course, but ever since had been driving various types and makes of diesel-engined fire appliances.

After half an hour or so driving around the station's fire ground, I had re-mastered the art of changing gear without the horrible clanging of gears so easy for the inexperienced driver to do on these quite difficult gearboxes.

On the next day duty, I was down to drive the pump escape to fires for the first time. I carried out the routine checks on the machine at 9 am on the change of watch, but it was not until about 11.30 am that the first fire call came in.

The bells went down and I jumped up into the driving seat of the pump escape, the dutyman came out with the call slip, and shouted out the address of the fire.

The call was to neighbouring Battersea fire station's fire ground as take machine. The appliance room doors opened and I drove out of the station.

After making the right hand turn out of the station, I attempted to change into second gear. The gear lever first of all refused to come out of first gear, and then for a while would not go into second gear. All this being accompanied by a horrendous clashing and ringing noise from the gearbox. I found this a bit embarrassing and disconcerting on my very first fire drive at Brompton.

The venerable sub officer sitting alongside me in the number one seat was visibly not impressed either. I kept the fire engine roaring along in second gear for a time, whilst I plucked up courage to try for the change to third gear. This time, the gear stick totally refused to come out of second gear. Even after several tries, it was still stuck solid.

By this time, we had arrived at a T-junction in the road, and turned right into the busy Kings Road. I kept the engine revolutions down a bit and tried for third gear once again. This time, it came out of second gear easy enough, but totally and absolutely refused to go into third gear. Each time I pushed the gear lever forward, it gave a loud ringing noise like the ringing of a giant bench saw. Thus, we proceeded down the busy and fashionable Kings Road, slipping into second gear occasionally to gain a bit of momentum, and then grinding and crunching away at the old third gear without success.

The venerable sub officer had by now given up ringing the appliance fire bell, whether out of sheer embarrassment, or the fact that I was making more noise with the gearbox than he with the bell I know not. Whether he did or not was academic, because from the position he had now adopted, lying almost flat in his seat, out of site of the public, he would not have been able to reach the hand bell, which was mounted on the cab roof, even if he had wanted to do so.

We turned left at a set of traffic lights heading towards the River Thames and Battersea. With the road speed and engine revolutions very low, I tried one more time for third gear. Then with a little clanging of gears only, she went into third gear. What a relief! In third gear, we should be able to get up to thirty miles per hour and at least arrive at the fire.

Ahead of me at about 400 yards distance, I could see one more major hazard to be surmounted. The busy Thames Embankment traffic crossed over the road we were travelling along. I could see the three lanes of traffic in each direction, thundering across the junction in the distance ahead of me. Having got into third gear only with great difficulty, I most certainly did not want to have to come out of it again. So I was planning my approach to the junction with this object in mind, to arrive at the traffic lights when they were green, and thus in my favour.

This of course is easier said than done, for at any busy road junction, there will be cars turning left and right and partially blocking the junction. This was inevitably what occurred. Not daring to drop below ten miles per hour, the stalling speed in third gear, and with the lights in my favour, the traffic in front of me snarled up. The only clear route through the junction was onto the offside of the road against the oncoming traffic flow. Then back onto the nearside again, threading my way through the traffic in doing so. All to be achieved with a minimum speed of not less than ten miles per hour lest I stalled the engine.

The comparative calm of the last twenty seconds or so had meant that the sub officer had just regained the seated upright position. As we entered into the first bend of the Embankment chicane, with the traffic scurrying in all directions around us, his sudden furious burst of renewed frantic bell ringing didn't help matters at all. Merely serving to confuse the poor motorists who were now busily engaged looking all around them, wondering no doubt where the devil did that fire engine come from, instead of proceeding forward out of my way.

We made it through the junction without mishap, more by good luck than judgement, leaving the tangled-up motorists behind us to sort themselves out in their own good time.

Then up and over the brow of Battersea Bridge, and we could see Battersea's two machines pulled up at the side of the road, we had arrived. The sub officer dismounted from the machine and slammed the door behind him without comment and stalked off to find the officer in charge of the incident.

All on my own in the cab, I tried to find out why the road gears would not engage properly and cleanly. The vehicle's clutch certainly seemed to be okay. Whilst the vehicle was stationary, it was possible to engage all four road gears. It appeared that only while the vehicle was moving did the trouble arise.

Then I spotted the problem, the power take-off that engaged the fire pump to enable it to work off the appliance road engine was in the operating position. In theory, it is almost impossible to change gear with the power take off engaged. Although I should have spotted the power take off was engaged as soon as I moved off on the call, because I was driving a new, or unfamiliar, fire engine I did not do so. But despite all the upsets, what pleased me was that even with the power take off engaged, I had still managed to engage not only second, but third gear also, quite a considerable achievement, of which I was quite proud.

It was this that was on my mind when the sub officer returned. I said to him, "Do you know what I have just done, Sub?"

To which he immediately replied, "Yes you have just knocked ten years off of my life, and if I'm not wrong, just about every tooth off every cog, off every gear, in that bloody fire engine."

I tried to explain to him about the power take off being engaged, and how difficult it was to engage even second gear with it so engaged, yet I had still managed to obtain third gear, but he was obviously in no mood for a discussion on technical matters, so I let it pass.

I did learn from this incident, and in the future never drove more than a few yards with the power take off engaged, without recognising the fact immediately. In future years whilst riding as officer in charge of appliances in the nearside front seat, I would invariably know before even the driver of the appliance knew, that the power take off was engaged. I have startled many a driver by informing him before we had even left the appliance room that his PTO was engaged, so fully did I learn my lesson.

It was 9.00 am on a fine Friday morning in spring; we were on day duties and had just completed roll call. We were now busy carrying out routine checks on the appliances and equipment, and I was driving the pump that day. In the back cab of the pump hanging up on racks would normally be carried three proto-oxygen breathing apparatus sets, one of which would normally be allocated to me.

*

Today, one of the sets was defective and awaiting spare parts. The two remaining sets were allocated to the two firemen riding in the back of the machine, both of them being senior and experienced firemen.

At around twelve o'clock, the bells went down and a call came in, the crews jumped onto the fire engines and started the motors. The dutyman came out with the call slips, shouting so that all the crews could hear, "Man collapsed in tank, Kings Road, Brompton's ground." The attendance for this type of incident would be two fire engines, plus one ambulance.

When we arrived at the address given on the call slip, it was a dry-cleaning shop in the middle of a row of shops at the Fulham end of the Kings Road. The two fire engines swung across the road to park outside the dry cleaners, facing the oncoming traffic. There was no sign of the person who had made the call, so the two crews nonchalantly dismounted and made their way into the dry cleaners. I jumped down to the pavement from the driving cab to finish rigging into my fire gear.

After around half a minute had passed, two firemen came dashing out of the shop, jumped up into the back of the pump, then disappeared back into the shop carrying with them the two oxygen breathing sets.

I had begun to think that the call might be a false alarm, and so had not bothered to go into the shop. A further twenty seconds went by and two more firemen dashed out to collect the breaking in gear, and hearth kit.

The hearth kit was a box containing general purpose building tools, hammers screw drivers wood chisels, cold chisels etc., which was stowed in the rear appliance lockers, telling me as they did so that they needed them to cut through a flat roof at the rear of the building.

It was all beginning to look quite interesting, and I was thinking it was about time I went in to have a look at what was going on inside.

Just then, the station officer came out and dictated an informative message for me to send to control over the radio as follows: "Workman collapsed inside metal tank at rear of dry cleaners, efforts being made to release." By the time I had sent this message, a further five minutes had gone by, and I was beginning to think I would have missed all the excitement.

I made my way into the shop, primarily to tell the station officer that his message had been sent. I passed through the front public part of the shop and into a room at the rear. This room was almost completely filled with a large square metal tank around ten feet by eight feet, and about seven feet in height, leaving a gap of around one foot between the top of the tank and the ceiling of the room.

As I entered the room, squeezing out of the gap between the tank and the ceiling was a fireman wearing breathing apparatus. I had obviously missed all the excitement; the breathing apparatus firemen were coming out. The fireman squeezed through the gap and tumbled to the floor and remained there in a heap.

It must have been pretty exhausting work in that tank, so I helped him off with his breathing apparatus. Saying nothing to me, he rose unsteadily to his feet and stumbled off out of the shop. That left one BA man still remaining in the tank, so I thought I would have a look and see if he required any assistance getting out of the tank.

I climbed the short ladder placed against the side of the tank and peered over between the top of the metal sides and the ceiling. As I did so, I became fully aware of loud banging noises above my head and saw that parts of the ceiling were beginning to fall downwards into the tank. I looked down into the gloom, and what I saw shocked me, there was the workman still lying unconscious on the floor and the other BA man was sitting cross legged unconcernedly beside him.

I called down to the fireman, "Ernie, are you okay?" He looked up at me and gave what I can only describe as a drunken, stupid smile, then raised his thumb in the air to signal that in his opinion he was okay, although it was pretty obvious to me that he was not.

As he had raised his head, I had seen immediately what the problem was, his nose clip to the breathing set was hanging down loose, and not firmly clipping his nostrils closed. Whatever it was that had rendered the workman unconscious, was slowly and surely having the same effect on him.

I jumped down from the ladder, and picked up the one remaining breathing set, the one the other fireman had discarded. Quickly checking the cylinder contents gauge, I saw that there was still a thirty-minute supply in the cylinder. I quickly threw the set over my shoulders and buckled it up, putting in the mouthpiece and the nose clip.

I was up the ladder and over the side into the tank, but not quite sure what I was going to do. It was difficult enough for a fully conscious man to squeeze between the gap between the top of the tank and the ceiling, let alone an unconscious one.

I dropped down into the tank and placed Ernie's nose clip back onto his nose, but the damage had been done. The noxious gases were now circulating inside his closed-circuit breathing set. I was aware of voices calling me from above. Looking up, I could see a hole in the ceiling and flat roof and faces peering down at me. The other firemen had managed to cut a hole in the roof about a foot square and were calling down to me. "Try to get Ernie to stand up, Dave, and we will try to grab him through the roof."

A simple request to Ernie to stand up was useless. He apparently thought the whole situation was one great big joke and hilarious. Shouting loudly and bad temperedly at him with much swearing and bad language finally did the trick. He stood unsteadily upright, although I think the only reason, he did so was to fight with me for being bad tempered and swearing at him.

Two strong arms appeared through the hole in the ceiling and grabbed hold of the two shoulder straps of his breathing set. Ernie rose gently up into the air towards the hole in the ceiling. His head and shoulders disappeared through the hole, then he snagged. The oxygen cylinder to his breathing set, sitting in the middle of his back, would not pass through the opening. I got my shoulders underneath his bottom and desperately pushed. For in my mind, he was blocking the only way out of this mess. Then above me, more desperate crashing of hammers and tools, the hole in the ceiling was being enlarged.

After what seemed like ages, Ernie's bottom and legs rose up and out of sight. Above me was a patch of daylight, framing the faces of the other firemen.

Now for the unconscious workman. I could not honestly remember how this man came to leave the tank. He wasn't a terribly big man, but I would have thought far too big for me to handle on my own, in his unconscious state. I know for sure that nobody came into the tank to assist me. I think his rescue must have been achieved by me lifting him semi-upright, and other firemen assisting via the gap at the top of the tank, he then finally being lifted clear through the hole in the ceiling. The firemen on the roof may even have dropped a line down, which I would have tied to him. The strange thing is that I have no recollection at all of him leaving the tank. Just of being very, very relieved that he had gone, so that I could now get out of the tank myself.

By now, I was feeling quite drowsy and lethargic, which I was assuming was exhaustion, due to physical exertion. So when the big strong arms appeared through the hole in the ceiling, grabbed hold of the shoulder straps to my breathing set, then plucked me out into the fresh air like a cork from a bottle, I was a happy, very relieved man.

I made my way back out to the street, threw my breathing apparatus set into the back of the appliance and then sat in the driver's seat to recover. I was told that both the workman and the other two firemen had been removed to hospital by ambulance suffering from the effects of the fumes. Strangely, I was not concerned at all with this. I just wanted to get back to the station and a nice, hot cup of tea.

When all the gear at the incident was made up and stowed back on board the machines, I clambered up into the driving seat and drove back to the fire station. There I did what I had done a thousand times before. I pulled out across the road in the usual manner, in order to reverse back into the appliance room. I reversed back towards the appliance room doors and misjudged by a mile. I pulled forward, and reversed back, yet again I misjudged by a mile. As I was attempting my fourth try at reversing, the other driver who had been watching came across to me saying, "What's up with you, Dave, you drunk or something?" He then suddenly exclaimed, "Christ! Your eyes, they're like piss holes in the snow, are you okay?"

This remark for some reason greatly amused me, and I started giggling out loud. For in my mind, I was actually trying to picture piss holes in the snow. Little black holes in the glistening white snow, tinged around with yellow urine stains. Now why should my eyes look like that? I giggled to myself. Then suddenly, the other driver was being quite gentle but very firm saying, "All right, Dave, you get down from the cab, I'll reverse the machine back in for you."

In a very short time, a third fireman was being ferried off down the road to St Stephens Hospital, suffering from fume inhalation myself. In the hospital, I met up with the other two firemen, who had already seen the doctor. They had been informed by him that if we had survived thus far, there was nothing to worry about. The fumes had been apparently petroleum based, and that we had all merely been as pissed as rats, (the doctor's words). The bad news was that we would in all probability suffer major hangovers. The workman however who had been in the tank for a much longer time, was in intensive care, and there were worries about him perhaps having brain damage. The workman subsequently made a full recovery and was discharged from hospital some days later.

The question that had been puzzling me was now answered by my questioning the other two firemen. Why was I, who had been wearing full breathing apparatus at all times, affected by the fumes?

When the first two firemen had entered the tank to effect the rescue, they were faced with a delay, as the other firemen were cutting through the flat roof. Strictly, against Brigade regulations, they had been removing the mouthpieces of their breathing sets and placing them in the workman's mouth to enable him to breathe fresh oxygen, at the same time holding their breaths to avoid breathing in the fumes in the tank. The two firemen had been doing this alternately.

This particular problem arose with the Siebe Gorman proto breathing set. In this type of set, the oxygen was trickled into the set and circulated around and around until it had all been absorbed by the body. The carbon dioxide in the exhaled breath being removed by special chemicals in the set. These chemicals only acted upon carbon dioxide and not petroleum vapours. As the collapsed workman exhaled into the mouthpiece, the petroleum fumes already in his lungs

84

entered the closed-circuit breathing set. They were in turn inhaled by the firemen when it was their turn to breathe. With both firemen gradually becoming befuddled, their safety procedures lapsed, and they began to inhale the fumes in the tank. Ernie, the fireman who had remained in the tank, had realised this, and replaced and clipped his mouthpiece back in his own mouth, but in his confused state had forgotten his nose clip. The second fireman realising that he was succumbing to the fumes had done the correct thing and got out.

Thus, unbeknown to me, the breathing set that I picked up from the floor and strapped on before I entered the tank was already contaminated with the petroleum fumes. These fumes had their slow but sure effect upon me, but in my case, I was totally unaware of it.

The above experience should really have been brought to the notice of the breathing apparatus training school, so that future firemen would not make the same mistake, for the practice of supplying oxygen to unconscious people this way was fairly common, especially at fires (although against laid down procedures).

Though the incident had ended successfully, the fact that three firemen were overcome by fumes was considered a bit of a professional cock-up, so no more was said about the matter.

There can be no doubt the two firemen's actions, even though they may have been at some risk themselves, saved the man's life. When the workman arrived at the hospital, he was in a critical condition. Had he not had those ten to fifteen minutes breathing pure oxygen in the tank awaiting rescue, he would have died, or at the very least been a cabbage for the rest of his life.

*

Drills and fitness training at Brompton fire station were a bit of a problem, having such a small drill yard. Neighbouring stations full sized drill yards could be used, but this would mean that for both Brompton's machines to drill together at a distant station, another appliance would be required at Brompton to cover the fire calls while we were away. All to be arranged days in advance, which of course for day-to-day routine training was too much of a chore. Of course, all this arranging was totally out of the question for our daily game of volleyball. So we made do with what we had, and perhaps had more testing drills for it.

To use the fifty-foot-wheeled escape in the yard entailed driving the appliance out of the front of the station into the street. There removing the escape ladder from the appliance, letting it right out in the carriage, then wheeling it through the appliance room into the tiny yard at the rear, winding the escape back up in the carriage so that it was upright again. Then finally extending up against the tower. If a fire call was received during the drill, the whole process had to be reversed in double quick time, to put the escape ladder back on the appliance.

Wet drills was the term used when firemen played with water and squirted real water through the fire hoses. This was achieved by again parking the fire engines out in the street, then coupling up to a fire hydrant about 30 yards away from the fire station. The hose then fed from the fire engine through the appliance room, up whichever ladder was in use, to be squirted from the upper floors of the tower.

The drills were of course carried out at speed, much to the delight of a sometimes-bemused public. "Excuse me, madam." As you dashed by laying out a length of hose. "Mind where you tread, sir." As the hydrant cover was removed, and the standpipe key and bar shipped. The local residents were quite accustomed to it and never gave a thought to our antics as they picked their way over the hoselines. Strangers were inclined to think that with all this dashing about and laying out of fire hoses in the street the fire station really was on fire.

Volleyball or fitness training was a different problem; we could hardly stretch a volleyball net across the road in front of the fire station and halt the traffic. So instead, we used to stretch the net across the narrow Dudmaston Mews, at the rear of the fire station. Then we would play our game of volleyball there, only occasionally having to stop the game and raise the bottom of the net to allow a car to pass by.

A ploy in this crude volleyball game was that the team who were in danger of losing a point when a car happened along would always try to stop the game to allow the car to pass, and perhaps save the point. Whilst of course, the opposing team would shout, "Play on, play on, let the bugger wait." Then when play did stop and the unsuspecting motorist made his way forward to pass under the net, he would be smiled at and given thumbs up by the team that had gained the advantage. Vilified and subjected to deep dark scowls and mutterings by the team that had lost the point or advantage. Most of the local residents, if at all possible, tended to avoid passing through the Mews at this time of the day.

Dudmaston Mews had a seamier side to its life. In the dark evenings, and some not so dark evenings, a business lady conducted her business there. Where her actual beat was, we had no idea, but Dudmaston Mews was where she actually did the business, as the saying goes. What's more, her favourite workstation was right outside the rear gates of the fire station. On boring nights when there were no fire calls, nothing good on the television, and we were fed up with card games or whatever, we would then look out of the rear station windows to see if the lady was working. She was always in the customer's own car, and usually viewed from the first-floor rear window. Quite frankly, other than the sight of an occasional white bottom, nothing much happened, other than in the fertile minds of bored firemen.

The first time that I was shown the performance taking place in the Mews, I was told very matter-of-factly by the fireman that when I got bored with watching, if I went downstairs and over to the outside toilet on the far side of the drill yard then listened through the open window, I would be able to hear the dialogue and sound effects as well.

On one particular dark and boring night, the firemen decided to liven up the proceedings by bringing up the searchlight from off of the appliance, then sticking it out of the window and shining it into the car where the lady was working. This we did, but with an entirely unexpected result. The lady calmly got out of the car, stood with her legs astride and her hands on her hips and shouted boldly up to the first-floor window, "I've told you bastards once before, if you want to watch, that's okay, but don't piss about, I've got my living to earn."

In reply, a voice rang out from the listening post in the outside toilet saying, "Sorry, darling, it won't happen again." This disembodied voice from nowhere caught the lady rather unawares, for she hadn't realised we listened to the proceedings as well. It appeared that the firemen on the other watches also suffered from boredom on nights and had thought of the searchlight gag first.

*

For a change, Brompton had been having quite a busy night, and we were only too pleased to get our heads down at around 1.30 in the morning. At around 2.00 am, the bells went down again, and the dutyman's voice was booming through the appliance room. "Running call," (meaning that the caller had run to the fire station and pressed the outside firebell), "to motor car on fire Old Church Street, Brompton's ground."

As the appliances turned out of the station, we could see the glow at the T-junction at the end of the road. As soon as we turned left, there was the motor car going from end to end. A hose reel jet was put to work with very little effect; a second hose reel was pulled off the machine and put to work.

The station officer, who was a bit terse because he had had a busy night and was losing out on his sleep, then shouted out, "Put a jet on the bloody thing, that will soon put it out." This in turn upset me, for I was the pump operator, and although it would only take one length of delivery hose to reach the motor car, the large quantities of water used would necessitate setting into the street mains, and the nearest fire hydrant was over a 150-yards or five or six-hose lengths away. All that hose to be laid out, made up, fresh hose put back on the appliance, wet hose hung up the tower, all at three o'clock in the morning and all for a piddling little motor car. If the guvnor was to hang on for another five minutes, the fire would have more or less burnt itself out, and we could have pissed on it and saved all that work. This was the considered if somewhat disgruntled opinion of the senior firemen and myself.

The jet was duly set to work, and it took about twenty seconds for the three-quarter inch nozzle to blast the fire out. Then to begin to fill the gutters awash with water. Out of sheer bloody mindedness, I had given them about 80lbs per square inch pressure at the nozzle, which rather tends to splash the water about and get everybody wet. Unfortunately, though, not the intended victim, the guvnor, he had somehow disappeared.

Somebody had been impressed with our efforts though, amongst the small crowd of onlookers was a very distinguished looking lady, the owner of the motor car. Apparently, we had been invited back into her house for drinks. I went to look for the station officer, for I was his driver and I wanted to know if he was going to accept the invitation or not. I knew already that he was going to accept, for I had seen the very distinguished lady who had invited us. Also, property in Old Church Street, Chelsea, cost an arm and a leg.

Our guvnor was a social climber, a snob and a newly made member of the funny handshake mob (the freemasons). The latter was proving a bit of a problem for him, primarily how could you impress people by being a member of a secret society, if nobody knows that you are in it? He overcame this by acquiring a special secret society signet ring, which had a flip over faceplate. One side being plain gold, the other side black enamel and embossed with a pair of gold tweezers, the masonic sign. He would constantly play with this ring in the mess and the station office, flipping the faceplate over and over, inviting questions as to what it was. He also was being constantly thwarted by the watch members, telling standby firemen and all strangers to the watch on no account to ask him this longed-for question. His wife had a prosperous hairdressing business, and he went everywhere, the Hilton Hotel apparently being his favourite. He spoke to everyone important. "I was just saying to Norman Wisdom last night" were some of his name-droppings in the messroom.

I asked the other driver where the guvnor was. "He's gone back to the fire station," he replied. This surprised me.

"Is he not going in for drinkies then?" I asked.

"Of course, he is," replied the other driver. "Didn't you notice?" he queried.

"Notice what?" I said. "That when he turned out to the fire, he had forgotten to put his teeth in. Now he's gone back to the station to get them," adding, "Can't go visiting the nobs with no teeth in, can he?"

This surprised me for I had not known that he wore false teeth. I would have thought it more likely to assume that he had gone back for a wash and brush up, and to clean his boots for such a forthcoming social event.

The pump escapes crew were sent back to the station, leaving the pumps crew only for the drinkies. We followed the lady into the house, and I could sense an impending disaster, for the house was most beautifully and tastefully furnished, all around were antiques and object d'art.

Included in the pumps crew were firemen Slocombe and Shankster, who at the best of times were not particularly smart firemen. Now after a busy night's firefighting, they were both decidedly mucky. If placed in the centre of a pristine white shag pile carpet, which was where they were now standing, and then viewed, they looked horrible.

The lady of the house appeared unconcerned, and enquired, "What would you like to drink?" Before Slocombe had time to say a large navy rum please madam, she came back with the words "tea or coffee."

"Christ," he muttered under his breath, "we could have got that back at the fire station." He persisted, "No chance of a little drop of rum in it, missus, is there?" The station officer's angry glare caused him to stammer out defensively, "I was only joking, only joking, madam."

In the middle of taking our orders for tea or coffee, she turned and called out in her well-bred voice, "Pepe." The firemen's eyes turned towards the doorway, and then rested on the floor, waiting for the dog to arrive. My aunt had a delightful little poodle called Pepe. To our complete surprise, instead of a dog, an immaculately dressed manservant wearing black coat, winged collar and striped trousers arrived. Remember it was three o'clock in the morning, and he could not possibly have been in bed dressed like that.

The tea and coffee arrived in separate pots, and was served into exquisite bone china cups, along with some pretty little biscuit things to eat. We could almost have been taking afternoon tea at the Ritz, except that this scruffy lot would never have got past the doorman.

We stood around in a circle drinking our tea and coffee, as we had not been asked to sit down. This was quite understandable; the chairs were upholstered in a very expensive looking pale pastel pink material. Already Slocombe was dripping dirty water onto the white shag pile carpet. The mere thought of him sitting down on those pretty pink chairs made me wince.

The guvnor was making witty conversation with the lady when we heard him enquire, "Would it be in order to smoke madam?"

"Yes of course," she replied. The guvnor pulled out his gold cigarette case, he had probably only chanced his arm with the smoking request in order to display this case, for he was inordinately proud of it. He offered a cigarette to the lady, for to better display the case, but she did not smoke. Slocombe and myself pulled out our tobacco tins and began to roll up ciggies. The other fireman, young Ray Burke, had recently taken to smoking the same brand as the guvnor and very cheekily cadged one off of him.

We all stood around like social lemons, and the guvnor continued to do most of the talking. Soon the problem arose of what to do with the cigarette ash, for there was no sign of ashtrays in the room. The pristine white carpet (except where Slocombe was standing) was out of the question. The guvnor plucked up courage and asked for an ashtray. Pepe was called for and produced a tiny ornate ashtray about the size of a half crown which he gave to the guvnor. Slocombe and I simply used the upturned lids of our tobacco tins as ashtrays.

This left young Ray Burke in a quandary; he certainly could not cross the group and use the guvnor's tiny ashtray. He certainly knew better than to ask senior firemen, such as Slocombe and myself, could he please put his fag ash in our tobacco tins. So, what was he to do, for his hand was becoming full of ash, and pretty soon he was going to need to stub the cigarette out. I was now completely ignoring the conversation; my mind was now taken up entirely with how was young Ray going to get out of this one?

All credit to him, for he solved it. Over in the far corner of the room, he had spotted an ashtray of an unusual design. This didn't fool him, for his mum had one just like it at home. He moved over to fetch the ashtray and held it in his hand, flicking his cigarette ash into it. The ashtray was in the shape of an upturned hand with the fingers open and mounted on a base. The lighted cigarette could be placed between the fingers of the hand and be held by it, which Ray had proceeded to do.

The problem that I could see was that Ray's mum's ashtray would have been made out of plaster, and no doubt prettily painted. The one he was holding in his hands now was an exquisite carving of onyx or alabaster or similar, with what appeared to be solid gold fingernails, one of the lady's precious object d'art.

By now, the lady of the house was closely and intently watching Ray. Slocombe and myself where both watching and waiting with anticipation. The party came to an abrupt end, as Ray very carefully, so as not to spill any ash on the white shag pile carpet, twisted and ground his cigarette into his ashtray.

The next morning, instead of being awakened by short rings on the station call bells at 6.45 am as was the routine, I found myself being shaken awake by the dutyman, who gave me the usual hot cup of tea, and told me to get up and make my bed up quietly. This being a change from the normal routine, I asked him what was wrong. He explained that due to the busy night, he had dozed off in the watchroom (a most heinous crime) and missed giving the 6.45 am bells. He was now hoping to get away with it by simply ringing the 7.00 am work commences bells as if nothing had happened.

I said, "You won't get away with that, the guvnor's bound to know."

To which he replied, "Not if you all put your beds away quietly, because I've sneaked in and given him a cold cup of tea left over from last night. Then when he wakes up and finds that his tea has gone cold, he will think that he has overslept, and missed the 6.45 am bells himself."

So ends a chapter in this book, and a chapter in the history of the London Fire Brigade itself: For the past three months, on a site facing the Kings Road, not a quarter of a mile away, workmen had been busily constructing a new fire station. The old A8 Brompton fire station was to close, and the new A8 Chelsea fire station was to open.

People of my generation will tell you that everyone can remember where they were and what they were doing on the day the Second World War broke out, and on the day that President Kennedy was assassinated. Well, I was not born on the day that war broke out, but on the day that President Kennedy was killed, I was working on day duties at Brompton fire station.

Chapter 6
Chelsea Fire Station – 1964ish

After serving at one of the smallest, oldest and most cramped fire stations in the London Fire Brigade, we were moved to the newest, possibly most spacious station in the Brigade.

The station had been built directly facing onto the Kings Road, Chelsea. It had a vast four bay appliance room, with automatically opening and closing appliance doors. The smart messroom on the first floor was larger than all the accommodation at Brompton put together. The kitchen was staggering; it had everything possible, acres of work surfaces, potato peeling machines, fridges, bacon slicers and huge commercial cooking stoves.

To crown it all, it had a large commercial garbage cruncher built into the sink, a thing not many firemen had seen before in those days. This alone gave us many happy hours, finding out precisely what it would, and what it couldn't crunch. It wasn't too efficient with knives and forks etc., but it could cope with the average beer can easily enough. The wooden spoon used to push the cans etc. down was easy meat and we got through a fair number of these.

The firemen's dormitory/locker room on the second floor was vast and spacious yet gave a degree of privacy. For the tall lockers had been placed as to divide up the room into small two bed sections. This gave the added luxury of having one's locker by the side of the bed, instead of some remote and distant place. In the messroom on the first floor, there was even provided a purpose-built bar, with metal shutters to secure it, and comfortable armchairs all around.

The station office cum watchroom was on the ground floor and overlooked the Kings Road. Now instead of the dutyman being incarcerated in a tiny cubbyhole out of sight, he could watch the busy world pass by outside the windows, and even had the office staff to talk to.

The station drill yard was superb, huge by normal London standards. It had room to park the on-duty firemen's cars, and still a vast area to drill in.

The drill tower was a modern concrete one, incorporating a staircase all the way up to the top, as opposed to a single external metal ladder on the older types. Running up the centre of the drill tower was the hose drying facility, and amazingly, it even had electric hoists – no more hauling aloft by hand of wet, heavy hose, which at times with the heavy hose-layer hose, would take three or four men to do.

There was one small disadvantage. To fill the big four bay appliance room, we were allocated an additional appliance, a hose lorry. These were not normally very popular appliances; they didn't get to go to many fires. When they did, and if they were used, there was a great deal of work involved, for they carried a mile of heavy-duty three-and-a-half-inch hose. All this had to be scrubbed clean and then hung up the tower to dry. (We could see now why they gave us the electric hose hoists.) Then once dry, stowed back into the stores or onto the machine again. Also with the hose lorry, we gained an increase in personnel, one leading fireman, and two firemen to each watch on the station.

This was the first new fire station to have been built by the London County Council since the war. They had splashed out a lot of money on it and were indeed quite proud of it. For the official opening ceremony which was some two months away, they were determined to have something quite grand. The highlight of the proceedings was to be a grand fire display in the drill yard, and as our watch would be the duty watch that day, we and firemen from other stations would affect the grand display.

We still had the same station officer as at Brompton, and he was determined that the Chelsea involvement in the display was to be the star attraction, and he elected that Chelsea station would perform the high-speed hook ladder rescue.

Perhaps because of my height and build I was pretty nifty on a hook ladder, and it was put to me and another fireman, Ray Worboys, also good on hook ladders, that we should uphold the new station's honour.

Hook ladders are light wooden ladders about four-metres long, with a metal hook at the top, and were normally used at the rear of terraced type buildings where heavier and longer ladders couldn't be taken. To use the ladder, the hooks were engaged into window openings and the ladder ascended, then the same single ladder was used to climb up the outside of the building hooking into the window openings on each floor. Because these ladders were very dangerous to use to all but the practiced and skilled, the normal method of rescue with them was to lower the victim down from the building on a rescue line.

Two-man hook ladder drill at Lambeth HQ
(Photo courtesy: London Fire Brigade)

From that day forth, every time we were on duty, Ray Worboys and myself would practice our hook ladder drills. Working together as a team, we soon became very slick at it, endeavouring all the time to cut down the time required to perform the drill. When ascending the tower, two men with one hook ladder, Ray would carry the heavy, bulky rescue line on his back. I would pitch the hook ladder up to each floor, then hold the ladder steady at the base whilst Ray scampered aloft and then sat astride the windowsill to the right of the ladder. I would then follow him up and sit astride the windowsill to the left of the ladder and facing him. The reason for this being that when I had to pitch the ladder to the next floor, being right-handed I always had my strongest arm outside. Using this method, we would ascend the tower to the fifth floor, then both climb into the tower at this floor. Ray would take the line off his back and throw it to one side; I would move the hook ladder to one side of the window opening.

Unbeknown to the spectators, up on this floor was another rescue line, carefully flaked out onto the ground, and the two running nooses were already positioned around the legs and chest of the person to be rescued (another fireman). This line had also already been carefully measured, so that when lowering the body, when the body was three feet off the ground, there was a knot in it to prevent paying out any further line. The reason for this being that the lower down was a high-speed lower, and if this knot was not in the line, there was some danger that the (live) body may not quite stop in time, and we didn't want him crashing into the ground in front of all those important people.

The live body was to cause Ray and myself further problems. We had been practicing week in week out, to shave seconds off the time of the drill. The problem was that the live body was not a volunteer, in fact he was not terribly keen upon being the body at all but had been selected because he was fairly light in weight, making him easier to lower, and he was a relatively junior fireman, and had thus been compulsorily volunteered. He had developed a nasty habit when we first lowered him over the edge of the windowsill, prior to the actual lower down, of refusing to let go of the windowsill, causing us to lose valuable seconds. He would choose this time of all times to engage in a conversation on technical matters, was the line correctly flaked out, was the line properly reeved beneath our feet.

As the day of the display drew nearer, we began to despair. There was not enough time to train up a new body, and the current body kept promising that next time, he would let go of the sill as soon as we were ready, but nevertheless, couldn't quite bring himself to do so.

Ray solved the problem one day quite by accident. We had been practicing the drill as usual, and had made an exceptionally fast ascent, the body went out the window quicker than usual, but despite his previous promises, the body refused again to let go. Ray out of sheer frustration struck the body's fingers with his clenched fist, and the fingers released their grip, the body went into free fall for about four feet. The line which was fed over the sill, then down under my left boot, thence up to my right hand, to gain friction and purchase, began to rapidly pay out. From my position checking the line, I could not see the body, but Ray, whose job it was, was rapidly calling out, fourth floor, third floor, second floor. Before he could call out ground floor, the check knot in the line had arrived into my hand and the body came to a halt inches above the ground, with the body complaining that his bottom had actually touched the ground. This would have been quite possible with the speed that he was going, due to the stretch in the line as I braked him. It was judged the fastest lower so far, by a long way, and the body had got the message, if he didn't let go, we had ways of making him do so.

Having dispatched the body, now came the piece-de-resistance, the descent from the fifth floor. We had consulted with older firemen who had experience of hook ladder competition drills in earlier times. They had explained to us how a rapid descent of the hook ladder was to be effected, and it was as follows:

From the sitting position astride the windowsill, the first man stepped down and onto the hook ladder, stepping down two or three rounds until the feet where clear of the top of the window opening below. Then he removed his feet from the rounds of the hook ladder and placed them up against the outside of the strings, or sides of the hook ladder. Then transferring his grip from the rounds to the strings of the hook ladder and simply sliding down it like a fireman's pole. The trick was not to simply slide off of the end of the hook ladder to one's doom, but halfway down to swivel one's body sideways and into the window opening, landing with legs astride over the window ledge.

As soon as one's bottom was safely on the window ledge, a shout would bring the second man down the hook ladder just as quickly in the same manner, to sit in the sill at the opposite of the hook ladder. The first man then cleared the hook from the sill of the floor above, and lowered it down, sliding it expertly between the palms of his hands, until the hook engaged on the sill of the floor he was on. This procedure was repeated all the way down the tower to the ground floor. After all this time, I forget the times taken for a good crew to effect a rescue by hook ladder from the fifth floor of a drill tower, and come back down again, but using the short cuts detailed above, I would not think four minutes excessive.

The equipment used would all be specially borrowed and treated, the hook ladder would be carefully rubbed down with sandpaper and varnished, so that it would easily slide through the hands, and not inflict splinter wounds. The line would be an older line, so that it would be supple and run through the hands easily. The stopper knot, that which prevented the body crashing into the ground, would only be tied after much consultation and deliberation. Then all this equipment would be locked away in a secure store, so that nobody but the drill crew could use or tamper with it.

Ray Worboys and I were quite pleased with ourselves. Our drill had reached a high state of perfection, members of the other watches would sometimes stay behind after duty to watch and admire the drills. Firemen performing standby duties at the station spread the word around the division, great things were expected of us.

One week before the great day, we were to have a dress rehearsal of the whole display, and the great Assistant Chief Officer, the famous Alfie Shawyer was coming to view the display. Alfie Shawyer was famous as a fireman's fireman, and when rising up the ranks, his command at fires was renowned, as was sometimes his strong language at fires.

Upon ACO Shawyer's arrival at Chelsea, our station officer was excelling himself, describing to Mr Shawyer the excellence of his very own hook ladder rescue drill. The station officer had apparently taught us everything he knew, and we knew that if we made a cock-up of this drill, the station officer would not talk to us for at least a month.

The great moment arrived. Ray and I were stood smartly to attention at the base of the drill tower. Ray with the rescue line strapped to his back, and the hook ladder already in position and hanging from the first floor of the tower.

A whistle blew, and we were off. I ascended the ladder first, for this would give me a second or two's rest before I pitched the ladder to the next floor. As soon as Ray's bottom hit the windowsill on the first floor, he would say, "Go," and the hook ladder would be disengaged from the sill and on its way up to the second floor.

Thus, we arrived at the fifth and final floor, slightly out of breath, but in record time. Ray threw aside the line from his back and I moved aside the hook ladder, and we turned our attentions to the body, who seeing our slightly breathless state, was looking quite agitated, which we both duly noted. At this point, we got an enforced rest, because we were supposedly putting the line that Ray has carried up with him onto the body, but in fact, of course a second line was already upon him, and flaked out on the tower floor. This enforced rest lasted about ten seconds, to make it all seem believable to the public. Then the body was placed onto the windowsill, the line reeved underneath my fire boot, but this time, we were taking no chances with clinging fingers that wouldn't let go. Ray gave the body a quick shove and launched him into space, a look of startled horror appeared on the body's face as he entered four feet of free fall. I checked the initial shock on the line, and then the line was passing quickly and smoothly through my palm, and Ray was calling out the floors as the body descended. Just as Ray called out, "Ground floor," the check knot arrived in my palm, and the weight went off of the line. The remaining line was gathered up and thrown out of the window, to crash down on top of the body below. It is possible with a little care to avoid the line crashing down onto the body, but this particular body had not performed too well and did not deserve this consideration.

The drill had gone well and very quickly so far, and we were determined to excel on the descent. I descended the hook ladder first and started the slide almost as soon as I was on the ladder, swinging cleanly into the fourth floor. Ray, not to be outdone, did likewise, shouting, "Go," as he crashed down astride on the sill opposite me. I raised the hook ladder a fraction and turned it around in my hands so that the hook was facing away from the tower. This was done so that when I lowered the ladder, the hook would not crash down into our skulls. Then the sides, or strings of the ladder slid through my palms, and with a deft twist of the hand, the hook of the ladder was engaged on the sill of the fourth floor. Within a second, I was out on the ladder and sliding my way down to the third floor.

Hook ladder drills carried out in this manner were of course slightly dangerous, but it was exhilarating, and we were making such superb time that we couldn't stop grinning at each other on the way down. In something like twenty to twenty-five seconds, we had descended from the fifth floor of the tower and were standing smartly to attention at the base. A short blast on a whistle told us to fall out, and we doubled smartly away from the tower, whilst noting from the big smiles on the station officer's face that all had apparently gone well.

After a short break to recover, we were summoned to meet ACO Shawyer, who when I met him, surprised me. This was not the old Mr Shawyer that I had heard about and seen occasionally on make-up fires, this was a new Mr Shawyer, he had taken on the mantle of great rank. He spoke to us very quietly saying that it was one of the slickest hook ladder drills he had seen in a very long time, and that it must have taken a great deal of time and practice to reach that standard. "Unfortunately" – and he used the word with feeling – "those days are past," he said. "Safety at work and drills is now everything, even though you might be happy to take the risks that you have just been taking, the Brigade cannot now let you. You will have to do the drill in the manner laid down in the drill book, ie no sliding down the strings, and you will do the drill at a speed that will take at least twice as long as you just performed it."

We could tell that he hated having to say that to us, and it was sad that it had to be said to us by the great Alfie Shawyer, but as the man said, "Times are changing."

Although we carried on doing the hook ladder drill at the display, it just wasn't the same. If we couldn't do it our way, then climbing up to the fifth floor of a building on hook ladders was boring, hard work. Some good came of it though, the body was a much more cheerful and happy man, for now we had time in the drill to ease him gently out, instead of violently ejecting him out of a fifth-floor window, and then lower him down at a gentle and sedate pace.

As the day of the station opening drew near, plans were being made. The mess manager enquired whether he would be required to do the catering. This brought smiles to the firemen's faces, for the thought of the Lord Mayor of Chelsea, and all the other big nobs, eating his special two-inch thick cheese and onion sandwiches, for he made no other kind, was hilarious. The station officer replied no, there was no expense being spared for this event, outside caterers were being brought in, and the finest of fiddly things to eat would be provided.

The big day finally arrived; tiered seating was erected in the drill yard for the important people. All the off-duty firemen and their families had been invited, and some even came. The display and the speeches all went off without hitch, and then came the great highlight! A momentous occasion in most firemen's lives, the eating of the free LCC food.

We had been watching the outside caterers prepare the food all day. It really was superb, basically a cold buffet, but of the very finest ingredients. All sorts of vol-au-vents, dainty smoked salmon sandwiches, cold asparagus spears and the likes, and not a cold sausage roll to be seen. What we had particularly noticed was that although the important people would be eating separately from us. Basically, we would be eating the same food, and there was plenty of it, the London County Council had really done us proud on this one.

At around 5.30 pm or half an hour before the shifts changed, all the important people had long gone and there were still masses of food left on the tables. I was surprised, although really not that surprised, to see Chester Slocombe working his way around the food tables with a black plastic bag in one hand. He was carefully selecting the finest of the remaining food and placing it gently into his plastic sack. Chester's kids were apparently going to dine off the finest in the land, for a few days at least.

*

It was whilst serving at Chelsea that I encountered my first serious RTA, or road traffic accident. The inner-city fire stations tend not to get too many calls to serious RTAs. Mainly because the inner London traffic is normally so congested and slow moving, that most accidents would occur at 30 miles an hour or less, therefore incurring not quite such serious damage to the vehicles. Such serious accidents as do occur mainly tend to happen when the volume of traffic on the roads is low, such as the early hours of the morning.

The accident was a result of what I call the 'Irish taxi driver syndrome', which is a story about a small town in Ireland, where there were only two cars. Each was driven by two brothers and one of them was the local taxi. A stranger had hired the taxi to take him across town, and every time the taxi came to a red light, the driver went straight through without braking. The stranger asked the taxi driver, "Wasn't it dangerous to go through red lights like that without stopping?"

The taxi driver replied, "Not at all sir, there are only two cars in the whole of this town, mine and my brother's."

On the return journey, the taxi carried on as normal going through red lights. Then it came across a green traffic light, and the driver screeched to a juddering halt from 40 miles an hour. The irate passenger said to the driver, "Why is it that you quite happily drive through red traffic lights at 40 miles an hour, and yet when you come to a green light, you screech to a halt?"

To which the taxi driver cheerfully replied, "Not bloody likely, sir, far too dangerous, my brother might be coming in the other direction." The call came in at around 4.30 am and was to a 'road traffic accident, person trapped, junction of the Embankment and Chelsea Bridge' A8 Chelsea's Pump and Pump Escape to attend.

The appliances drove out of the appliance room over the Kings Road, and straight into Oakleigh Street directly opposite, from where we could already see Chelsea Bridge. From around halfway down Oakleigh Street, and in the early dawn light, at the junction of the Embankment and Chelsea Bridge, we could see an object in the middle of the road, and the whole road junction appeared to be bathed in white. As the fire engine thundered along the road towards it, the whiteness puzzled and unnerved me slightly, so that I eased off the accelerator. Then as the appliances drew up at the scene, it could now be seen that the object was in fact an overturned fully laden milk float. Also, that what appeared to be white paint was the spilled milk from a hundred broken bottles.

Leaning up against the milk float, ashen faced was the driver. He was clutching what appeared to be a broken arm, which apart from other minor cuts and bruises appeared to be his only injury. So we turned our attentions to the other vehicle, which was a newspaper delivery van. This vehicle was firmly embedded around the granite stone buttresses of Chelsea Bridge.

A small group of firemen were gathered around the front of the vehicle. As I walked over to them, a fireman dashed past me carrying a line, and the station officer called out to me to reverse the pump back up to the rear of the newspaper van because they were going to try to pull the van back and away from the Bridge buttress using the fire engine. I had done this sort of thing before, and the best way to effect it was to drive nose on to the vehicle to be towed. For then the operation could be carried out in reverse gear (the lowest gear on a vehicle) and at the same time, the driver could see what was happening. The line was attached first to the van and then to the fire engine. I engaged reverse gear, took up the slack in the line, then slowly went backwards. Then with a great rendering and scraping of metal, the van came slowly backwards from the bridge buttress.

I first removed the line from the fire engine and parked the machine out of the way, then returned to the rescue. As I approached, I could see that nothing was happening. The firemen were just standing around in a subdued manner doing nothing. Then as I walked around to the front of the van, it was obvious why. Upon the van's impact with the solid buttress, the driver had been thrown forward, breaking the windscreen with his head. His face had then slammed down onto the metal lip into which the windscreen would fix, virtually cutting his head in half across the line of his eyes. There was very little blood, so he must have died instantly of his horrific head injuries.

We spent around a further half an hour at the scene, removing the body for the ambulance men, then cleaning up the broken glass and milk from the roadway, waiting for the police to complete all their measurements of the accident scene. We pulled the damaged vehicles to the side of the road for the police, then returned to the fire station to have a very subdued breakfast. It's strange but had we released that driver alive, the breakfast table would no doubt be buzzing with conversation. We had just put the same amount of work and care into releasing the body, but cadavers just don't seem to count the same.

*

The Irish taxi driver syndrome! It appears that many people who are up and about before 4.00 am in the morning in London, think that they are the only ones on the road and drive accordingly.

A group of the younger firemen had been sitting around in the messroom late at night, discussing Chester Slocombe. They had observed with much humour that Chester's nose, which was rather small and upturned, reddish in colour and dimpled with small hairs growing out of the dimples, reminded them all of a strawberry. That henceforth, he should be called strawberry nose. Nobody so far had plucked up the courage to call him that name to his face, for although Chester knew he had a problem (the drink) and usually kept a low profile, he was in fact a very witty and intelligent man.

One day one of the younger firemen, a married man who had fertility problems, and thus had adopted two young children, actually did it! He called Chester to his face 'strawberry nose'. He did it in good humour and with a smile on his face. Nevertheless, with baited breaths, we stood and awaited the response. When it came, it almost destroyed the young fireman. It was one of the most cutting vitriolic put downs I have ever heard. For in a low hissing voice, Chester simply said to the young man, "Fuck off, sawdust bollocks."

One Thursday evening (the night before pay-day), Chester was quietly watching the world go by in the Kings Road, from the window of the first-floor recreation room. During the course of that day, somebody had given me in my change a Dutch guilder, instead of an English florin, or two-shilling piece. The two coins being almost identical in size and shape. At that time, the coin would buy a pint of beer, or twenty cheap cigarettes. I called over to Chester, and when he turned around, flipped the coin in the air and placed it on the window ledge. Then saying to him, "I will play you table tennis for this, Chester," knowing that he would have no money in his pockets on a Thursday night.

A big smile came over his face, for he could usually beat me at table tennis, despite his size.

After that followed three of the most energetic games of table tennis I have ever played. Chester was literately steaming with the exertion of the games. At the end of three games, I had actually beaten him, which was not what I had intended to do. So I challenged him again. "Make it the best of five games then, Chester." So off we went again, this time Chester had to win both games to get the coin. I really was on superb form and took him to match point on both games. I then deliberately served into the net, to let him win the match. With a huge grin

103

of triumph on his face, he went over to the windowsill to collect his money. He picked up the coin, examined it, then gave a roar, "You bastard, Wilson. You've just made me sweat my bollocks off for half an hour for a foreign coin."

"Sorry, Chester," I replied. "But I never said it was a two-shilling piece, did I? I just said 'I will play you for this'." He saw the funny side of it, and I bought him a can of coke in the canteen.

The next evening after roll call, he came up to me all smiles, saying, "That foreign coin you palmed me off with, well I soon found a vending machine to take that, twenty cigarettes it was worth. I was not at all surprised, I had known full well when I gave it to him, that he would somehow find a way to realise its value."

*

November the fifth, Guy Fawkes night, or bonfire night. In the early 1960s, this was the busiest night of the year for the Fire Brigade.

A special bonfire night routine was implemented in the London Fire Brigade. At around 1800 hours, the breathing apparatus, which at that time was only carried on the pumps, was switched over to the pump escapes. The Brigade even brought in a special bonfire report form. A very much simplified type of form that took a fraction of the time to complete, as compared to the standard report. Such was the large number of these fires we attended.

For the duration of bonfire night routine, pump escapes would only attend building or structure fires. The pumps in turn would deal with the numerous bonfire calls.

The watch mess manager would have provided an evening meal, which would not spoil easily, such as a stew or the like. For there would be no telling at what time crews would get their suppers. Some stations that usually had a great number of bonfire calls on their own station's fire ground would make great piles of sandwiches to sell at cost price to appliance crews called in to the station to assist them.

The bonfires themselves would often be organised on a street basis by local inhabitants. If there were a bomb site or waste ground nearby, they would build the fire there. If not, they would build the fire in the centre of the road, and that was partly the problem. The local councils would then have to spend thousands of pounds in repairing the melted asphalt damaged by the bonfires.

The number of bonfires in a district varied in accordance with the standard of living of the population. Working class areas of London would have a bonfire in almost every street. Some of them quite elaborate affairs, with barrels of beer and pianos all out in the street.

Street bonfires that were not a threat to property were not routinely extinguished by the Brigade, but only at the request of the police. This is where problems arose, for the fire Brigade, normally jolly good fellows in the public's view, now became the villains of the piece. For we were now about to extinguish their bonfire which had taken a great deal of effort to build and put an end to their jolly street party.

In the past at this type of incident, stones had been thrown at the firemen, and their hoses slashed. So the Brigade had adopted a safety routine. The basic idea being that if things got ugly and out of hand, the appliance should be able to drive away immediately and without delay.

If the bonfire was in the middle of the street or road, and blocking the street, the appliance would reverse down the street in order to be facing in the right direction for a quick getaway. The hoses would not be plugged into the fire engine, but instead plugged directly into the street fire hydrants, the pressure from the water main only being used to extinguish the fire. Thus, in the event of a quick retreat being necessary, this equipment could be simply abandoned.

Before we even entered the fray, sufficient policemen needed to be present to cover our retreat, for there would sometimes be two or three hundred irate members of the public wanting to take revenge upon us. Not surprisingly, this was not a popular duty with the crews, who had they been off duty, would in all probability have been joining in the fun themselves.

On one particular bonfire night, we had been ordered to assist on A12 North Kensington's fire ground. We had spent most of the night until midnight extinguishing lists of bonfires on that fire ground. As it turned out, we were only too grateful to purchase thick corned beef sandwiches and cups of scalding hot cocoa – cocoa, unlike tea, can be kept hot for a long time and not spoil. We returned to our own station at around 12.45 in the morning, buying fish and chips on the way, not much fancying a stew that had been cooking for seven hours.

On this particular night, I had been temporarily promoted to the rank of acting leading fireman, and thus in charge of the appliance. During the course of the evening, we had extinguished around a dozen or so bonfires, all on North Kensington, or Kensington's fire grounds.

The next morning, it was my duty to pass the details of the calls we had attended during the night over to the fire stations on whose fire ground they had occurred, in order for that station to complete the necessary fire reports. I was on the telephone to Kensington fire station and had just announced rather grandly, "Acting Leading Fireman Wilson speaking, and I have a list of six calls I attended on your fire ground last night." I then went on to add cheerily, "You will no doubt be pleased to know that they were all bonfires." I was in fact thinking of the paperwork that this would save their office staff. Back over the telephone came a weary, worldly-wise senior voice saying sarcastically,

"Yes, and I bet you was pleased they was all only bloody bonfires too." No doubt referring to my lowly acting leading fireman rank.

*

Upon hearing that you are a fireman, one of the questions that people invariably ask is, "What is the biggest fire you have ever been to?" It being a common belief that the bigger the fire, the more exciting, impressive, whatever, it must have been. This is simply not so. Even from training school days, young firemen are told that the fire which invariably gives most job satisfaction is not the ten, twenty, or thirty-pump fire over the other side of London, but a four-pump fire, persons reported, on your own station's ground.

Firstly, in order to gain some idea of the magnitude of fires, you first need to understand that fires are classified by the number of pumps required to attend the fire in order to extinguish it. Thus, ten-pump fires, twenty-pump fires etc., is seldom ever the number of pumps required to pump water to extinguish the fire. Instead, it is an indication of manpower required to put the fire out, ie the number of firemen plus their equipment that is needed.

The minimum number of firemen required to man a pumping appliance is four, it can be as many as six, but most of the time it is closer to four. Thus, an order from the fire ground to make pumps ten is not a request for ten pumps to pump water, instead an order for not less than forty firemen plus all their ancillary equipment carried on the pumps, to attend the fire.

The biggest fire that I ever attended in my career occurred whilst I was stationed at Chelsea. It was classified as a sixty-pump fire and was in the days of the London County Council, when in the whole of London, there were only around one hundred pumping appliances.

The fire occurred at the Bishopsgate Railway Station in the City of London in around 1964/65, just before Christmas.

In the early hours of the morning, Chelsea's pump with myself driving was ordered to standby as fire cover at Bethnal Green fire station. This was rather unusual, Bethnal Green was a long way from Chelsea, right over the other side of London in fact. To be ordered to stand by all the way over there was a bit like being told you were going to the seaside for the day.

The first real indication that there was a really big fire burning came as I turned left onto the embankment to head towards the City of London. Above the roar of the road engine, I could hear the station officer seated next to me saying something about a sunset. I raised my eyes from the road and looked at the sky ahead. There, sure enough, was what appeared to be a beautiful sunset. But where a sunset shouldn't be! Certainly not at only 1.30 in the morning. I might be a city lad but even I know the sunsets in the west, and that doesn't mean the west end of London.

Switching the appliance radio to the channel used for really big fires, we were given the answer. Some unknown senior officer was busily engaged in making pumps forty, at Bishopsgate Railway station.

The City of London was normally pretty quiet at this time of the morning and devoid of traffic. We made our way through the city at a leisurely pace, for we were only ordered to stand by at Bethnal Green for fire cover, and not proceeding to a fire. The only other traffic on the road seemed to be fire engines, and they were going in all directions. Some like ourselves proceeding to stand by for fire cover, others judging by their speed and noise, all bells ringing, to the forty-pump fire itself. A casual observer would have been puzzled indeed as to the location of the fire with all this activity. For at one point a fire engine, lights on, bells going, came down the same road as we were travelling along, only to disappear in the opposite direction.

We arrived at Bethnal Green to find that another appliance had arrived just before us, also to stand by as fire cover. They had already discovered where the tea, sugar and milk were kept and a brew-up was in hand. So, we lounged around for about half an hour drinking tea and talking, then getting fresh hose up into the appliance room for the Bethnal Green crews upon their return. Then the station fire bells rang, and Chelsea's pump was ordered on to the now sixty-pump fire.

When the call came in, both crews were in the first floor messroom, this being a strange station a frantic search began for the pole house doors.

Now it was the custom on fire stations not to wear boots/leggings above the ground floor. This was in the days when we used to clean the fire stations ourselves, thus for obvious reasons.

When on standbys, we seldom had our shoes with us and couldn't comply.

I found the pole house doors first. I raised my hand, released the safety catch, pushed the doors open against their springs and stepped onto the pole. Nothing happened! I had my legs twined around the pole in the usual manner, but it appeared that something had cancelled out gravity. I was puzzled, and with seven or eight firemen behind me, all champing at the bit to use the sliding pole, somewhat agitated, but nevertheless firmly stuck to the pole.

My mind was racing, had I discovered anti-matter? Then it dawned on me, my black waterproofed leggings were sticking firmly to the metal pole. As the laws of friction had already been discovered and defined, I lost interest. I simply untwined my legs and slid down, using my hands only to brake me at the bottom.

Upon our arrival at Bishopsgate Railway Station, or more correctly upon our arrival in the vicinity of the station. For we could get no closer than 300 yards because of the congestion of parked emergency vehicles, police, fire, ambulance etc. Because of the distance that we were parked away from the fire, we were relieved of the usual crafty fireman's routine at large fires of keeping his fire engine as far away as possible from the actual fire. So that upon our return, we would still have a full complement of hose and gear.

Firemen at a fire in need of hose or equipment invariably go to the nearest appliance and take their requirements from it. The problem with this system is an administrative one, especially if the incident occurs in a different division. It can sometimes take months for this same equipment to find its way back to its home station, if ever! So prevention is better than cure. Little did we know, but later that night, we were going to experience the grand slam of equipment losses.

We reported to the control unit and whilst waiting to be given a job detail, stood and gazed at the fire. It was certainly the biggest fire I had ever seen; it was awesome, in both sight and in sound. From where we were standing, it appeared to have engulfed the whole of the vast main line railway station. The flames were leaping hundreds of feet into the air and lighting the sky for miles around.

We were shortly given a job detail and ordered to relieve another crew on a ground monitor. This was a device for holding and directing very large jets of water onto fires, with nozzle sizes of two inches plus. These monitors were very useful on this type of fire, for they threw a great weight of water a long distance onto the fire. Once they were set up and working though, there is not a great deal of work involved, other than winding handles to change the direction and height of throw.

About thirty feet away in front of us, the station perimeter wall of around twenty-five feet in height had been pushed outwards and collapsed. This allowed the outer walls of the burning station itself to be seen, some thirty yards away. It was through the windows of this outer station wall that we spent the next five hours squirting water. Thousands and thousands of gallons of water disappeared through those windows, yet it appeared not to make the slightest bit of difference to the fire, and I soon got bored! Unless the actual position of the ground monitor had to be moved, it really needed just one man to wind the handle to direct the throw. So we soon worked out a rota, one man to work the monitor, the rest to smooch about, go to the canteen van or whatever. Thus, it seemed I spent the rest of the sixty-pump fire just smooching about or what-evering, with just an occasional spell of long-distance water squirting.

One good thing about very large fires is that they tend to act as Brigade reunions. Firemen, old mates that perhaps had been at training school together, firemen that had served together at other fire stations, years ago, then all being dissipated to the far corners of the London Fire Brigade, would turn up, usually in the vicinity of the canteen van at some big fire. Some would still be firemen, some others very exalted in rank. Nevertheless, all would meet, and hours could be spent discussing the in-between years.

*

At around 9.30 to 10.00 am, a strange crew was seen making their way along the outside perimeter wall, calling out, "Chelsea! Chelsea's pump crew." This was our relief crew; the fire had been subdued quite considerably by now, or almost burned itself out, whichever version was preferred. We quickly instructed our relief crew on what our duties had been, the whereabouts of the canteen van and any other information that might make the duty more comfortable, then departed to find our own fire engine.

Here we encountered the first major problem of the sixty-pump fire. Someone had pinched our fire engine! We returned to the control unit and reported this to them. They were not at all surprised to hear this and suggested that we pinched somebody else's fire engine. Adding that was the only way, other than by public transport, that we would get back to our station.

Bishop's Gate Railway Station Fire 1964
(Photo Courtesy: London Fire Brigade)

The problem had arisen earlier on in the fire. As the first crews had been relieved, these men would have been the first crews to arrive at the scene in the early stages of the fire. Thus, their appliances would be right up the front of the huge jam of fire engines – in some cases even trapped behind the falling walls at the fire. These crews had been instructed to take any available machine and to return to their stations, which they had duly and gratefully done. Unfortunately, the thing snowballed, and as a result very few crews got to go home in their own fire engine. At least the one we got was a warm one; it had obviously just arrived carrying a relieving crew, for the engine and cabs were still warm. So we set off, arriving back at Chelsea fire station at around eleven o'clock. Just in time for stand-easy, but two hours late in going off duty and leaving the day watch crew to attempt to locate and retrieve our own fire engine.

So that was a sixty-pump fire, admittedly we had gone on to the fire late, after most of the hard work of laying out hose lines had been already done.

The fire was still burning brightly when we arrived but after the initial period of awe and wonder, being restricted to just one tiny corner of the fire, because of our duties on the ground monitor, boredom and the feeling of what can we do next soon set in.

The next night, we were again ordered on to Bishopsgate as a relief crew. The building was still smouldering, and because of the dangerous state of the structure, firemen had not been able to enter and had continued firefighting operations from a distance.

It was only then that we could gauge the extent of the fire. A huge mainline railway station, with all ancillary buildings, hundreds of laden goods wagons, dozens of railway delivery lorries burnt out. Walls collapsed everywhere, all the metal roof supports twisted and sagging. The whole railway station would need to be put into rubbish skips and taken away. As our county Fire Brigade colleagues would sarcastically say, well done lads, that's another fine car park you have created there.

One interesting sight that we saw on the second visit was that of a fire engine completely surrounded by collapsed buildings and walls, so that it could not be removed. The machine, which was a Dennis fire engine, had the blue plastic to its flashing lights melted by the heat of the fire and running down the sides of the roof. The whole machine in general was badly scorched. Every single piece of gear and equipment had been stripped from the appliance. Almost as if they were expecting to abandon and sacrifice the poor fire engine to the flames. Yet the fire engine stood there all alone and thundered and pumped away even now. Charged suction hose led into the machine, and charged fire hose led out, and the pump thundered on. Yet there was no sign of a pump operator, or attendant fireman. It was obvious that somebody came by occasionally and gave it a little drink of diesel fuel and topped it up with oil and water.

Dennis fire engines had always been one of my favourite makes, after seeing this one pumping the night away, that was doubly so. A thought passed through my mind. The fire might have been a bit on the boring side for me, but I bet the pump operator of this particular fire engine had an exciting night.

So that was it! The biggest fire I ever went to in my whole career. Even now, I think it probably still holds the record of being the biggest single fire in London, since the war blitz. Yet I was soon bored with it. Give me a four-pump fire, persons reported on my own station's ground any day, just like they told me in training school.

At around this same time, they were building the Royal Garden Hotel, on A10 Kensington's fire ground. An enterprising fireman at Kensington fire station had obtained the security/night watchman contract. He was employing his fellow firemen from both Kensington and Chelsea fire stations to do the work in their off-duty time. He was paying a very good rate of pay, and so firemen were falling over each other to do the work.

As this fireman was a friend of mine, I was his representative at Chelsea fire station. Part of my duties was to collect the wage packets off of him and distribute them at Chelsea fire station. I normally received and paid out these wage packets on a Friday. The fireman at Kensington would despatch them to me, via the Fire Brigade divisional van, the van which delivered the Brigade's internal mail on a daily basis.

On this particular Friday, the van had come and gone with no wage packets being delivered (delivered of course in a plain sealed envelope, addressed to me). The Chelsea firemen were now becoming agitated, they had bills to pay and no money to pay them with. Off duty firemen had come into the station to collect their part-time job money and were becoming irate. I had telephoned Kensington fire station several times, but the money had not arrived there yet. Then at long last, around 3.30 pm, the station coin box telephone went, and the message was passed to me that the money had arrived at Kensington fire station. They would do their best to get it to Chelsea before we went off duty.

Firemen can be very resourceful and innovative, especially where money is concerned! At around 3.45 pm we received a fire call to Queens Gate, on Chelsea's fire ground but bordering with Kensington's. This meant that two machines from Chelsea and one from Kensington would attend. I was driving the pump with the station officer sitting alongside me.

When we pulled up outside the address of the fire, I found just the station officer and myself looking for the fire. Most of the other firemen were peering down the road, in the direction of Kensington fire station. I thought nothing of this at the time, until Kensington's pump pulled up at the address. Then I saw a line of firemen queuing up by the rear cab of the Kensington machine. Then I saw little brown paper envelopes being passed out of the open rear cab window, I got it in one! I never did find out who made that false alarm call. I did know that if a man was enterprising enough to organise the security on a huge building project, then merely delivering the wages on time should not be too much of a problem.

*

This was the period when England was swinging, and swinging most of all down the Kings Road, Chelsea, where I spent most of my social hours, in the pubs and cafes. In the past year, two very important things had happened in my life. The first was that I had applied and been accepted for a posting to Soho fire station and was about to leave Chelsea. The second, in the previous year I had met my wife to be, and she was about to immigrate to Australia with two friends. So it was make-your-mind-up time for me, I proposed, she accepted and I was now about to be married.

I arranged a going away from Chelsea party at a local pub in Fulham and informed all my mates in the surrounding fire stations. Around fifty attended, and the landlord of the pub didn't know what had hit him, but he was quite pleased, for firemen are big spenders, especially on beer. Then in the midst of the noisy proceedings I called for quiet and informed them all that this was in fact my stag night, I was getting married in two days' time.

A little old man of around seventy was playing the piano, and every now and then he would stop playing and offer to fight anyone in the room. Somebody would buy him another drink and he would forget about fighting and play again. The word got around Walham Green that the Cricket was lively tonight, and pretty soon the place was bursting at the seams. Lots of pretty girls for the firemen to dance with.

Before I had left home, my mother had warned me, "Don't bring your drunken mates back with you tonight; remember Pat's staying with us."

My wife's family had moved away from London the day before, and my wife was staying at our house until the wedding.

At around 10.45 pm, I could see the beer glass going from fireman to fireman around the pub. I knew only too well what that was for, a collection to buy take away beer for the party. Where would the party be held, my house of course. I went outside to the toilet, and then sneaked out of the pub through the other bar. I was a little bit drunk, and giggling to myself as I left, I had fooled that lot.

My house was about five minutes' walk from the pub. When I got home, I was very pleased with myself, telling my mum how I had thwarted my mates and done a runner, before they could follow me home with all the beer.

The doorbell to our flat rang, damn! I had forgotten that half of them knew where I lived anyway. I hid behind a curtain and the plan was my mother was to tell them that I had not yet come home. She disappeared out of the room. Five minutes later, she reappeared, saying, "You can come out now, Dave."

"Have they gone then?" I queried.

"No," she replied. "They are all coming in." It was not that my mother was easily intimidated, quite the opposite in fact, just that most of them also knew my mother from the fire station socials. They had cheerfully and cheekily informed her, "Mrs Wilson, if we can't come in and finish off the party, we'll hold it right here in the street." So my mother, being a sensible lady, allowed them all in. The party went on till the early hours of the morning.

So came the end of my time at Chelsea fire station, at least I went out laughing!

Chapter 7
Soho Fire Station – 1965

The old Soho fire station was in Shaftsbury Avenue, just off Piccadilly Circus. If looked at carefully it was architecturally a very strange building. The ground floor was to all intents and purposes a standard London County Council, three appliance bay fire station. One-half of the first floor blended in nicely with the ground floor. The left-hand side of the first floor was of a crude concrete construction.

The reason for this peculiar construction was that the building had been partly demolished during the Second World War by a bomb. The bomb killing several firemen on duty at the time. The fire station had originally been three or four stories high. Following the bomb blast, it had been tailored down to its one and a half remaining stories. The temporary, (subsequently permanent), concrete construction added to one end later.

It was nevertheless a very busy and happy fire station, thus the reason for my request to transfer there. The station was a three-appliance station, pump escape, pump and turntable ladders. The station's fire ground embraced the whole of what was commonly known as the West End and was London's entertainment centre. It contained theatres, striptease clubs, London's Chinatown, also many of London's tourist sights and venues. To the west of the fire ground were Mayfair, Pall Mall and the Ritz hotel, a very plush area which made the whole fire ground very varied and interesting.

Over the period of the next few months, the blue watch Soho firemen and myself were getting used to each other. I had arrived as a fully qualified fireman, motor driver, and turntable ladder operator, (I had qualified whilst at Chelsea). Having only had service at two relatively quiet stations, my firemanship and character had yet to be assessed by them. My character assessment had been assisted by the fact that a lot of them had the same habit as myself, of liking a

115

beer or two after day duties. As with every other fire station I had served at, there was a pub within twenty-five yards of the fire station. This particular hostelry was in fact the very next-door building to the fire station.

After a time, I had attended various four pump and other fires with the watch. Mostly, I had been driving an appliance, which would only demonstrate that I was a good driver and pump operator.

In the small hours of one morning, we had been called to a fire in one of the side turnings off Shaftsbury Avenue. The building was a four-storey terraced building with a shop on the ground floor and a basement below and with an open basement area in front of it. The shop on the ground floor was smoke logged, so the door was forced to gain entry.

Ongoing into the shop, there was plenty of heat, but no sign of fire. After much crashing around in the smoke-filled shop, we could not then find our way out of it, neither to gain access to the upper floors, nor the basement.

This was a peculiar feature of the properties in the Soho district. An experienced fireman upon entering a house would instinctively find his way around, even in smoke or in the dark. Most types of property have a basic layout, ie stairs to the right or left of the house, centre stairs going off a passageway etc. The properties in Soho had all been divided, and sub divided, with partition walls. Then each unit was invariably provided with its own locked door, all no doubt in order to provide more revenue for the landlord. But the end result for the firemen was that they were virtual rabbit warrens, or likened to a maze, where at every turn you have to hack your way through the tall hedges.

Inside the shop, we had just decided that because of the heat level the fire must be in the basement, when a basement window cracked in the heat and fell out, releasing the hot smoke and gases in the basement, making it then abundantly clear where the fire was.

By the time I had made my way out of the ground floor shop, a ladder had been placed down into the basement area. The ladder was resting against the basement railings, at ground floor level. A branch on the end of a charged length of hose had been passed through the railings and was waiting to be taken down into the basement. Standing on top of the ladder in the smoke and heat zone was a young fireman hesitating. I said tersely to him, "Go on then, get down the basement."

He nervously replied, "I can't. It's too hot."

When I was released from driving duties, I liked to be at the sharp end. I was already a bit peeved that this young fireman had beaten me to be first on the ladder. "Right, get off then," I snapped at him, which he hurriedly did, and I took his place on the top of the ladder. He had not the experience to know that this was the hottest place to be. The sooner I descended the ladder, below the rising heat, then got down on the deck the more comfortable it would be for me.

On the floor of the basement area, the branch was passed down to me. I immediately opened up the branch to check that it was working. Then I approached the door to the basement. The door had two glass panels in it, so using the heavy branch I broke the panel nearest to the door lock. Reaching in through the broken panel, I felt for the lock and turned it, then moved the door a fraction until it opened. I was aware that two other firemen had joined me in the basement area, and shouted to them, "Get ready to lighten up the hose, I am going in."

I pushed open the basement door and moved inside, it was very smoky and hot, like an oven, I could not see any flames, but I could hear the noises of the fire. So I opened up the three-quarter inch jet and directed it at the ceiling, as I did so swinging it around. This deflected the jet of water off of the ceiling and down onto the contents of the room. If it did not actually reach the seat of the fire, it would at least reduce the room temperature. I did this for around thirty seconds or so, until I thought it was safe to proceed without the worry of a flashover. Then, calling to the firemen behind me to lighten the hose, I crawled forward blindly into the room.

I was now about six feet into the room. In every direction, I was meeting obstructions. I couldn't see for the smoke was very thick, but I seemed to be in some kind of a storeroom. Every time I opened up the branch, the water bounced back onto me from some obstruction. Every twenty seconds or so, I called out to the firemen behind me, "Lighten up the hose." Then crawled forward and around obstructions, directing the water jet at the ceiling, hoping it would reach the still unseen fire, for although I was down on my belly at floor level, the heat was still fierce.

I had other firemen behind me a minute or so before, but now I seemed to be on my own. I presumed they were lagging behind to ease the hose around obstructions. As I made my way around one final obstruction, I could now see a dull red glow through the smoke. At last, something positive to point the jet at. Before opening up the jet, I took a good look at the fire. I seemed to be at the doorway of yet another room, which is where the fire was burning. I pointed the jet at the dull glow in the smoke and opened it up.

After around twenty seconds or so, I was back in total darkness as the visible fire was extinguished. This was the reason that good firemen, before they opened up with the jet, took a good look at their surroundings. I now tried to move forward into this room but the hose was too heavy to drag on my own. So I called back loudly once again, "Lighten up the hose." But there was no response. I repeated the call, but still there was no response. I moved as far forward into the doorway as I could, and then proceeded to drown the unseen fire with water. Swinging the jet backwards and forwards, up and across the ceiling, over and over again. It was only when I could stand fully upright, without feeling the tightening of my cheeks and ears, that told me the heat had dissipated, that I could relax and shut down the jet.

I now realised that I was in fact all on my own. I called back to the other firemen, "Hello there, where are you?" but got no reply. Now I began to worry where were the other firemen, did they know something that I didn't, was the building going to fall down on' me? Firemen will never retreat from a fire leaving their mates behind without a damned good reason. I thought it best if I made my way out to find out what that reason was. In the smoke and dark, I crawled on my hands and knees following the hose between my legs. I followed its meandering path all the way back to the basement area, meeting nobody on the way.

I then climbed back up the ladder through the smoke and steam that was still gushing out of the broken basement window to finally emerge at the top in the bright light of an appliance searchlight trained upon the building. There I was spotted by one of the younger firemen, who with an amazed look upon his face said to me, "You're missing."

"Yes, I know," I replied tersely. "Missing all my fucking mates who were supposed to be helping me, where are they?"

"No, no," he repeated. "You're supposed to be missing in the fire; the breathing apparatus crew is just going down to look for you."

"Tell them not to bother," I said acidly. "I'm out, and the fire is more or less out, and the sooner we get a hose reel back down there to finish it off, the sooner we all go home."

The explanation was, that the two firemen who had followed me down the ladder were younger, relatively inexperienced firemen. Up to a point, they did a very good job, because feeding forward the heavy large diameter hose in the heat and smoky conditions, especially with only two of you, is arduous work.

But because they had to feed hose forward around every bend and corner, they dropped a long way behind me. Being relatively inexperienced, the heat especially worried them. They then called forward to me, but I did not hear them. Probably because the jet was in use and crashing noisily into all those unseen objects. They then decided the safest and correct thing for them to do was to make their way back outside and report me missing.

The fire did not go as well as it might have done, but from my point of view, it had been a good fire. It had established me high in the pecking order of firefighting qualities on my new watch.

*

Almost every building on Soho's fire ground had a basement, and some of them were very large basements indeed. The British Museum for example, had a really massive, frightening basement. Consequently, a large number of Soho's fires involved basements, which are very difficult fires to extinguish. Putting out basement fires is like trying to put out a roaring fire in a domestic hearth. But in order to do so, you first have to enter by the chimney, then climb down the flu itself to put out the fire.

One underground fire which Soho was famed for involved the deep underground shelter at Goodge Street, Tottenham Court Road. This shelter was in fact a converted tube train tunnel, deep in the ground. We were down there one day on a familiarisation visit, and I was very impressed!

After descending some hundreds of steps, we emerged into the tunnel. The tunnel lights were switched on, and they were placed alongside and down each side of the tunnel. The tunnel was so long that these two rows of lights seemed to merge into one in the far distance.

The tunnel, or deep shelter, had been used as a troop transit centre during and after the Second World War. The fire had started in a feeding centre, or canteen, halfway along the tunnel.

The thought of having to walk a quarter of a mile in breathing apparatus, in dense, thick smoke, without being able to see your hand in front of your face, then to lay out hose and carry all the gear the same distance in a total blackout is quite frightening.

There were other kinds of tunnels on Soho's ground. These were underground service tunnels. They ran underneath Piccadilly Circus, Shaftsbury Avenue and Charing Cross Roads. They were approximately eight to ten feet in diameter, and about six to eight feet below ground level. They contained mainly essential services, such as sewers, telephone cables, water pipes, electricity cables and the like. Once or twice a year, the firemen would go down them on familiarisation visits, and they were quite interesting. The entrance would usually be made via a grating in the middle of a traffic island, just down from Soho fire station.

As we proceeded along, light and ventilation were admitted via further gratings on the traffic islands along the route. There was much competition amongst the firemen to arrive at these gratings first, as there may have been money or other goodies dropped down them through the metal gratings. The unsuspecting public tended to stand on these gratings, waiting for a break in the traffic to cross the road. Unfortunately, not the ladies quite so much, because their high heels tended to lodge in them. A shouted remark from below of "Hey you are standing on my head" would produce some amusing scenes, as the public then looking down would see a group of firemen peering up at them from deep in the bowels of the earth.

*

Because Soho was such a popular fire station, firemen tended to stay there for very long periods of time. In its time, it has had some very extrovert characters on the watches. Fireman Heaton – Ward, sometimes known as Heaton Hyphen Ward, or Doc Ward. He had been in the Brigade since World War Two and at Soho fire station most of that time. He was called 'Doc' because he was a trained chiropodist, and this was indeed his part time employment. Not only was he called Doc, but he spoke like a doctor. For a fireman, he spoke exceedingly good Queen's English. So much so, some even called him a toffee-nosed bastard.

He would of course treat any fireman with foot problems for a small consideration. He delighted in showing any interested fireman the contents of his locker. A sort of black museum, which included various grotesquely shaped toenails and the like, that he had removed from people's feet.

It was not unknown for divisional headquarters, when ordering firemen to stand-by at other fire stations, to send to Soho the ordering, "Order your

120

chiropodist to standby at A1 Manchester Square." Which meant that some fireman at that station had fixed it with division for Doc to standby in order to attend to his feet.

Eric (the mole) Prosser, another very long served fireman, so called because he used to spend nearly all his time on duty down in the bowels of the station, ie the basement. He was also known as the Appy man, because when on duty, it was his job to tend the apparatus, which was the Brigade's name for the coke fired boilers, usually situated in the basements of fire stations.

The Appy man was not always 'appy' though, in fact at times he could be downright miserable. Especially so, if someone had interfered with his boilers, or his opposite number on the other watch had not filled up the coke lockers before going off duty.

Off duty, Eric was a theatre fireman, and he worked for at least two theatres. He was I think divorced, and had no immediate family, and his whole life revolved between his two theatres and the fire station. He ran a kind of mini employment agency, and firemen in the division wanting part time work as a theatre fireman would only need to telephone Eric, who would know of, or locate suitable employment, all at no charge to the fireman.

Eric would spend hours in the basement, tending his boilers, or doing his own domestic chores such as washing and ironing. He was addicted to loud music, and literally everywhere he went in the basement, he had with him a portable transistor radio, always it seemed turned on at full volume (he was forbidden to use it above the basement level though). On two occasions to my knowledge, this radio drowned out the sound of the fire call bells, and Eric missed fire calls.

George, 'miserable in the morning' Phillips was another older fireman, in around his mid-forties at the time. George was a quiet, affable man, happiest when driving the Maguirus turntable ladders. He had, so I was told, been a prisoner of war for a large part of the Second World War, and just hated to get up in the morning.

The station officer on the other hand was just the opposite. He would come around at 6.45 am turning on all the lights and shouting cheerfully, "Shake your feathers, shake your feathers."

George in return would growl back in a deep, meaningful, bitter tone, "Raus, raus, fucking raus to you all." Which I was given to understand translates as,

"Good morning all," in German. George of course having learnt his German in the prison camps.

*

It was at a small house fire in the Shepherds Market area of Soho, that I discovered another strange quirk of Soho's character. That it was possible to rent out a very plush, expensive, bed sitting room without any other facilities whatsoever, such as kitchen, bathroom etc.

We had attended a small fire in such a bedsit, which was furnished to a very high standard. I was attempting to open all the windows to let the smoke out. I cleared the smoke from the main room and was searching for the ancillary rooms, kitchen bathroom etc., but there were none. I commented to another fireman how strange it was that the dwelling consisted of a bedroom only. He replied, "It's not a dwelling, you silly sod, it's a knocking shop," further explaining, "a prossie's parlour (brothel)." He walked over to a bedside table and opened a drawer in it, and then said, "Here, look at this." I saw that the lady of the house obviously purchased her condoms in bulk.

*

Soho had its seamier side, ladies of the night, strip clubs, mucky book shops and because they operated outside the law, any disputes they had between themselves also would be settled without recourse to the law. In extreme cases, this very often took the course of setting fire to your opponent's premises.

Around this time, there was obviously a feud going on between the operators of the mucky bookshops (pornographic purveyors). Over a period of months, we had a number of fires in these premises, including several four-pump fires. One of the premises I attended must have been a wholesaler, for down in the basement were almost as many books as would be found in a small public library. All stored as on library shelves, except that there would be up to two dozen copies in mint condition of the more popular books. There were books in that cellar to cater for just about every perversion and deviation you could possibly imagine. I had thought I was worldly wise, but some of those book's subjects surprised even me.

Soho had its bad points also from a fireman's point of view. This was the very large number of calls to people shut in lifts. Although releasing people from lifts can be very satisfying at times, it does tend to become rather routine work. In Soho, nothing seemed to be straightforward. With most of the property in Soho, the building would have been there before the lift, so the lift, lift shaft and lift motor room would somehow have to be squeezed into the building. Each lift installer seemed to have his own pet way of doing this. The installing of lifts into buildings had been an ongoing project over the past-fifty years or so, resulting in the variety of designs and makes of lifts and the method of installing them being enormous.

To release people from a lift, you had first to find the address, then find the lift shaft within the building itself. Somewhere in the building would be the lift motor room. This is where Soho's lift installers excelled, in hiding the lift motor rooms.

The usual place to put the motor room was directly above the shaft. This was not always possible due to the design of the building. When hydraulic lifts were introduced, the lift motor could be, and very often was, placed anywhere within or without the building. One small advantage of hydraulic lifts was that the motor room could even be placed on the ground floor of the building. Thus, saving the arduous walk up many flights of stairs. Unfortunately, Sod's Law says that you will not know that the motor room is on the ground floor until you have walked up many flights of stairs and found it not to be at the top of the building. Then, and only then, will it become patently obvious that the lift is a hydraulic lift, and the motor room is on the ground floor.

Only when the lift motor room was found, could the actual task of releasing the people from the lift begin. Many happy hours have I spent, playing the game of 'find the lift motor room'.

*

Rubbish fires, Soho was literally plagued with these. Because of the multi-occupancy commercial use of the buildings, the generation of rubbish or refuse was immense. The rubbish was cleared away by the local council every night. The local trades' people would pile it on the pavements in cardboard boxes, plastic sacks or dustbins every night for collection by the council. Then almost every night the local, or visiting, pyromaniacs would set fire to it. Not just one rubbish fire, but very often a trail of them, from Shaftsbury Avenue to Oxford Circus, as they made their pyromaniacal way back home, via the Oxford Circus tube station. If the rubbish was placed in the doorway, or up against the building itself, and most of the occupiers knew better than to do this, the rubbish fire could spread to the actual building. Many of Soho's four pump and even larger fires have in the past had this origin.

The area between Shaftsbury Avenue and Oxford Street was probably one of the most traffic-congested areas of London. During the daytime, its narrow streets would be filled with general commercial traffic, servicing the restaurants, clubs and offices with which the district abounded. At night-time, it would be filled with the general public visiting these establishments. After eight o'clock in the evening, all parking discipline evaporated. The general theory being that once you had stopped your car, if there was still room for one other car to pass along the road, then that was a suitable parking place. This theory worked quite well, until vehicles larger than private cars wished to use the road fire engines.

The firemen at Soho fire station were, in my opinion, the best motor car bouncers in the whole of the British fire service. When a motor car was causing an obstruction, for example parked on a street junction so the appliances couldn't turn into that street, it would be bounced up onto the pavement. To do this, as many firemen as were available would start to bounce the car on its road springs at one end. When the car was at the peak of an upward bounce, on a given word all the firemen would lift the car upwards and sideways, by as much as a foot. This bouncing was repeated quickly and at the front and rear of the car, and within the space of a minute the car would have been moved sideways, and up onto the pavement.

The normal attendance for a fire call in that district would be the three appliances from Soho. The pump escape, pump and turntable ladders. The first two appliances were standard machines, and negotiating the narrow-congested streets was difficult enough for them. But the turntable ladders were around thirty-five feet in length, and four feet of this length overhung at the front of the vehicle. Just getting to fires at Soho could be an art form.

Three appliances proceed down a narrow street to a fire to find a car is double-parked and there is nowhere to bounce it to. A fireman produces his axe, smashes the quarter light, opens the driver's door and sits in the car. The rest of the crew push the car along the street until it can be pushed clear. The appliances proceed forward. At a road junction, another car is parked so that the appliances cannot turn. The crews jump down from the fire engines and this car is quickly bounced up onto the pavement; all this is done without orders being issued. The appliances proceed forward once again. Another car is double-parked, the quarter light is broken to gain access, but the car's doors are security locked, and the vehicle has a steering lock, and the car cannot be bounced sideways. The three fire engine horns are making a cacophony of noise in an effort to attract the driver. In the meantime, four firemen have gone to the water locker on the first machine and are now making their way forward on foot. They are carrying a standpipe key and bar, lengths of hose and a branch. If all else fails, they will set into a street hydrant, and using the pressure in the street mains, fight the fire until the appliances arrive.

*

Part of the reason for my application for Soho being accepted was that I was a qualified turntable ladder operator. Fortunately, as far as my posting was concerned, they did not look deeply into this. For I was qualified to drive and operate Merryweather turntable ladders, and the turntable ladders stationed at Soho were of the Maguirus make, which meant of course that I could not operate them.

Arriving for night duty one evening, as I entered the appliance room, to my surprise instead of our Maguirus ladders, was a set of Merryweather turntable ladders. The Maguirus ladders had been involved in a traffic accident during the day and taken off the run, the Merryweather ladders were a spare set. The duty board for that night had been amended, and my name was now down to drive the turntable ladders. After roll call, and as soon as we had finished our tea, I asked to have the ladders out in the drill yard. I felt my ladder operating skills were a bit rusty, and wanted to get in a bit of practice, and for an hour, I practiced to my heart's content.

At around eight thirty, the bells went down and the yellow indicator light in the appliance room came on, denoting a turntable ladder shout. When I jumped up into the cab, I saw a piece of paper stuck with Sellotape onto the windscreen and on it were written the words 'Palace canopy'.

The Palace Theatre was directly opposite the fire station, on the other side of Shaftsbury Avenue. It had along the side of it a canopy which overhung the pavement, provided I believe, to keep the public dry as they queued to go into the theatre.

This piece of paper had been stuck on the windscreen by the other ladder drivers to remind me, tongue in cheek, not to make the same mistake that so many other turntable ladder drivers not used to Soho had made. That is, as I pulled out of the station and across Shaftsbury Avenue to then turn right, not allowing for the canopy's overhang. Remember that the actual ladders stick out four feet in front of the appliance. Failing this, I would join the long list of Brigade ladder drivers that had all at some time demolished the overhanging canopy outside the Palace Theatre.

At one thirty in the morning, a special service call was received at the station. The call was as follows, 'To assist police, man threatening to jump, Charing Cross Road. Silent approach, Soho's pump and turntable ladders to attend'. Silent approach meant to approach the incident without sounding the bells or horns.

On arrival, the address was a row of shops six storeys in height, with residential accommodation above. We were met by the police, who told us they had been attempting to arrest a man in a fifth floor flat over the shops. He had locked himself into the flat and threatened that if the police attempted to break in, he would throw himself out of the fifth-floor window.

The police asked if it would be possible for us to put a ladder up and block the window opening, so that the man would then be unable to get out of it. They stressed it must be achieved at the first try and done quietly.

The only ladder which would reach the fifth floor was of course the turntable ladder, which I was driving for the very first time. I positioned the ladders into place in front of the building and very carefully sited them on the road to reach the fifth-floor window. A man in a white shirt occasionally appeared at the window and shouted out of it. This was the alleged villain, and this was the window to be blocked.

The turntable ladder's ground jacks and axle locks were lowered into place, and with the power take off to drive the mechanical ladders engaged, all was ready.

At this point the station officer, with George Phillips by his side, came over to me and said, "Now look here, Wilson, we are only going to get one shot at this, now if you think you can't do it, George here will do it," indicating George at his side.

126

That was exactly what I needed, just as I was facing my first real test of my ladder operating skills on the fire ground and under stress – to know that the guvnor had no confidence in me. He was in fact telling me that although he did not really have the power to prevent me working the ladders, he would be far happier if George, the more experienced ladder operator, did so.

I quietly replied, "Thank you, but I think I can manage, guvnor."

The plan had been agreed with the police; they would keep the man talking at the door of the flat, then give me the signal to proceed. I would quickly and quietly block the window with the head of the ladders and when I had done so, they would break into the flat and grab the man.

I was standing up high on the operating platform waiting for the start signal. When the signal came the big searchlight clicked on, illuminating the window. I engaged the elevating clutch and the big ladder began to lift up off of its gantry. As soon as the ladder was clear of the gantry, I engaged the training lever and the ladder began to turn across the chassis to face the building. The ladder was now directly across the chassis, and the ladder elevated and aimed for the window above the fifth floor. I moved the big speed lever into high speed and began extending the ladder up into the air. The ladder increased in length, its ladder pawls clicking loudly away as it did so. I felt sure that even if the man could not hear the noise of the engine, he must surely hear the noise of these loudly clicking ladder pawls, but he apparently did not. The ladder was still extending upwards, and I made some small adjustments to the training across the chassis.

I now noticed that there was a policeman leaning out of the window directly above the one I was aiming for. He was frantically signalling with his hands that the ladder was already high enough. I knew more about this subject than he did, and kept the ladder extending directly towards the agitated policeman. The policeman had given up his signalling in despair – to him the ladder was already far too high to effect the window block. Only now did I start to depress, or lower, the ladder into the building.

What the policeman did not know was that as the ladder was lowered to the building, it would lose most of this apparent excessive height as it crossed the pavement and basement area. I had in fact deliberately kept the ladder slightly short in length, so that as it entered the window opening, I could increase the length, and thus completely block the window. I pushed down on the depressing lever to lower the ladder into the building. This was where I faced the moment of truth. The ladder dropped beautifully and neatly into the window opening, with only inches to spare below the top sill. As the ladder came to rest, behind it in the room appeared the man in a white shirt. The man was now desperately attempting to squeeze out of the window, around the sides of the ladder. I pushed down on the depressing clutch lever and the big ladder tightened up firm against the bottom windowsill and was now immovable in the window opening – the man was trapped.

After the ladders were all made up, and I was waiting to return to the station, George Phillips came over and said to me, "Dave, was I relieved when you said that you would do it. I haven't used Merryweather ladders for years; you did a fine job, far better than I could have done." Such praise from the master! Considering that this was the first time I had operated turntable ladders in anger on the fire ground, I was quite pleased with myself. This my very first operational ladder job, was to remain the most exacting one of my whole career. Some were to follow that were more dangerous or exciting, but none that ever required such precision operating, with only one attempt.

*

I had heard that a New Year's Eve on duty at Soho fire station could be pretty lively, but I had not realised just how so. Until around eight o'clock, it was just like a normal busy Saturday night in Soho. Happy crowds swirling back and forth along Shaftsbury Avenue outside the fire station. A few run-of-the-mill calls, people shut in lifts, etc. Then from nine o'clock onwards, the crowds began to get really thick. Happy people making their way from pub to pub, no doubt on route to Trafalgar Square to see in the New Year.

The drill yard was full to capacity with cars, as visiting firemen had called in at the station to say hello and scrounge a free parking place. At eleven o'clock, the pavements were thronged with people, all travelling in one direction, Trafalgar Square. Many of them now slightly drunk, and, calling up to the firemen as we peered over the balcony at the first-floor level.

Inside the station, the bar was open. The bar was situated in the recreation room, which was the concrete but placed at first floor level following the bomb damage. The bar itself was a little window that opened out onto the snooker table in the recreation room. Inside the window was to be seen but a single beer pump. In the recreation room were gathered most of the on-duty firemen, some

128

civilians, mainly visiting off duty firemen, celebrating the New Year in the West End, and also some friends of the firemen on duty.

Also, there was Frank. Frank was a retired fireman who lived locally and used the fire station as his local social club. Frank was to be found in the recreation room most nights of the week, depending on which watch was on duty, some watches being more socially inclined than others.

At around half past eleven, a fire call was received to Covent Garden vegetable market, which was a three-machine attendance. The pump escape, pump, and turntable ladders, with myself driving the ladders, turned right out of the station for Cambridge Circus, then turned right again for the Charing Cross Road. This road led directly down to Trafalgar square, and had been closed to traffic and was now filled with a seething mass of good humoured, happy people. The crowd hindered our progress, and when we eventually arrived at Covent Garden, it was as we had half expected, a malicious call.

After sending the stop message, we set off on the return journey back to the fire station. We were now in the thick of the crowds, and with no horns and bells going, the fastest we could proceed was a very slow walking pace. The crowds were shouting happy New Year, offering us drinks from their bottles and climbing up onto the fire engines. There was nothing we could do about it but lay back and enjoy ourselves in the happy atmosphere. The turntable ladders that I was driving were the Merryweather mechanical set, a rather old-fashioned open style machine with no cab, and the ladders were literally festooned with people. The leading fireman in the left-hand seat had a most delightful pretty young lady sat upon his lap. She was ringing his bell for him (the appliance bell, of course).

The tradition on most fire stations was on the stroke of midnight, on New Year's Eve, to run the appliances out onto the station forecourt and ring the bells and sirens for around thirty seconds. On this New Year's Eve, we were stuck in a solid crowd of people in the Charing Cross Road. So we sounded the horns and bells right there, to tumultuous cheers from the crowd. Upon arrival back at the fire station, before we could reverse back into the appliance bays, we had to evict all our passengers. Quite a few of the ladies thought that a ride on the fire engine included an invitation to a party. When at last we got rid of the passengers, with much kissing and happy New Year's greetings, I made my way back up to the recreation room and bar on the first floor, and found a party going on.

The recreation room was full of people, all the visiting firemen, off duty firemen, on duty firemen's friends and the like had all returned to the fire station to continue celebrating. Frank, the retired fireman, was busy behind the bar serving them beer.

The party carried on for some hours. At one stage, every other lady present seemed to be wearing a policeman's helmet, the owners of which were distributed around the room, happily supping pints of beer.

The party came to an abrupt end at around 3.30 am, when to great cheers from the visitors, a fire call was received at the station, which turned out to be a rubbish fire which had spread into the adjacent building. This kept us away from the station for more than an hour, so that when we returned, all of our guests had drifted away.

To adapt the words of a well-known song, 'The party's over my friend, time to call it a day. Put on your fire gear, ride your red engine, now you must earn your pay'.

*

With the Merryweather turntable ladders on the run, I began to drive them on a semi-permanent basis. George Phillips loved his Maguirus ladders and didn't care much for the Merryweather set and made no objections to me driving them most of the time. After actually fighting fires, ladder driving and operating became my first love.

On the ladders you didn't get any rubbish fires, or lift jobs, you only got calls to real fires. If, when you got there, the ladders were not likely to be required, ie a basement fire, you could join in the fire fighting. Then at make-up fires, one of the first indicators that most of the fire fighting and excitement were over would be the loud request, "Ladders away, Guv," which invariably meant that the ladder driver was fed up and wanted to go home.

Most of the property in central London was four stories high or more, and the ladders received a great deal of use. Smoke issuing from a roof, put the ladders up to have a look; person locked out of fifth floor, send for the ladders; difficult chimney, request attendance of turntable ladders. The Brigade's policy was that the ladders were there to be used, so use them. Of course, every pitch on the fire ground, ie person locked out, was worth a dozen simulated pitches on the drill ground.

Driving the Merryweathers was a pleasure and skill of its own. The open cab, the long bonnet sticking out six feet in front, the ladders themselves resting on the gantry above the driver's head, and then protruding out and over the bonnet, the big steering wheel which was not power assisted and at slow speeds took all one's strength to turn. The gear change lever, big and solid, like the top sawn off a bofors gun. The crash (no synchromesh) gearbox, which required at times a wait of almost five seconds in the neutral position before the next gear could be engaged. Lastly, the pedals. The brake pedal was a big six-inch diameter rubber covered disc, set on the right. The clutch pedal was again a big six-inch diameter disk set to the left. Hidden away in between the two of them was a tiny little accelerator pedal.

Driving them was like driving a ship. With the big, solid chassis, she swayed and rolled with every camber in the road. With the helmsman (driver) seated so far back from the front of the ship, the wheel had to be turned long before the turning was reached. Stopping them on wet roads was exactly like a ship. Great distances had to be allowed to bring the thirteen tons of metal to a halt without locking the wheels, or she would glide on unstoppable, until the momentum ran out, or she struck something even more solid than herself. They even had a ship's bell, a great big, upturned silver bucket of a fire bell, suspended on the nearside and rung by hand by the officer in charge.

With the mechanical ladders of German design, the Metz and Maguirus, the driver operated them standing on the ground at the rear of the ladders. But with the Merryweather ladder, the driver stood up on high, on the actual turntable itself, where he could be better seen and admired by his public. He was provided with great big levers, like railway signal box levers, to push and to pull for fast and slow speeds. Separate levers for each movement of training, elevating and plumbing. The Merryweather mechanical turntable ladder driver was, and could be seen to be, a true artisan.

The mechanical turntable ladders were the last of an era and were now being replaced by hydraulically operated ladders. These new ladders included such luxuries as fully enclosed and heated driving and crew cabs; power steering; power brakes; hydraulically operated ground jacks and axle locking devices. Though these new ladders were indeed far superior to the old mechanical ones, for myself and many other ladder drivers, it was similar to the passing of the age of steam – a sad, nostalgic time.

*

One Saturday afternoon we had been called to assist ambulance crews to evacuate a casualty at Piccadilly Circus, the pump and turntable ladders to attend. A workman had been working on the illuminated signs at Piccadilly Circus and had electrocuted himself. The ambulance crew required our assistance to remove him from the building roof, which was six floors up.

The turntable ladders were positioned and set up. Behold there was I, in broad daylight, in the middle of Piccadilly Circus, with all the traffic stopped, hundreds of people watching, standing up on high on the ladder turntable about to perform my party piece – if only my mum could have been there to see me.

The workman had been secured into a Niel Robinson stretcher, carried by the ambulance, (similar to a mountain rescue stretcher). A rescue line 220 feet in length was fed through a pulley at the top of the first ladder extension, one end of which was brought to the rear of the ladder. The ladders were elevated and then extended up and over the roof of the building. The Niel Robinson stretcher was connected to the line, the slack was taken out of the line from below and the line reeved around a friction bollard. The ladders elevated up and clear of the building, then trained, or turned away from the building. The line was then allowed to run over the friction bollard, which effectively braked its descent. The casualty descended to the ground to be borne away by the ambulance men. Unfortunately, for me, no cheers or standing ovations, nor calls for encore. Once the show was over, the cosmopolitan London crowds simply drifted away.

*

For many months now, I had been suffering one of London's greatest problems, finding somewhere to live for my wife and myself. We had a great deal of money saved up, but mortgages on properties were almost impossible to obtain.

Some months previously, at a Brigade function, my wife had been told that the Reading and Berkshire Fire Brigade were offering houses in order to attract firemen transfers to that Brigade. I had applied and been accepted, and now with some apprehension was about to leave the grime and smoke of London for the fair county of Berkshire.

Chapter 8
Reading and Pangbourne Fire Stations - 1966

From one of the busiest metropolitan fire stations in the country, I was now riding in my off-duty time out of a rural village retained fire station – transformation of lifestyle indeed.

My transfer to the Reading and Berkshire Fire Brigade in 1966 involved a full 48 hours per week on duty as a fireman in the town of Reading. Then, when off duty from my new house in Pangbourne, a small riverside village of around 2,500 people about six miles to the west of Reading, I would ride as a retained fireman out of Pangbourne fire station, being called out to fires by a bell in my own house and a loud wailing siren above the fire station. When I first heard the siren, it brought back old memories. I didn't know whether to run for the fire station or run for the public air raid shelters.

Caversham Road fire station, Reading, was my new full-time station. The terms full time, whole time, part time and retained being the terms used to differentiate between the two kinds of firemen in county brigades. Whole time being the firemen whose main occupation was with the Fire Brigade. Part time being those firemen, usually in small communities, whose main occupation would be something else, ie butcher, baker or candlestick maker. Just to confuse matters a little, my title would be whole-time part-time fireman, or full time retained. To sum it all up, when I was off duty at home in Pangbourne, and the siren sounded or the bell in my home rang, I then jumped up on Pangbourne's fire engine and got paid some extra money.

My first day on duty at Reading fire station did not start well. I had assumed that only London had traffic jams and had allowed what I thought was a safe journey time of twenty minutes to get to work. Then, as a result of Reading's unexpected traffic jams, arrived ten minutes late for duty.

Caversham Road fire station was, by London standards, a handsome and spacious fire station, built in the late 1930s as the headquarters and only fire station of the then Reading Borough Brigade. Reading had since amalgamated with Berkshire, to form a big county Brigade.

The station was a two-storey high, three bay station, but the appliance room was so large that it could accommodate six appliances, three of them turning out through the rear appliance room doors.

The appliances stationed and on the run at the station were my old favourite, the Dennis F11 petrol machine as a pump escape, a set of Merryweather hydraulic turntable ladders, another appliance as a pump and a breakdown/rescue lorry, which attended road traffic accidents and the like.

My first days on the fire station, I was like a fish out of water. On the fire ground, I was an experienced fireman, but on the station, I was a new boy all over again, having to re-learn and adjust to the county fireman's ways. Added to this, there was some animosity over the big city firemen pinching there, the local firemen's, houses.

I had been posted to the blue watch at Caversham Road. This by chance happened to be the drinking watch, the sociable watch. The watch where if anything was going to happen, usually of a calamitous nature, then blue watch was where it happened. They seemed to be still living back in the days of the old Reading Borough Brigade, and Reading is famous for amongst other things, its brewery.

On the first floor of the station above the appliance room was the bar, or social club. The bar would have done credit to any pub. Fully stocked with a range of draught beers and lager, rows of bottles of spirits fed through optics or measures. Crisps, peanuts, bottled beers and of course the inevitable packets of three, were all available. For someone who had been used to a single beer pump, or a few cases of beer in a cupboard under the stairs, this was staggering.

After around 8.00 pm of an evening, especially Friday and Saturday evenings, the bar would fill up with what were then strangers to me, and an evening's drinking would begin. The sub officer, who was second in command of the watch, would be there from beginning to end, and never without a pint of Guinness in his hand. Some of the other regular visitors, I was later to find out, were the officer in charge of the division and third in command of the Brigade, who usually appeared after the local pubs had shut, and the officer second in command of the division, and overall command of Caversham Road fire station. Life on a county fire station was going to take a bit of getting used to.

*

Soon after my arrival, it was decided to assess my driving skills they wanted to see how I would cope with the traffic in the town centre. So we set off, with the sub officer in charge, in the turntable ladders.

I do not know what they were expecting, but after the back doubles of Soho, the wide spacious streets of Reading were a piece of cake and I was henceforth deemed to be a Brigade driver. They tested me under the wrong conditions though, for a turntable ladder fire call in Berkshire could be of twenty miles distance or more. My lack of driving skills, if any, would be driving along major roads at seventy miles per hour for long periods, with the bells and horns going.

Firemen are I think, probably the same the world over. Before many weeks had gone by, I had settled down and was one of the watch. I had to watch my tongue though, for they had their own sense of humour and were already beginning to imitate my cockney accent. It was very hard not to compare their ways with London ways. They would then mimic my accent saying, "You're not in fucking London now, boy," and of course, they were right.

*

Monday night at Pangbourne fire station was drill night, and it was on a Monday night that I first reported there, taking with me my second set of issued fire gear to hang on the gear pegs there.

With me on that first night were two other new whole time retained firemen reporting for duty at Pangbourne. The first had, like myself, transferred from London, Peckham Road fire station in southeast London. The other, and now my new next-door neighbour in Pangbourne, had transferred down from Glasgow Fire Brigade. This small, rural village fire station now had to assimilate not one, but three ex big city firemen into their ranks.

The fire station itself was quaint; it stood in the main street of the village. It was a single-storey building made out of corrugated iron, with a small brick-built lecture room, and office at the rear. There was no drill yard, the crews travelled to Reading in the appliance to practice ladder drills and the like.

135

Two machines were stationed at Pangbourne, a water tender ladder, similar to a London pump, but it carried with it 400 gallons of water. Also, a personnel carrier, which was used to ferry additional manpower to the fire ground. The sub officer in charge was a garage mechanic, and his dad, a gardener by trade, was the leading fireman. They were all very proud of their little station, and indeed to be firemen, and they made us very welcome, but they had some quaint little ways.

The very first fire call I attended with them was on a Sunday morning when the siren and the bell in my house sounded at around 11.00 am. The call was for the water tender ladder to a rubbish tip alight about three miles out of Pangbourne. A call they had obviously attended many times before.

On our arrival, we found a deep pit half filled with household rubbish which was smouldering and giving off thick clouds of smoke. There was a hydrant very close by, and the routine was to run the hose directly off the hydrant to the fire, which was quickly done.

I then saw to my surprise that the appliance driver, who was the manager of the local ironmonger's shop, had removed his fire helmet and was now wearing a Tyrolienne type hat, with a very large pheasant feather stuck in it. He also appeared to be lighting some kind of fire himself. He explained to me, "We are usually here for at least a couple of hours, so I thought I might as well get the kettle on for tea." In a back locker on the machine, they apparently carried all that was necessary to produce a cup of tea, anytime, anywhere.

This being a Sunday morning, there was no hurry to return to the station (retained firemen are paid for their time). Not until one o'clock that is, when two firemen, Bert and Maurice, would apparently want to go off down the local pub.

At one o'clock almost on the dot, we left the fire station. I joined Bert and Maurice, in the 'Star'. The 'Star' being the local pub that was just across the road from the fire station, for a quick pint or two. Isn't it amazing? Yet again, there was a pub only yards away from the station I was serving at. There they told me that prior to my arrival, they were the only two on the station who liked a drink. The rest of them, they said, would get pissed on half a pint of light ale, adding, even though that had been diluted with the tears they'd shed into it, crying about how much it had cost them. They carried on telling me, "The other thing that annoys the rest of them is that if the station gets a fire call whilst we are in here, we've even got time to drink our beer, and still be first in attendance at the fire station."

*

At Reading fire station, Mick Clements was a big man, over six feet tall and very sturdily built. He was in the messroom shouting out in a loud voice, "Where's that little cunt from Fulham?"

I tapped him gently on the back and said quietly, "Right behind you."

He turned and apologised, saying, "Sorry, mate, I didn't know you were there." That was Mick's style shout first, think afterwards.

Mick was a townie, that is born and raised in the town of Reading. Despite the fact that Mick had applied for and been refused the house that I now lived in, we became firm friends. Although we had both been born in towns or cities, we had a common interest, a love of the rural life.

Mick got me a part time job working in Reading cattle market as a drover alongside himself. On the first day at the cattle market, Mick gave me a stick and then instructed me to drive a pen of black Aberdeen Angus cattle to the auction ring, saying to me, "Just tap them gently on the heels with the stick to keep them moving." I followed behind the cattle and tapped the rearmost one gently on the heel with the stick. It replied with a swift and vicious backwards kick narrowly missing me. *A nasty tempered one*, I thought to myself. So I moved over to the other side of the bunch, and gently tapped the rearmost cow there gently on the heel. Again, a violent backwards kick, which I again narrowly avoided. I was now very much on my guard. Standing well back, I tapped yet a third one on the heel. As I now expected, it kicked back at me. I thought to myself, for one cow to kick backwards was not unusual, for two to kick back was extraordinary, for three to kick backwards, someone was taking the piss. I turned and looked behind me, Mick Clements and the other stockmen were convulsed with laughter. Some joke! Those backward kicks, had they connected, could have broken my leg.

When all the penned cattle had been taken to the auction ring and returned to their pens, Mick came up to me and said, "That's it, Dave, we're finished now."

"Good," I replied. "Are we off home now then?"

"No, not yet," he said, "follow me." He led me through to the back of the market where the stock loading ramps were. "Wait here for a while," he said. "We might get a bit more work." After a wait of ten minutes, Mick said to a farmer who had been trying without success to get four large sows to enter his trailer, "Want a hand, mate?"

"Yes, please," the farmer replied.

Ten minutes later, after a lively bout of pig wrestling, we were half a crown richer. Over the next half an hour, we made another five shillings helping to load various reluctant beasts onto lorries and trailers. Then we retired to the market café for a stockman's breakfast, a huge fry-up which comprised some part of the anatomy of just about every species of animal that had passed through the market that morning.

*

Caversham Road fire station was in the centre of Reading. One day whilst on day duties, the sub officer said to me, "Have you seen Mick Clements, Dave?"

"No, Sub," I replied.

"Well, when you do see him, tell him to take his bloody sheep back, it's here again."

"Sheep, Sub?" I queried.

"Yes, sheep, it's on the lawn again eating the bloody grass."

I went around to the side of the fire station where there was a small lawn, and sure enough, there was a sheep eating grass. When I found Mick, I asked him, "What's all this about your sheep?"

"What sheep?" he asked.

"Well, there's one on the side lawn eating the grass," I told him.

"Oh bugger!" he said. "It's out again; it's the Judas sheep from next door."

Next door, over the other side of the railway tracks was the slaughterhouse, or abattoir, (where Mick also had yet another part time job). The Judas sheep was the one that led all the other innocent sheep into the killing pens, from whence only it emerged alive.

Mick explained, "This is the only grass for miles around, and it keeps escaping to feed on our lawn. Every time it does that, I have to sneak it back again, because if they find out it keeps escaping, it will make one final trip through the killing pens." (He was a big softie at heart, was Mick.)

*

The fire bells sounded at Caversham Road fire station, the call slip said 'Cow in a ditch rear of the fire station, breakdown lorry to attend'.

"Cow in a ditch in the middle of town?" I queried to Mick Clements. "They must mean horse surely."

"No, it will be a cow," said Mick.

The small slip road at the side of the fire station led up to railway shunting yards. About 150 yards up this road was a man waving us down. The breakdown lorry pulled to a halt and we jumped out. There at the side of the road, at the base of a steep railway embankment, was a deep drainage ditch, half full of mud and oily water. Behold, there in the ditch was a cow!

The breakdown lorry had a large crane on the back; the lorry was reversed back so that the crane was overhanging the ditch.

Mick Clements had appeared from the rear cab of the breakdown lorry, wearing only trousers and vest and carrying in his hands the animal rescue slings. He then went down into the ditch to join the cow in the murky water. Mick's job would be to feed the animal rescue slings under the front and rear of the cow. These could then be attached to the hook of the crane, and the animal hauled clear.

Whilst he was attempting to do this, the cow was struggling strongly. The man who had waved us down was obviously the owner of the beast. He was most anxious for the safety of the cow, and kept on saying, "Don't damage it, lads, don't damage it."

At last, the slings were connected to the hook of the crane, and we were ready for the lift. The owner though was not satisfied, calling out, "Mick, move those slings farther apart, spread the load, we don't want to damage the beast." Mick it seemed knew everybody.

At last, with a great sucking sound, the cow came clear of the mud. The breakdown lorry was gently driven forward, and the cow lowered softly down onto the road. Whilst it was still in the slings, the owner came forward and quickly looked it over and seemed satisfied as to its condition. Then to my utter amazement, he produced a humane killer gun, put it to the animal's forehead, and promptly shot it dead. Its falling weight being held by the slings still around it.

Mick had emerged from the ditch covered in mud and slime, just in time to see the animal shot. I turned to Mick, shocked, and said, "For Christ's sake, Mick, he's been going on about not damaging the bloody thing and now he shoots it."

Mick was unruffled, saying, "That's Alf Meade, the owner of the slaughterhouse, that cow was on its way for slaughter when it escaped. What Alf had meant was don't damage or bruise the animal, because that would affect the value of the meat."

The crane of the breakdown lorry raised the carcass up in the air, a slaughterhouse lorry reversed underneath. The carcass was lowered onto the lorry and driven off to the slaughterhouse.

Back at the fire station, Mick told me that was the kindest thing to have done to the cow. The animal would have been under great stress after its ordeal in the ditch, and to then put it through the slaughterhouse routine would have been inhumane. The next day, the fire station mess received a huge joint of beef, delivered to the fire station by a grateful Alf Meade.

Some months later while riding with the Pangbourne crew, and called to a cow in a ditch, I realised just how much I had learned alongside Mick Clements.

The cow was stuck in a muddy, shallow ditch in the middle of a field. The animal came out of the ditch fairly easily, using fire hose as animal rescue slings, and lots of manpower. Once the cow was out of the ditch, we needed to hold it still whilst we checked it over for injuries, but the cow thought otherwise.

During all these operations, I had taken a somewhat back seat. Thinking these Pangbourne/country lads had been doing this sort of thing for years. But to my amazement, once the cow was out of the ditch, not one of them knew what to do next, other than to physically wrestle with the cow. These were all village lads, and when you are raised in a city, you tend to think that people that live in the country know all about cows, pigs, sheep and the like. It just isn't so. I had in my limited time in Berkshire more experience with stock than all of them put together.

I moved forward to the cow, placed the thumb and forefinger of my right hand into the cow's nostrils and pinched them tightly together. She stood as quiet as a lamb. Cattle have very sensitive noses, hence the ring through the bull's nose, and if gripped like this can normally be held quite still. After a cursory examination, the cow was considered to be undamaged. I released my fingers from the cow's nose, then with a loud complaining moo, she galloped off into the sunset.

*

140

I had by now settled in quite well at Caversham Road, and I think the Reading lads were quite pleased with their new cockney fireman. They had taken a keen interest in cockney rhyming slang. I think they were under the impression that Londoners talked it all the time. They all knew that 'apples and pears' meant stairs, and that 'barnet' meant hair. Although they didn't know the rhyme was 'barnet fair', but they were keen to learn. They would learn a slang word from me and practise on their friends.

"Nice bit of Tom you've got there, Fred," Jack would say.

Fred replies, puzzled, "Tom?"

"Yes. Tom! Tomfoolery," adds Jack gleefully.

Fred, ever more puzzled, again queries, "Tomfoolery?"

"Yes, tomfoolery, jewellery, you've got a nice watch Fred, cockney rhyming slang didn't you know."

It all started to get a bit out of hand; they were endeavouring to learn obscure rhymes to catch me out. The boldest of them had even taken to calling the station officer 'Guvnor'.

I was going to give them one they would not have heard off. In the county brigades, the pump was called a water tender ladder, although I had always persisted in calling it the pump.

On a fire station a common enquiry was, "What are you riding today?" which meant, "Which fire appliance are you riding today?"

The next time I was asked that question, I replied, "The camel."

"Pardon?" was the reply.

"You asked me what I am riding," I said, "and I am riding the camel." The man walked away with a puzzled look on his face.

Later another fireman approached me and said sympathetically, "I hear you are riding a camel today Dave, is that right?"

"Quite correct," I replied.

"Any special sort of camel?" he queried.

"No," I replied. "It could be a dromedary, or a Bactrian, it doesn't matter."

He paused and thought, then said, "What exactly is this camel that you are riding then?" so I explained.

"Camel, camel's hump, camel's hump – pump!" A big smile lit up across his face.

"I've got it, cockney rhyming slang for the water tender, sorry I mean pump."

This was one rhyming slang I had invented myself, for I had never heard the pump called a camel before. Yet amazingly enough, years on, back in the London Fire Brigade, I was to hear the term being used by even them. It could only have travelled all the way to London via the Fire Services College of Knowledge at Morton in Marsh, deepest Gloucestershire.

*

In my early days at Reading, I had heard the term 'shadow manning' but was not sure exactly what it meant.

I was riding the pump escape when the bells went down. I made my way to the appliance room and the indicator lights were showing BL, which meant that the call was for the breakdown lorry. The breakdown lorry was parked in one of the rear appliance bays and turned out to calls via the back appliance room doors and the station yard.

I stood watching, waiting for it to proceed on its call. A fireman dashed by with his fire gear in his arms and shouted to me, "Come on, Dave, you are on this shout."

"No, I am not," I called back. "I'm riding the pump escape."

"That's right," he replied. "And you are riding this one as well."

I was puzzled, how could a man ride two fire engines at one time? Well apparently, he could, it was called shadow manning. The sub officer made this abundantly clear to me, as he told me to "Stop pissing about, and get your arse and fire gear on the breakdown lorry quick."

For an ex-metropolitan fireman, the breakdown lorry was a revelation, for its call out area was the whole of the county of Berkshire. It was like going on a charabanc outing, we kept going, and going, and going, all through the main highways and leafy lanes of Berkshire. It was only the noisy two-tone horns and bells that spoiled the illusion of an idyllic day out in the country. I made a mental note that next time I did one of these trips, I must try to have a packed lunch and possibly a bottle of beer to hand.

The ride finished somewhere, I know not where, in deepest Berkshire, when the radio crackled into life with the message, "Breakdown lorry not now required, return to base."

It was a beautiful summer's day, and the sub officer said to the driver to take us back the pretty way. The pretty way took us forty-five minutes to return back to Caversham Road. Unfortunately, it being past lunchtime closing, all the pubs were shut, or it could have taken even longer.

*

The Reading lads had their own sense of humour, and standard little jokes to play on the younger firemen. At the side of the fire station on the little patch of green where the sheep occasionally grazed was a pond with goldfish in it. On a Saturday morning, one of the junior firemen would be told that it was his job today to change the water in the goldfish pond. He would be shown how to pump the water out of the pond using a stirrup pump (hand pump) so as not to damage the fish. The water was to be pumped into buckets and poured down a nearby drain. When the water level had been reduced to around three inches, he was then to report back to the senior fireman. This exercise would take him at least an hour.

When he reported back to the senior fireman, the senior fireman would look at the pond, and say, "Good, now we have to remove the fish before we drain the pond completely. Go into the kitchen and tell Auntie Vi that you want the straining basket out of the chip pan. Then use the basket to catch the goldfish and place them into buckets of water. When you have done that, finish draining the pond."

Auntie Vi, the station cook, was a big, buxom lady of around fifty-five years of age. She had never married but had been the cook on this fire station for around twenty-five years, and no one, but no one, mucked Auntie Vi about!

When the spotty young fireman entered the kitchen and told Auntie Vi that he would like the chip basket please, Auntie Vi had seen it all before. "You would like my chip basket, would you?" she repeated.

The young fireman said, "Yes please, Vi."

Then auntie Vi says, "If I ask you why you want my nice, clean, sterile chip basket on this a fine Saturday morning, you wouldn't be going to tell me that you want to put it in that filthy mucky pond out there, to catch bloody goldfish with, would you?"

"Why yes, Vi, how did you know that?" said the startled young fireman.

"How did I know that?" shouted Auntie Vi. "I know that, because those silly buggers are still playing the same bloody silly tricks now that they played twenty-five years ago, now piss off out of my kitchen." Auntie Vi, despite the image that the name conjures up, really did speak like that, honestly!

*

Around this period in time, I had a little minivan, which was my own and my family's means of transport. The little van had seen better years, money was tight and I tended to nurse it along, not being able to afford a new car.

One evening, after day duties, I got into the van to drive home to Pangbourne. I started up the engine and engaged first gear, let out the clutch and nothing happened, the car stayed stationary. I checked the car was in first gear, let out the clutch again, nothing happened. I began to worry. I then engaged reverse gear, let out the clutch, nothing happened. I am not the world's best mechanic, but this clearly indicated a major transmission breakdown, and likely to be expensive enough to write the car off. I tried both procedures again, this time pressing the clutch pedal up and down in between each movement, but again nothing happened – calamity!

I got out of the car to find one of the firemen who did part time work as a mechanic. He came over to the car, raised the bonnet, peered in, shook his head, and said, "Yes, you have definitely lost all traction. Whilst the car is in this condition," he said mournfully, "it will never move again." He looked at my face, which was a picture of gloom and despair. Taking pity on me he said, "There is one thing you could try."

"What's that," I said, raising my hopes.

"Try looking underneath," he said.

"That won't help much if the traction is gone, will it?" I argued.

"Just try it," he insisted, so I looked underneath. There I saw to my amazement, but unmitigated relief, that the front of the car had been jacked up, then lowered back down onto blocks so that the front wheels, and this was a front wheel drive car, were a fraction of an inch off the ground. I looked around the drill yard and station and there were all the grinning faces. You just can't beat an old joke; all you need is a new face to play it on.

*

Just inside the front door of my home at Pangbourne, up almost at ceiling level, was a large bell, just like the call bells in the fire station. This was my house bell for retained fire calls. It was tested every morning at 7.00 am, whether I was at home or not.

It was a very noisy bell, for it had to awaken me in my bedroom on the floor above. With a young baby in the house, and me away from home often on nights, my wife was getting a bit fed up with it. For not only did it ring every morning at 7.00 am, but every time Pangbourne received a fire call. Even when I was on night duty at Reading, the dreaded bell would ring.

One of the Pangbourne firemen presented me with a switch and told me how to wire it in so that I had an on/off switch by my bedside. All very illegal to muck about with the post office equipment, but then they didn't have to live with their bloody great bells clattering twenty-four hours a day.

From around 7.30 am until around 10.00 pm, a big siren sited on a pole above the fire station would also sound for one minute when a fire call was received. This was for the firemen working away from their homes and around the village in the daytime. Upon hearing the house bell or siren, the retained firemen would make their way to the fire station as quickly as possible. All methods of transport were used, cars, cycles or on foot.

On arrival at the fire station, the firemen took one of six tallies off a board, and the first six men to arrive at the station rode the appliance. The reason for the tallies – in the past, it was the first six firemen on board the appliance that would ride the machine. This had led to some interesting little disputes, as two, three, four firemen had fought each other to get on board the fire engine first. So keen were they to ride that fights had allegedly broken out. Apparently, the most dangerous part of the fire calls was actually just getting on board the fire engine. So a new system had to be found, hence the tallies.

It must be explained that although retained firemen did give up their time to do this sometimes-dangerous job, they did get a very fair turnout fee, which sometimes added to the competitive spirit to get on the fire engine.

One fireman had the nickname 'Mad Jack Ericson', but not because he was mad in a mental sense. Instead, because he rode his cycle like a bloody lunatic when attending fire calls. He lived around a quarter of a mile from the station, and usually attended fire calls on his bicycle, speeding like a demented Olympic racer to get to the fire station first, in order to get a ride. At the side of the fire station was a small access road, and the cycles would normally be leant against the station wall in this road. Mad Jack, if any other fireman was close to him in the race to the station, would leap off his bicycle and leave it to career down the access road all on its own, whilst he rushed into the station.

A fire call had been received at the station, and Mad Jack had done just that! His bicycle had sailed on serenely on automatic pilot, whilst he had dashed into the station to grab the last tally.

The sub officer being the officer in charge of the station had a privilege. He was allowed to park his car in the single car parking space at the rear of the station.

Whilst Mad Jack was rigging in his fire gear this same day, the sub officer came hurrying into the station and called out crossly, "Who has left his bicycle lying out in the road?"

Jack had been warned about this habit before, and so was on the defensive. "Sorry, Sub Officer, it was me," called back Jack. "It won't happen again, I promise."

The sub officer then shouted out, "Oh no, you're not sorry, you are bloody well broken hearted, if you but knew it. It won't happen again either, 'cause I've just run it over with my car."

Poor old Jack allegedly suffered from a little-known medical condition called brassicitus, which was aggravated or induced by tinnitus. Tinnitus is the more common complaint; this is the medical term for ringing in the ears. The name brassicitus is taken from the name for the cabbage family, or the brassicas. Jack was normally a very intelligent, pleasant, well-mannered man, but upon suffering a sudden attack of tinnitus, the ringing of bells in his ears, or even the siren above the station for that matter, this would invariably induce upon him a sudden and even more severe attack of brassicitus.

Brassicitus is more commonly known in the fire service as 'cabbage head'. This complaint makes a man totally unable to act or even think reasonably. Brassicitus (cabbage head) is to be found at all ranks and levels of the fire service. It always and invariably follows an attack of tinnitus (ringing of bells in the ears). Thus, Jack was not alone in his sufferings.

When the siren above the fire station sounded, the whole village was aware that a fire call had been received at the station. Everybody took extra special care in crossing the village roads. Local motorists on seeing flashing headlights behind them, instead of then endeavouring to obstruct a road hog, would realise it was a retained fireman on his way to a call and pull over. On a busy week for fire calls, ratepayers would feel they were getting value for money from the fire rate. On later seeing the firemen in the village, they would then get the gossip on whose house had caught fire and the extent of the damage.

At around ten o'clock at night, the siren would be switched off. The authorities perhaps assuming that all good firemen would be at home, or tucked up in bed by that time, and respond to their house bells. The problem was that the local pubs didn't shut until 10.30 pm, which left a gap of an hour before the firemen were back in their homes. Some brigades solved the problem by allowing a fire bell in the pub itself. In other cases, the firemen solved the problem themselves by leaving the following instructions with fire control. 'In case of fire on our patch, telephone the Queen's Head and shout fire!'

Pangbourne did not suffer that problem, there were but three of us that used the 'Star' across the road from the fire station regularly. The fire station could be seen from the pub windows, and if the automatic lights came on in the fire station, it usually indicated that a fire call had been received. Many was the time the three pubgoers had waited for the rest of the crew to arrive, all seated on the appliance fully rigged in fire gear before the first non-imbibers crashed through the door out of breath.

I have responded to the siren on foot, on bicycle, by car and by canoe. I was canoeing on the River Thames at the time when the siren sounded. I have responded by hitch hiking. I was half a mile out of the village when I heard the siren and flagged down a passing car. I have even responded by fire engine.

I was out for a walk with my wife and young daughter, along a country lane about half a mile out from the village. Behind me, I heard the sound of a heavy vehicle, and moved off the road onto the verge to let it pass. When I looked back, I saw to my surprise, that it was Pangbourne's fire engine. I had not heard the siren over the station sound, calling out the crew. This was not too surprising, for the distance that the siren would carry varied very much with the weather and wind conditions. The fire engine pulled up alongside me and the sub officer shouted across, "Jump on, Dave."

"I can't, I'm out for a walk with my family, and I haven't got any fire gear," I replied back.

He shouted, "You've got to get on, we only have three in the crew." The fire engine was not supposed to leave the station without a minimum crew of four. I jumped up into the back cab, saying sorry to my wife who was left behind looking quite cross.

Once on the fire engine, the sub officer told me the call was only to a motor car alight. They thought they would chance it with a crew of three.

We drove along for around five minutes, when over the top of some trees we saw a big cloud of black smoke. As we approached, a farmer waved us into a field. There we saw a motor car on fire from end to end.

I now had a problem, I had no fire gear, I was dressed in trousers, shirt and wellington boots. I said to the driver of the machine, "I haven't got any fire gear; you fight the fire, I will operate the pump." A look of utter bewilderment came across his face. Perhaps not surprisingly, for I had never seen this particular fireman do anything other than drive the appliance or operate the pump. The other members of the crew were the sub officer and the sub officer's dad, who was one of the oldest firemen I had ever seen. The sub officer's dad, who was the leading fireman on the station, usually helped lay out the hydrant at a fire, then stood in the road directing traffic around it. These two firemen were now the only two working hands at this fire.

To my amazement, it was the sub officer who actually extinguished the fire. His dad helped by lightening up the hose from a respectful distance. The driver, whom I had replaced as pump operator, actually stood and talked to the farmer during the whole of the proceedings. He still carried on this conversation, even whilst the poor old sub officer's dad and I made up the hose. The driver was from a respected family in the village, and was inordinately proud of the fact that he was a fireman, he was a nice, pleasant and likeable man, but a fireman?

*

On a lot of these Pangbourne fire callouts, I was at a bit of a disadvantage. At the time, I had an old black Labrador dog called Whiskey. Now Whiskey very much liked to ride in my little minivan. In fact, he was very loath indeed to miss a single chance to ride. So every time the fire bell rang in my house, before I could respond, I first had to make sure the dog was secure inside the house. That dog was no fool; he associated the ringing of the fire bell with exciting rides in my car.

One day the fire bell rang, Whiskey was secure in the rear garden, which was surrounded by a six-foot high fence. I set off in the van for the fire station. I negotiated various turns and junctions before leaving the estate where I lived, then onto the long, straight road that led towards the fire station, I checked my rear-view mirror. Sure enough, there screeching down the middle of the road behind me was a great big black Labrador. He had jumped the six-foot garden fence, so eager was he to ride. He reminded me for a while of the previously mentioned 'Mad Jack'.

I turned left and screeched to a halt outside the fire station on the main Reading Road. As was the custom on hearing the siren, a small crowd of people had gathered to watch the fire engine leave. I don't know what these people could possibly have thought when a small mini-van screeched to a halt outside the fire station, then the driver hurriedly got out, rushed around to the back of the van and threw open the rear doors, then to immediately disappear off in the direction he had just come from and seconds later appear back in view, dragging behind him a big black dog which was roughly thrown in the back of the mini-van, the doors being slammed behind it. The driver himself then to promptly vanish into the fire station. The locals would know well enough what was happening, for both Whiskey and I were well known in the village. It must have seemed a strange carry on though, to strangers in the crowd.

In later years when I had transferred back to London, I travelled up to town by train, leaving my car behind. Whiskey would sometimes camp out underneath the car for days at a time.

On one occasion, we went to the Isle of Sark for our holidays, the only occasion that we did not take Whiskey away with us. Instead, he stayed with a neighbour for the fortnight. On our return, I asked had he behaved himself whilst we were away. The neighbour told me that for the first two days we were gone, the dog disappeared. The neighbour was frantic and searched everywhere. At last, she found him, he had made his way to my allotment/vegetable patch, dug a great big hole in the middle of the potatoes, then camped up there for two nights until he was found. Later, when I went to the allotment and saw the size of the hole he had dug – about one metre deep, one metre wide, and two metres long – this caused me some deep thought, and then I told my wife, "If I die before that dog, don't whatever you do, let him see me go into my grave. Because if you do, as sure as eggs are eggs, the bugger will come and dig me up again."

We had received a call at Pangbourne to a tractor overturned, one man trapped. One machine from Pangbourne was attending, plus the breakdown/rescue lorry from Reading. I had only attended one of these incidents previously whilst on duty at Reading fire station, but I knew – the prognosis was not good. At this time, tractors were not required to be fitted with safety cabs.

Tractor drivers work normally on their own, in the middle of lonely fields. By the time, their predicaments are discovered and help arrives, they are very often crushed to death, or simply asphyxiated by the weight of the tractor bearing down on them.

We had been driving down country lanes for around fifteen minutes before I heard the sub officer call back from the front of the appliance that we were there. Looking out, I could see a tractor completely overturned in a ditch at the side of the road. The tractor was resting partly on its front bonnet and partly on its high rear mudguards. A lady driver told us that the tractor had pulled over to let her pass in the narrow road, when without warning, the tractor suddenly slipped down into the ditch and turned over and that the driver was still alive. The tractor had no safety cab, and the fact that the driver was still alive was surprising and good news.

I scrambled down into the ditch and I could see the driver, who was trapped underneath the tractor in his cab. It was difficult to make out which bit of the driver was which, there seemed to be so much of him in such a small space. I spoke to him. "Are you all right, mate?"

A deep voice from somewhere under the tractor said, "Yes, I'm fine, just get me out."

After about a minute's study, I could now make out roughly which way his body was positioned. One thing was abundantly clear – this was a very big man, in a very small space. I had no idea how we would get the man out at this time, but one thing was obvious, the steering wheel was going to be in the way.

I called for the Cengar equipment, which was basically a compressed air operated reciprocating saw. When it arrived and was set up, I squeezed underneath the tractor and began cutting away the steering column. This was a long and difficult job, the saw blades kept breaking because of the difficult access to the column.

Eventually, I was underneath the tractor and in the cab area with the trapped man, who was remarkably cheerful considering the predicament he was in. When a saw blade broke, which they constantly did, I would have a short rest and a pause, whilst the other firemen changed the saw blade for me.

During one of these breaks, the trapped man said to me, "You lads had better get your fingers out, it's still coming down."

"What's coming down?" I asked him.

"The tractor," he replied. "It's sinking down slowly into the mud of the ditch."

I set back to work cutting through the steering column, but now time was of the essence. I was trying my hardest not to break the blades and thus lose time. I still had no idea how we would get the man out once I had cut through the steering column, just that before anything at all could be done to effect a rescue, the column would need to come off.

At long last, the blade went right through the column, and the man said straight away, "That's better, the pressure is off me now." I had cut the column as low down as possible, to give us the most room. I passed the saw, steering wheel and column out to the other firemen outside, and turned my attention to the trapped man, asking him if he was injured in any way.

"No," he replied, which I thought quite amazing, as there was a heavy tractor perched on top of him. I then asked him if he could move his legs, yes, he could move them. Although the man was very cramped in the tractor cab, it was only his legs that appeared to be trapped beneath the front of the tractor. If he was uninjured, perhaps he could get himself out with a little help.

I had by now squeezed right behind him in the space between the two large tractor wheels, so that I could grip him under both arms. I then told the man, "When I say go, you give a backwards kick with both legs, and I will pull you at the same time." We did this, and I asked him, "Did you move at all?"

He said, "Yes. I moved backwards a bit."

We repeated this for about five minutes, him giving backward kicks with his legs and me giving mighty tugs at the same time. After this time, he had emerged about a foot backwards into the cab. I was now particularly keen that he should be rescued soon, before the tractor sank into the mud anymore, because he was now blocking my way out from the cab and I was effectively trapped with him. We were both now so cramped inside the ever-decreasing space in the cab that I could not pull him backwards anymore.

I think it was at this point that I became a little bit apprehensive, as the tractor settled yet lower in the mud. What had I done? I had helped to dig my own grave! I had manoeuvred the big man into such a position that I could not now possibly escape myself. So far as I was now concerned, this had definitely become a self-rescue operation on my part.

I helped him twist his head and shoulders so that the firemen outside could grip him under the arms and assist his efforts to free himself. After a further five minutes of pulling and tugging and him kicking with his legs, he finally emerged from underneath the tractor, safe and uninjured, mainly through his own physical efforts. I then crawled out behind him and saw for the first time what a large man he was. He was over six foot tall and weighed around twenty stone. It was very hard to believe that this huge man had just emerged unscathed except for a few bruises, from that tiny space underneath the overturned tractor. Even harder to believe that I had been in there with him.

An interesting note to this story is that when back at Pangbourne station, I heard the sub officer comment, "We handled that job all right without any help from the Reading lads."

When I was next on duty at Caversham Road, Mick Clements said to me, "I heard you did well the other day, Dave, us Reading lads saved the part timer's bacon again." It would seem I had mastered the impossible, I was considered both by the whole time, and the retained firemen, to be one of the lads.

*

One thing that Pangbourne and Reading fire stations had in common was that the western region of British Rail, the old Great Western Railway, ran within yards of both stations. Both Reading and Pangbourne prospered when the railway was built through both the town and the village.

In the days of the old steam engines, the old hands would tell of the many embankment fires they attended in the hot summers, all started by sparks from the steam trains. But now, the whole region had long since converted to diesel trains, and only occasionally would we go onto the railway tracks to fight fires.

One fine summer's afternoon a fire call was received at Reading fire station to a diesel train alight on the permanent way east of Reading railway station. The appliance went to several locations looking for the train, but we could not find it. A radio call to fire control requesting that British Rail give a better location of the train finally brought results. But the nearest we could get to the train by road was several hundred yards. Between us and the train were around four railway tracks, over which we could not stretch our hose. The train, although issuing smoke through its engine room vents, did not seem to be dangerously on fire.

The plan was to cross the tracks over to the train, make contact with the driver, and if he required our assistance, then get him to move the train to a location where the road crossed over the railway, about a mile down the track, then extinguish the fire there. Mick Clements and I set off over the tracks to meet up with the train. Mick set off first, followed closely by me.

Halfway across the four sets of tracks, Mick was about fifteen yards in front, when he stopped and turned around. I think he wanted to talk to me. As I approached him crossing a railway line, I jumped up onto the line then off again down to the ballast. He suddenly shouted loudly with horror in his voice, "Dave, what have you just done!" His voice was so very intense that I stopped dead in my tracks then looked quickly behind me to see what could have happened. I could see nothing.

"What do you mean, what have I done? I haven't done anything," I said.

He was speaking very slowly with a shaking voice, "You have just stepped onto a live electric rail," he said.

"Don't be daft," I replied. "This is the Western region; diesel trains."

"Oh no, it's not," he said. "These two tracks are where the Southern region comes into Reading. These two tracks are electrified, that's the Western region over there, where the diesel train is standing."

I still did not believe him – how could I step on a live rail without being electrocuted? Yet when I looked closely at the rails I had just jumped upon, they were all mounted on porcelain insulators, they were electrified all right.

That was probably as close as I have ever been to death. On a beautiful day, on a silly little nothing fire. Remember old Dave Wilson? Yes, wasn't he the silly bugger that stood on a live rail? The reason I didn't die? The reason I didn't go up in a flash of blue light, and a big puff of smoke? Mick was wrong, I did not step onto a live rail. I can only surmise that I jumped onto a live rail. I landed with one foot only on the live rail, then sprung off the rail again using the same foot. At no time did I have one foot on the rail and one foot on the ground, thus completing the electrical circuit to earth. Rather like when birds perch on high voltage transmission lines, they survive because they don't complete the electrical circuit to earth. Nevertheless, my obituary, had the need arisen, would probably still have included the words 'silly bugger'.

*

I seem to be a man that does things the hard way. When I had initially applied to join the London Fire Brigade, I had to apply twice. I had now made my second application to transfer back to the London Fire Brigade. I had been turned down on my first application, because I was living in a Berkshire Fire Brigade house, which I would have needed to vacate if I left the Berkshire Brigade. I had since borrowed enough money from my family to put down a deposit and buy my own house in Pangbourne. I was now awaiting a reply to my second application for transfer back to London.

The straw which finally broke the camel's back, and me to transfer back, was as follows. In my quest to top up the low fire Brigade wages, I had started a chimney sweeping business from my home. Financially, this did very well, and did not interfere with my retained duties. It was against Brigade regulations though, to run a business from a Fire Brigade house. I had anticipated if caught, to face a charge under discipline regulations. When eventually someone reported me to the Brigade, the divisional officer informed me that if I did not cease the business, I would be thrown out of my house. Then adding, did I know that I needed permission to even install a telephone in my house? At that point, I decided it was time to go.

When in the future people asked me why I could not settle in the Reading and Berkshire Fire Brigade, I could only answer, it was not one big thing but rather a thousand little things. The firemen that I met in Reading are still my firm friends, but I think that once you are a cockney fireman, you remain a cockney fireman.

One thing was sure; I was going to miss the county brigade's social life. At Caversham Road fire station, we were playing host to a visiting party of German policemen, who were accompanied by an equal number of Reading police force. It was one o'clock in the morning, and the bar was crowded, most of the guests were as pissed as parrots. They were still calling for pints of Guinness, which they (the Germans) pronounced as 'Gwiness', when finally, they were persuaded that they ought to leave. Some of the policewomen decided they would leave via the sliding pole, which led from the recreation room/bar to the appliance room. Whilst the policewomen were receiving instructions on how to descend the fireman's pole, all the male guests had been quietly ushered away to the appliance room below, there to witness the rare and privileged sight of police lady's stockings, suspenders and knickers, as they descended the sliding pole to resounding cheers. A perfect end to a perfect evening, to a slightly imperfect transfer.

My transfer application back to London had this time been accepted. It was a sad time. If all the compliments that were now given me had been given me before my application, I just might have stayed. But as Mick Clements said in saying his goodbye, "Well, you're back off to the smoke then, Dave."

Chapter 9

Southwark Training School (Again) – 1969

Once again, I was to walk through the narrow archway entrance to Southwark Training School. I had spent four months there for my initial recruit training two weeks for breathing apparatus training, another two weeks training as a motor driver and yet another two weeks qualifying as a turntable ladder operator. Now on my transfer back to the London Fire Brigade, they had decreed that I must now spend another five weeks at Southwark.

It would appear that at that time, they considered that any fireman that had transferred away from the London Fire Brigade needed his head examined. So the Brigade had allocated five weeks to examine it in. Five weeks to teach me that which I could have equally as well taught them – that my driving skills had not deteriorated driving through all those meandering country lanes. Then the breathing apparatus refresher course, to check that I could still find my way around the infamous Southwark smoke chambers, rat run.

I think I was deemed a bit bolshy, because I told them if they really wanted to see how quickly I could negotiate the rat run, then let them really set fire to the bloody thing, then see how long it took me to get out.

The squad of five to which I was assigned was given the grand title of 'Transfers and re-enrolments' – which meant myself and one other fireman had transferred back to the London Fire Brigade. The other three firemen had resigned from the Brigade and then subsequently re-enrolled.

In charge of the squad was Temporary Station Officer Clarkson, a man who had joined the fire service on the same day as me, then spent three months of recruit training in the same squad. He greeted me cheerfully, not even realising that I had transferred out of the Brigade. He had I think after basic training, spent only two years on a fire station, then set out on the promotion route, via various

156

office jobs and headquarters postings. He had always said that one day he would be the chief officer, which he ultimately was.

Two of us from the squad had now to retake our driving qualifications and were ordered to report to the motor driving school. There to my surprise, the test was to be taken in my old favourite fire engine, the Dennis F11 petrol machine. The other driver was ordered to take the test first, no practice run or the like, just jump up into the driving seat and show us what you can do.

This fireman, having driven diesel machines with synchromesh gear boxes since leaving motor school, never stood a chance. He crashed nearly every gear. He was duly failed and he was heartbroken.

My turn came, I really would not have minded if I failed this driving test. I had a lot of firefighting experience that I had missed through being the driver to make up. I did not stand much of a chance of failing the test either, other than actually throwing the test, which I could not do on principle, for they had a Dennis F11 on the run at Reading which I regularly drove, thus I had kept my hand in.

During the course of the actual test, I did not snick a single gear; I could see the examiner was suitably impressed. He would normally only examine trainee drivers, who would be bound to crunch the odd gear or two. The result was, I was now once again a Brigade driver. He gave the game away afterwards by saying, "If you could trundle turntable ladders around the back doubles of Soho, I wasn't expecting you to fail." He had obviously looked up my record card.

Whilst in Berkshire, I had passed the national written examination for promotion to the rank of sub officer. The next step on the ladder to promotion would be to take the practical examination for promotion to this rank. I noticed that the practical examinations where being held at Southwark at that time.

I approached Station Officer Clarkson, told him I had passed the written exam and could I be included in the practical examinations currently being held. I think he may have pulled a few strings, for old times' sake, for I was told it was a bit irregular, but yes, I may take part.

I had thought there was not much chance of me passing the sub officer's practical exam, as I had not prepared for it. I had intended that it would be a good dress rehearsal for next year. If you want to pass examinations, training centre is the best place to be. Training centre staff set the syllabus for these practical examinations, and in some cases actually conducted them.

Besides being able to demonstrate a thorough knowledge of pumps, pumping, and fire service equipment, a candidate for sub officer rank had to be able to impart this knowledge to recruit firemen. He had to be able to instruct recruit firemen in how to perform basic hose and ladder drills, then to supervise them whilst they did so. His knowledge of breathing apparatus and breathing apparatus procedures must be graded excellent.

I was attached to training school, albeit temporarily attached, therefore the instructors gave me their full assistance. I was given squads of recruits to practice my drill instructions on. I was given a whole morning's instruction by the breathing apparatus instructors. Any assistance I asked for to assist me in passing the exam was given.

The examination took one whole day, divided into six examination subjects. At the end of that very long day, I walked out through the archway of the training school, totally and absolutely mentally and physically drained. Then I joined the rest of the examinees in the Goldsmith's Arms a few doors along from Southwark fire station, to rest and recuperate.

It was ultimately worth all the effort, for a month or so later, promulgated in Brigade orders were the words, 'Fireman David Wilson, attached to A21 Paddington fire station has passed his sub officer's practical examination'.

I was the only one in the squad that had a turntable ladder qualification to re-take. This time, they allocated a whole three days to re-familiarise myself and take the examination.

By now, the mechanical ladders had been phased out of the Brigade, so I was to re-take the exam only on the Merryweather hydraulic ladders. Again, the Reading ladders had been a Merryweather hydraulic set, so I had been driving and operating the ladders the whole time I had been away from London.

The sub officer in charge of turntable ladder training was a very senior instructor in the training school. He wasn't too far off of retirement age and had been doing this job for years. I had joined a squad of three firemen who were in the middle of their turntable ladder operator's course.

On the first morning in front of the three other firemen, he said to me, "Right then, old Wilson, let's see what you can do. I want you to put the head of the ladders into the seventh-floor window of this drill tower."

I sat on the operator's seat and pressed the loading pedal with my foot, this increased the engine revolutions to bring the hydraulic pressure up. I then elevated the ladders up from their housing. As the ladders came clear of their housing, I pressed the training bar with my right knee – this turned the ladders around across the chassis. As soon as I had elevated high enough, I pressed the right-hand lever to extend the ladders. I now had all three ladder movements in synchronisation, so that the ladders elevated, turned and extended up to the window in one continuous synchronised movement.

Whilst I was doing this, the sub officer momentarily had his back to me, talking to the squad. He could see by the looks on the squad's faces that something unusual was happening, so he turned around to see what it was. To his amazement, he saw that I was just about to rest the head of the ladder onto the seventh-floor windowsill.

"How did that get up there so quickly?" he snapped.

I didn't answer straight away, for I was engrossed in the fine adjustments as the ladder actually entered the window opening.

One of the trainee ladder operators answered his question. "It was brilliant, Sub, he just carried out the three operations of elevating, training and extending all at the same time."

A big smile of self-satisfaction came across the sub officer's face! "Now I see!" he said grimly. "You have got into nasty little Berkshire ways. You have been operating the knee-training bar with your knee, haven't you? Not as the London Fire Brigade instructs, with your hand, you are a very naughty boy."

Merry weathers had designed the ladders so that the training of the ladder could be done with the knees, leaving the hands free for the other two operations of elevating and extending. The London Fire Brigade thought otherwise and insisted that the knee bar be operated with the hand.

Later, when the sub officer found that I had eight years' service, and was an ex-Soho fireman, and had used the ladders operationally countless times, he mellowed towards me.

The time came for me to re-qualify. The examining officer – an assistant divisional officer – told me to extend the ladders to the seventh floor of the tower and position the ladders alongside the tower so that a man could walk up them and step off onto the tower. I did as he asked. He then walked all around the ladders holding his thumb up in the air, like an artist, gauging perspective. He came back to me and said, "They are three feet too high."

I then walked around the ladders without holding my thumb up, came back and said to him, "No, they're not, they're spot on."

Being an assistant divisional officer in training school, he was not used to people arguing with him. But then, he was not really used to dealing with qualified and experienced ladder operators either, so I stuck to my guns. After a minute or so of debate, which was beginning to get quite heated, I reminded him what the original order was. That I should extend the ladders to the seventh floor of the tower, and alongside the tower, in order that a man should walk up them and step onto the tower – he agreed, but still insisted that they were three feet too high.

I played my trump card. I explained to him that at the angle of elevation which the ladders were at, when a man walked up them to the top, the weight of the man would cause the ladders to sag down the three feet, thus enabling the man to step off safely onto the seventh floor. He appeared dumbfounded; he had never heard of this one before. The matter was resolved by the summoning of a recruit fireman, who was instructed to go up the ladder and prove the matter one way or the other. Fortunately, for me, the ladder did sag with his weight, as I had known it would. The recruit stepped safely off the ladder onto the seventh floor of the drill tower. I was then duly if somewhat grudgingly, re-qualified as a turntable ladder operator.

For the rest of the time, we five firemen, all with between four and ten years' service each, sat around and scratched our bottoms. The station officer would visit us once a day to brief us on what he thought our daily routine should be. If it sounded interesting, or informative, we would comply. Occasionally, he would arrive with a Brigade minibus and take us to the Brigade stores to draw more equipment or uniform. From the end of the first week, the squad had been autonomous and self-disciplined, and in the main part, we occupied our own time.

Finally, the end of five weeks, and the full five weeks we served. At last, we received our postings to our new fire stations. I was very pleased with mine, I was being posted back to the 'A' division, my old division and A21 Paddington was to be my new station.

A21 Paddington was a newly built station, with one of the busiest fire grounds in London. It was also divisional headquarters for the 'A' division – I had never served at a divisional station before.

As a bonus, for I was still living in Pangbourne, my train to work ran directly into Paddington railway station, a mere eight minutes' walk from the fire station.

Chapter 10

Paddington Red Watch – 1969

A21 Paddington was a brand-new station; it had only opened a month prior to my being posted there in 1969. It was a large four appliance bay station, four-storeys high, the top storey being accommodation for senior officers. It included all the new design features of the Chelsea fire station, but as it was intended as a divisional headquarters station, a few more as well.

The basement included a large smoke/humidity chamber, intended for divisional smoke training. The ground floor was the large appliance room, and the station/divisional watchroom. The station office was on a mezzanine floor, between the ground and second floors, overlooking the large appliance room. All the station accommodation was up on the second floor, messroom, dormitory, kitchen, recreation room etc.

There was a breathing apparatus charging room, where the BA cylinders were re-charged, this employed two full time firemen seconded to divisional headquarters. On the ground floor of the station was a separate wing for divisional headquarters, divided into rooms for divisional staff and senior officers. The station had a large square-shaped drill yard, and a seven-storey concrete modern drill tower.

Paddington's fire ground ran roughly along the line of the Bayswater Road, to Marble Arch. Then along both sides of the Edgware Road to Maida Vale, and included the large triangle of land inside these two roads. Running through all this was the Regents Park spur of the Grand Union Canal. The station was built not a hundred yards from its picturesque attraction, 'Little Venice', the canal's fashionable basin for canal boat enthusiasts.

The appliances at the station were pump escape, pump, turntable ladders and emergency tender. Then attached to 'A' divisional headquarters, three staff cars, two general purpose lorries and a divisional fire control unit. All these vehicles would have drivers and crews to man them, being part of the compliment of firemen at the station.

A21 Paddington fire station had replaced an old, small London County Council station, called Edgware Road. Edgware Road had been a pump escape and turntable ladder only station. At times, as few as six firemen would have been on duty on the station, but now at the new Paddington, up to thirty-six was possible. The majority of these firemen would have been posted in from other fire stations, some of them unwillingly.

The watches also included a disproportionate number of junior and recruit firemen. This I think was the reason for my posting to Paddington, with my nine years' service, I was a relatively senior fireman.

Life on a big divisional station was different, there being so many firemen on duty, they tended to break down into subgroups. The crew of the emergency tender, (six firemen) would tend to stick together as a group. The old Edgware Road firemen formed yet another group. As the station had only been opened for a short time, the watches had not yet had time to gel together.

There was one thing in Paddington's favour, the old Edgware Road fire ground which Paddington had inherited had been a very busy ground. If there is one thing good for morale on a fire station, it's lots of fire calls.

At this period in time, Paddington was a very busy fire station, ten to twenty calls a night not being unusual. These calls would be shared out amongst the four fire engines stationed there, the turntable ladders and the pump invariably taking the lion's share, around ten to fifteen a night.

At around this time, a lot of Paddington was being pulled down in slum clearance programs, which generated a lot of rubbish and derelict house fires. Thirteen in one night was my personal record, whilst riding the pump one night. That was not counting other calls we attended in between.

This was where my love of the turntable ladders was really cemented. The turntable ladders didn't go to rubbish fires, didn't go to people shut in lifts, with all those stairs to walk up. The turntable ladders only went to real fires involving high buildings. Then, when in the ladder driver's opinion, all the excitement was over, all he had to do was shout 'ladders away, guv', and off he went back to his nice warm fire station.

I was now approaching thirty years of age, supporting on my meagre wage a wife, two small children, a big black Labrador and an exceptionally large mortgage. Yet I was still only a gash hand or common-all-garden fireman after nearly ten years' service. It was time to pause for a midlife crises. I did a bit of soul searching and decided that I really ought to worry a bit more. I didn't worry enough, that was my problem, I was too easy going. I reasoned that if I had worried more all of my career, I could have been at least a station officer by now, albeit a somewhat neurotic one.

That was it, I decided I was going to be more conscientious, and worry more. What should I worry about, that was the new problem – this caused me many worries. I really couldn't think of anything special to worry about. So after a week or so of worrying about not worrying, I decided to give it all up and not worry at all, just carry on as usual. Thus, ended my early midlife crisis.

Because I had passed the promotion examinations to the rank of sub officer, I was now doing a lot of acting-up in the rank of acting leading fireman. This involved carrying out administrative routines in the station office, and when attending fire calls riding in charge of one of the appliances.

We were on day duties, and I was temporarily promoted to the rank of Acting Leading Fireman and was riding in charge of the turntable ladders. At 2.00 pm, straight after lunch, the stand-by driver who was driving the ladders decided it was such a pleasant day that he would like to road test the ladders, which in effect really meant it was such a nice day that he felt like going for a drive. Permission was sought of, and given, by Brigade control and we left the station. The appliance radio was switched on, for if any fire calls came in, we would be mobilised to the fire by radio.

We set off for the Edgware Road, around Marble Arch, along the Bayswater Road, then turned right into Queensway. I had done this route before with standby drivers, they took this way because it had more pretty girls per mile than any other route.

As we turned right into Queensway, the appliance radio crackled into life. "Alpha 213, Alpha 213, priority over."

"Looks like we've picked up a shout," I said to the driver. I acknowledged the call, "M2FH, from Alpha 213 go ahead over."

Then, came back, "Order your turntable ladders to a fire at 32 Cornham Avenue, A21 Paddington's ground."

I acknowledged receipt of the fire call, then said to the standby driver, "Okay, I know the address, I will direct you to it."

As we turned into Corrham Avenue, I saw that the pump escape only was already in attendance. They were parked up on the right about 200 yards away, and as we approached, I could see smoke issuing from the top of the building.

The building had a semi-basement and was two storeys in height. It had a room built into the roof, which was where the smoke was issuing from.

As we approached the fire, I said to the driver, "Looks like you might have a chance to use the ladders here. Make sure you park up so that if we need to, we can get the ladders to work."

Jumping down from the turntable ladders, I could hear the engine of the pump escape pounding away and saw a hose reel tubing snaking off into the building. I was looking for Acting Leading Fireman Mathews, who was in charge of the pump escape that day. I wanted to find out whether the turntable ladders should be extended to cover any eventualities that might occur.

Acting Leading Fireman Mathews was a much younger fireman than me and had far less time in the job. But by being in charge of the pump escape, and being first in attendance at the fire, he was nominally in charge of the fire.

When I found him, he was up a short flight of steps at the entrance door to the house. He was busy rigging in a proto breathing apparatus set. Before I could ask him my query about the turntable ladders, he said to me, "Quick, get a set on Dave." (Meaning a breathing apparatus set.)

I replied, "But I'm in charge of the ladders, you might want to use them."

"Never mind that," he snapped. "There's two kids involved in here, get a set on quick."

I dashed away to the pump escape to get a proto breathing set out of the back cab. I slipped the set over my shoulders and jumped down. As I walked back to the door of the house, I pulled my head harness from my pocket and put it upon my head. Arriving back at the door to the house, I was still clipping up and adjusting my set. Mathews was now fully rigged and waiting for me.

"Hurry up," he repeated. "There are two kids in there."

I clipped my mouthpiece up to the head harness, put on my nose clip and began the starting up routine. Mathews was now beside himself with impatience. "For Christ's sake hurry up, there are kids in there."

I had not yet even buckled up my breathing set body belts, when Mathews grabbed me and physically pulled me into the house, leaving behind there at the head of that short flight of steps, my fire helmet.

We made our way up a flight of stairs to the first floor and turned left onto a landing; it was smoky at this point but did not warrant breathing sets.

Along the landing, we found two firemen laying down on the floor and fighting a fierce fire in the front room of the house with a hose reel jet. They were pointing up a second flight of stairs, indicating that the children were up there.

Mathews went up the stairs first, he went about two thirds of the way up, reaching the level of the top of the door where the fire was coming from. At this point, he would have entered the zone where the heat was spilling out from the burning room below and rising to its highest level. He turned quickly and crashed back down the stairs past me. I followed him down to find out what the problem was. He was down on the floor with the other two firemen, with his mouthpiece out, and saying, "It's too hot, it's too hot, we'll never make it up there."

Now Mathews was less experienced than me – just because he couldn't make it didn't mean that I couldn't. So I turned back up the stairs on my own. When I reached the point where Mathews had turned back, the heat coming from the room struck me. It was fierce but not excessive; I had experienced similar heat levels before. Seeing as there were children involved, I pushed on forward up the stairs.

When I reached the top of this flight of stairs, something happened I had never encountered before – all the hair on my head began to frizzle up. I thought at first that it was on fire, but when I raised my hands to my head, it was not on fire, but felt to be standing upright. It felt like a demon barber was applying a hundred lighted tapers to it, all at once.

I went onto the landing and crawled left along a passageway to see if I could get out of the rising heat coming up the staircase enclosure. But conditions there did not improve. I knew that I could probably continue to crawl forward under these conditions, but I would not be able to search properly once I got there. I was also worrying about the crew below me; they were all relatively inexperienced firemen. Would the fire beat them, and chase up the stairs behind me? Reluctantly, I decided to retreat, and I hated retreating. I made my way back down the stairs and joined Mathews and the crew below.

I crouched at the foot of the stairs for around two or three minutes, by which time the hose reel jet had subdued the fire somewhat. I touched Mathews on the shoulder and indicated with my head that we should give it another go. This time, I led the way up the stairs. This time at the head of the stairs, the heat was still pretty fierce, enough to sting my ears, and taughten the skin on my face, but this time my hair behaved itself and did not frizzle up.

We carried on forward and began searching the smoke-filled room above the fire. Underneath a bed, we found a little child around two years of age, unconscious. Mathews carried the child back down the stairs for other firemen to deal with. In the far corner of the room, between a bed and a wall, I found another child, this time around three to four years of age, again unconscious. Mathews had by now returned, so I gave this child to him to take below whilst I carried on searching.

We found no more children in the room, or the house, and the two that we had found were removed to hospital by ambulance.

When we got back to the fire station, neither Mathews nor I spoke about the fire, he had his reasons, I had mine.

The following day in a national newspaper, was a large photograph of one of the children we had rescued. The picture was of only one of the children, the other had died in the fire. The story that accompanied the picture said the usual things – child rescued from fire by brave, heroic firemen…etc., etc.

I have hated the memory of that fire ever since. For you see, the reason my hair stood up on end, the reason my hair felt like a hundred burning tapers were being applied, the reason I never made it into that front room to search at the first attempt, was that I was not wearing my helmet. A fireman never goes into a fire without his helmet, yet I had gone into the fire without mine, and it had possibly cost a young child his life.

Mathews had rushed me into the fire, and I should have known better. With my helmet on, I am convinced I would have carried on past the rising heat zone without turning back and found that kid three or four minutes earlier. If one child did survive that fire, then both children could theoretically have survived. Never ever again, did I go into a fire without my helmet firmly upon my head.

*

The kitchen and mess at Paddington would have done credit to a medium sized hotel. It had every modern convenience, except one, a potato peeling machine, which the mess manager, Martin Walker, never to ceased to complain about. He apparently hated peeling potatoes. Two civilian cooks were employed, one came in early to cook the breakfasts, the other started later in the day. With the station and headquarters personnel, plus ancillary employees, as many as fifty meals would be prepared at peak times on day shifts. On day shifts, the mess could be as busy as a small factory canteen.

In the evenings, the mess reverted to being a simple fire station mess, with Martin Walker, the mess manager, providing and cooking meals for on duty station personnel. Paddington's mess differed slightly from other stations in that it ran a supper club. Martin would provide the ingredients for a supper which around eleven o'clock in the evening the firemen would cook for themselves, all for a nominal payment. It was very often something simple like cheese on toast, or a bacon sandwich, with tea or coffee.

One evening, I was feeling hungry and decided to make myself a bacon sandwich. I set the bacon on the stove to fry and found a loaf of bread. It was the usual procedure to cut the bread into slices on the new, shiny bacon-slicing machine, which I had never worked before. This machine was state of the art, and must have cost a fortune. It could have shaved a gnat's whisker in two. I placed the loaf of bread on the carrier, set the blade to around three quarters of an inch cut, stood back and pressed the button. To my surprise, instead of the blade passing the loaf of bread, the loaf of bread moved past the blade. It made a neat cut lengthways down the loaf of bread. I quickly pressed the stop button and had a quick re-think. I turned the loaf around and tried again, another neat cut down the length of the other side of the loaf.

When in doubt ask, so I asked one of the younger firemen, who found it hard to believe that I could not manage such a simple task. He turned the loaf around so the uncut end would be sliced, set the machine in motion, and two slices came off, it was so obvious I felt a complete idiot. I left the loaf of bread clamped into the machine and carried on making my sandwich.

The next morning at 6.45 am when I came down to the mess for my early morning cup of tea, Martin Walker was in the kitchen surrounded by a group of firemen, all looking at the bacon slicing machine. I heard him say loudly, "There you are, it's done it again, fucking amazing!" Then again, in a loud irritated voice. "Somebody's buggered up the bacon-slicing machine, who used it last?"

Amongst the group of firemen gathered there, it was decided that the last person to use the machine was me, and I was duly summoned to the kitchen. "What have you done to this machine?" Martin demanded.

"Nothing," I replied. "It worked all right when I had finished with it last night."

"Right, watch this then," he said. He switched on the machine, with the loaf of bread still clamped to the carrier. The carrier passed over the blade, and the slice of bread fell off, but it was in three separate pieces.

"How did you do that?" I asked him.

"I didn't bloody well do it," he said irately. "The machine did it. You were the last one to use the machine and you've knackered it, what did you do to it?"

I again replied, "Nothing. I didn't break the machine, do it again, cut another slice," I requested.

"I don't need to," he said, "it happens every bloody time," but nevertheless pressed the button to start the machine. The carrier passed over the blade, and the slice of bread fell off in three separate pieces, once again. "Fucking amazing," said Martin once again. "How the devil does it do it? I can't see how it can possibly cut it in two directions at once."

Then I remembered that when I was trying to make the machine work the previous night, I had made two cuts along the length of the loaf of bread. It would be these two cuts that were responsible for making the slices fall off in three parts, not the machine itself. The machine had worked perfectly well, cutting its way along the loaf of bread until it reached my two lengthways cuts. Then, hey Presto! The bread started to fall off the machine in three pieces.

I apologised to Martin for forgetting to tell him about this. He was so relieved that his bacon-slicing machine was still working, that he simply brushed my apology off. Later, I heard him discussing with another fireman just how he planned to use the technique to play a joke on his opposite number, the mess manager on the blue watch.

*

Ivor Rice was the sub officer on the red watch. He was a big genial man of around fifty years of age; he was easy going and soft. In some ways, an ideal balance to the station officer, who was over strict and rigid. Ivor normally rode the emergency tender, a job for which he was well suited, for he would seldom be in overall charge of an incident. Things seemed to happen to Ivor on the fire ground that did not happen to the average sub officer.

Ivor always carried with him to and from duty a rolled umbrella. This was considered by the reprobates on the watch to be a little bit effeminate. They decided to teach him a lesson. They went through the station office, and then

168

through all the staff offices below, emptying the contents of the hole punch machines into a paper bag, which they then emptied into his furled-up umbrella.

Then they waited and waited, for days, weeks, Ivor said nothing, not a cheap. Nor could any information be prised from him. "Do you ever open that umbrella, Sub?" He simply smiled at them. "You must open it when it rains, Sub, surely?" Another big smile from Ivor. Ever since they had emptied the punch machines' contents into his umbrella, they had been imagining the outcome. Ivor would be standing in a bus queue when it came on to rain. He would open his umbrella, and the thousands and thousands of little circles of paper would cascade down to stick all over Ivor and the other members of the bus queue, what a wheeze! But Ivor would not, nor ever did say anything. He just would not give them the satisfaction of knowing what had happened, such was Ivor.

The station officer was on leave, this meant that Ivor was now in charge of the station and would ride the pump. On this day, I was acting leading fireman, and in charge of the pump escape. The bells went down and we were called to a basement fire at Westbourne Grove, on Paddington's fire ground.

When we arrived at the address, it was a retail shop, but there was no sign of any fire. We sauntered into the shop and spoke to the shopkeeper. "We have been called to a fire at this address."

"Oh yes," he said, "it's down in the basement, through that door," and indicated a door on the left, just inside the shop.

I approached the door and opened it. As I did so, a blast of hot air hit me full in the face. I dropped down onto one knee and slammed the door shut, at the same time calling out for a hose reel. When the hose reel was brought in, I checked that it was working and laid down on the floor in front of the door. Another fireman stood behind the door and opened it about six inches. As he did so, I blasted the hose reel jet through the opening. I kept the hose reel jet directed through the six-inch gap, and after minutes, the smoke and heat began to die down.

I was now lying on the ground in front of the fully opened door. In front of me, a flight of steps led down into the basement. From underneath the steps, and roaring through the open treads, a huge jet of flame was issuing. It was patently obvious from the roaring noise, and the colour of the flame, that this was a gas main alight.

Ivor had disappeared, so I asked the shopkeeper, "Is there any other way to get down into the basement to turn the gas off?"

"No," he replied, a bit too cheerfully I thought. "That's the only way down to the basement."

Ivor arrived back at my side with a big smile on his face, and said cheerily, "I've sent the stop message, Dave." This simple statement took my breath clean away; I couldn't believe it. Here we were, with a bloody great gas jet belching up the stairs. We couldn't hit it with the hose reel jet, and even if we could, we would finish up with a basement full of explosive gas, which would be ten times worse. We couldn't get down the cellar to turn the gas off, because the fire wouldn't let us. On top of all that, Ivor had sent the stop message, which in effect tells control, 'Everything is under control; we don't need any further assistance'. Nothing could be further from the truth; we were in the mire. If we couldn't get down the stairs to turn off the gas, the only alternative was to send for the gas authority. They would then take hours to turn up, have to dig up the road and cut off the gas there. This could take many, many hours. All the while, we would have to be spraying water into the basement to prevent the gas jet re-igniting the basement fire.

Desperation took over – something had to be done. I sent a fireman out to fetch the anti-flash gear.

The anti-flash gear comprised of an asbestos hood and gloves, protection against flash burns, when dealing with compressed gas cylinders. I put on the hood and gloves, then to the fireman who was spraying water down the basement to stop the gas jet flame spreading, I indicated that he should spray me all over with water.

The basement floor was about twelve steps down. I was going to have to go down that staircase like a rocket. I held my breath, then launched myself forward.

Because of the limited vision in the anti-flash helmet, and the brilliant white glare from the gas jet, after about the third step I stumbled and fell the rest of the way down the staircase. I landed up in a sprawled heap on the basement floor, and amazingly, I hadn't felt a thing. When I say I hadn't felt a thing, I mean of course the heat from the flame. I certainly felt most of the stairs on the way down, and the basement floor was solid concrete. The firemen above were calling down to me anxiously. I was more or less in one piece, and more importantly, totally un-singed.

Once down below and underneath the roaring flame, it was relatively safe. The basement was lighted by the glare from the gigantic gas jet. I could see the on/off valve to the gas pipe beneath the stairs, but the valve lever was missing. I called back up for a mole wrench to be thrown down to me. The mole wrench came clattering down. I put the anti-flash hood and gloves on again, to protect me from the radiated heat, then simply crawled below the jet and turned off the valve using the mole wrench. The roaring gas jet died away, then simply disappeared.

I went back up the steps and emerged on the ground floor. Ivor, his face beaming, said to me, "Well done, Dave."

Although Ivor was the sub officer, and I was just an acting leading fireman, I snapped at him, "Don't fucking do that to me again."

"Do what?" he replied, astonished by my outburst.

I am even now convinced that he had no idea what he had done wrong. What he had done wrong of course, was to send the stop message before the fire was under control. If the fire had then gone out of control, and more machines had to be requested, this tended to heap humiliation and ridicule on the whole station and personnel. Thus, I had tried that little bit harder, and gone that little bit further, to extinguish this particular fire, than perhaps I would normally have done. Next time, if there was to be a next time, I vowed to make sure Ivor went down to turn off the gas supply. Then he would know what he bloody well did wrong, he probably knocked ten years off my life.

*

One of the younger, and junior, firemen on the red watch at Paddington was a fireman called Roger Chapman. Roger was the sort of person that the words, cheeky, streetwise, humorous, irrepressible, cockney wit, would be needed to describe. He was a popular fireman on the watch with both the junior and senior firemen. I think of the previous descriptions, irrepressible comes strongest to mind, he just would not stop joking and messing around.

At around twelve midnight, the pump escape, pump and turntable ladders had gone out on a call to smoke issuing from a roof near Paddington main line railway station. I had remained back at the station, for on this shift, I was riding the emergency tender.

Calls to smoke issuing were pretty common and were fairly routine calls. They often turned out to be steam issuing from boiler vent pipes, chimneys out of sight from the ground, smoking excessively or a dozen other causes. Occasionally, they could be a roof or building going well.

I was waiting in the watchroom for the first message to come over the teleprinter. After the appliances had been away for around twenty minutes, the teleprinter chattered into life, and the message 'alarm caused by smoke issuing' came over the printer. A routine nothing to do fire call. I waited on in the watchroom, and ten minutes later, the appliances reversed back into the appliance room.

As I was now considered to be a prospective leading fireman, I would do the routine paperwork for fire calls. I went out into the appliance room to see the leading fireman in charge of the pump escape and confirm the details of the fire call. Whilst I was there, I subconsciously noted that the mood of the firemen was quiet.

Back upstairs in the station office, I was typing out the fire report for the incident. The station officer, accompanied by the leading fireman and Roger Chapman, passed through and went into the station officer's private office. After five minutes, they came out again, Roger was looking pale, ashen and dirty, and thoroughly dejected.

The station officer was saying, "Now you are sure you are all right, Roger?"

"Yes, guvnor," he replied quietly.

"Would you like to come off the run for the night and go to bed?" said the station officer.

"Oh yes please, guv, that would be great," replied Roger. Something very serious had occurred, Roger Chapman would never, never, normally volunteer to come off the run.

Back upstairs in the mess, Martin Walker told me the story. The call had been a fairly routine one. A passer-by in the street had seen smoke issuing from the roof of an office building. At twelve o'clock, the office block was locked up and secured. It was decided to use the turntable ladders to gain access to the roof and check for the source of the smoke.

The office block was in fact a terrace of old Victorian houses, converted into one unit for use as offices. It was six stories high and had a flat asphalt roof.

Roger and two other firemen went up the turntable ladder onto the roof to look for the source of the smoke. The roof was divided into sections by two-foot-high brick walls rising above the asphalt roof. These were the dividing walls of the old, terraced houses, extended above the roofs to act as a firebreak. Intended in the case of a serious fire in one of the houses to prevent the fire spreading along the whole terrace of houses.

Roger was following along behind one of the other firemen. They were making their way along the whole length of the roof, looking for the source of the smoke. The first fireman jumped over the two-foot wall and proceeded on forwards over the roofs. Roger was about ten feet behind the first fireman, and slightly to his left. Roger jumped over the two-foot wall and proceeded downwards! Straight down into the open maw of a four-foot-square boiler flue which went from the basement to the roof of the building.

Roger was later to tell us that all he remembered was the ground being taken from under him, and the sensation of falling. He reached out with his arms instinctively, to protect himself, and his hand struck an object which he clung on to. The object he clung on to was one of the metal rungs cemented into the walls of the chimney to enable maintenance workers to gain access to the inside of the chimney. Roger clung to the metal bar, stunned, and his next memory was of a bright light above him. The first fireman had come back looking for him and was shining his torch down the chimney.

The second fireman was puzzled, he had not known where Roger had gone. He also had been unaware of the boiler flue until he came back looking for Roger. He said he didn't realise it was a boiler flue himself until he leaned over it and smelled the smoke. He then knew instantly where Roger had gone and was horrified. Before he had shone his torch down the flue, he had called out, but heard no reply. So when he did shine his torch down the flue, and the beam of the torch picked out Roger, clinging to the side, he could not at first believe his eyes – it was a small miracle.

The next morning, Roger was still a bit subdued, but by the time the next tour of duty started, was back to his normal self.

When a fireman off the blue watch asked him what the weather was like in Greenland, Roger replied, "How the bloody hell should I know?"

The fireman then told him, "I thought you might have known," as somebody had told him that Roger was a bit like Father Christmas, always popping up and down chimneys Roger managed a big smile.

*

I had now completed yet another two-week course at the Southwark Training School and was now qualified to ride the emergency tender stationed at Paddington.

It was around 2.30 am that the call came into Paddington station, and before the clamour of the call bells died away, the blue appliance indicator light came on in the appliance room ceiling, denoting that the fire call was for the emergency tender. A cheer came up from the firemen not riding this machine – ET shouts were few and far between – and in the wee small hours of the morning, as far as the other firemen were concerned, they could have them all.

The call slip read 'Spillage of chemical, The National Heart Hospital, on A22 Manchester Square's fire ground'. As all the other firemen cheerfully and happily went back to bed, the emergency tender clamoured off into the night. The ET was attending this incident because at that time, only the emergency tenders carried the full chemical protection suits and equipment.

The Heart Hospital lay somewhere behind Oxford Street and quite close to Manchester Square fire station. Thus, when we arrived the Manchester Square firemen were already in attendance and dealing with the incident. Nevertheless, firemen being the inquisitive creatures they are, we, the ET's crew decided to investigate.

After a long, winding, circuitous route, we finally arrived upon the second floor of the building in what appeared to be a storeroom full of glass jars and carboys. This room I dubbed the pickle room, because it was full of pickled people bits. Then, because this was a heart hospital, most of the pickled people bits comprised of human hearts.

As I entered the storeroom, I saw two firemen mopping up some liquid from off of the floor, then squeezing the liquid into a Brigade chimney bucket. Then I saw a man in a white coat talking to a temporary sub officer, the officer in charge of Manchester Square's attendance. This temporary sub officer I knew from way back – it was my old mate, Jim Smith.

The conversation went as follows:

"Tell me again, what is the technical name for this stuff that has been spilt?" said Jim.

The man in the white coat answered, "It's a mixture of nitric acid and glycerine, we use it for preserving human hearts."

A hint of surprise crept into Jim's voice as he said, "What, it's nitro-glycerine then?"

The man in the white coat being a doctor or scientist was more precise, saying, "Yes, I suppose you could call a mixture of nitric acid and glycerine, nitro-glycerine, but it's only a weak solution and we use it for preserving human hearts."

Jim turned to his driver who was standing beside him, message pad ready in his hands, and said, "Right, take a message," then proceeded to dictate.

"From me, at 'Ere," (Brigade colloquialism for, 'From Temporary Sub Officer Smith, at the National Heart Hospital'), "approximately one gallon of nitro-glycerine spilt on floor, mopping up in progress." This the driver duly wrote down upon his pad.

I waited for a few seconds not quite believing what I had heard. Also knowing that Temporary Sub Officer Smith, besides being a most excellent piano player at Brigade socials, was also a bit of a wag. Finally, I said to him, "You are not really going to send that message, are you, Jim?"

"Why? What's wrong with it?" He snapped back tersely.

With a big grin on my face I told him, "Well, Jim, for a start, if that really was a gallon of nitro-glycerine down there on the floor, I for one would not be here talking to you. I would be around the corner three streets down, with my hands over my ears waiting for the big bang. Secondly, I don't think the powers that be would approve of this gung-ho method of dealing with liquid high explosive. They would almost certainly descend upon you in large numbers, despite the time of morning."

Jim's face creased as he considered this, then amended his message. 'From me at 'Ere, approximately one gallon of heart preserving fluid…', etc., etc. He obviously feared senior officers more than he feared nitro-glycerine!

Chapter 11
Paddington Red Watch (2) – 1969ish

One of the unusual features of Paddington fire station was the fireman's sliding pole. Because of the very high ceiling height of the appliance room, the sliding pole descended from what was in effect the second floor of the fire station to the ground floor. In effect, it was a drop of around thirty feet, as high as an average two-storey house.

The fireman's sliding poles seem to fascinate members of the public, they are intrigued by them. Whenever there are guests on the fire station (especially ladies), or the fire stations are opened to the public on open days, it will not be the latest piece of technical equipment they wish to see, but the fireman's sliding pole.

Firemen use them as a matter of routine, without giving them a second thought. Contrary to Brigade instructions, the firemen would occasionally slide down them with a cup of tea in each hand, rather than use the stairs.

Used correctly, they are much safer than the stairs to use. Without the poles at Paddington, up to thirty firemen would come rushing down the four flights of stairs every time the fire bells rang. A far greater hazard than making their way one by one down a sliding pole.

The poles are not without hazards though, but not the dangers the public expects. Workmen and guests on the station are one of the biggest hazards. Firemen will automatically and without thought, use a sliding pole to get from one floor of the station to another. The problem arises when you are conducting a workman or guest to another part of the station. Saying to the workman, "Follow me, I will show you the way." It is only when you are halfway down the sliding pole that you remember he is following behind, then hope to Christ that he isn't. For if he is, he will come tumbling out of the sky and smash down on top of you.

The doors to the London Fire Brigade pole houses were on springs, and automatically closed behind you as you passed through them, and then locked shut. The catch to open them was at arm's length above the door to the pole house. The combination of these two safety devices has probably saved the life and limb of many a tradesman, unwarily following a fireman around a fire station.

Firemen do sometimes have problems with the sliding poles. It is the custom on almost every London fire station not to wear fire boots above the ground floor. When an appliance has been ordered to stand-by at another fire station for fire cover, the crews will arrive with only their fire boots. Then they will of course go above the ground floor wearing them.

The problem then occurs if a fire call is received, for the firemen will seek out the nearest sliding pole, reach up to release the spring doors, grip the sliding pole with their arms and legs, and then nothing happens. The fireman stays stuck to the sliding pole; the plastic material of his waterproof leggings will not slide against the metal of the pole. There may be three or four firemen wanting to use the pole, and they will expect the first fireman, once he is on the pole, to disappear immediately from sight. When he doesn't, but instead remains clinging to the pole, and the other three firemen all pushing forward, it can become dangerous, with two firemen trying to get on the pole together. The fireman who is stuck will be told that the problem is his leggings and to release the grip with his legs and slide down the pole using his hands only.

I did injure myself on one occasion I was using the sliding pole. Whilst on night duty at Paddington, it was around 1.00 am, I was in the messroom on the second floor talking to a group of firemen. I had just lit a cigarette when the bells went down. I went over to the pole house and waited my turn to go down the pole, there was another fireman waiting behind me.

When descending the pole with a cigarette in your mouth, all that needed to be done was incline your head slightly to the left or the right to keep the cigarette clear of the pole.

This time, as I went down the pole, I was turning my head to try to see the appliance indicator lights mounted up in the ceiling. These lights showed which appliances would be attending the call. As I turned my head across the pole, I pushed my lower lip forward and my upper lip back to tilt the cigarette backwards and keep it clear of the pole. But the cigarette went too far back and touched the end of my nose then stuck there, causing extreme pain. I braked to a sudden halt on the pole in order to use one hand to remove the cigarette from the end of my nose. Fortunately, the fireman following me down the pole was looking downwards and came to a halt with his feet inches from my head.

Suspended fifteen feet up the sliding pole, we had a conversation.

"What the bloody hell did you stop for?"

"I burnt my nose with my cigarette."

"Sod your nose, I nearly bashed your brains out with my boots, get a move on down."

To my friends and family at home, the nasty little burn on the end of my nose was explained away by the simple answer that I did it on a fire call, which of course I did.

One of the biggest dangers involving sliding poles is when careless firemen leave objects below them for the unwary to slide down and crash into or onto.

One of the older firemen at Soho fire station had a pet name for these individuals. He used to call them Vlad.

"Hey, Vlad, don't leave that broom underneath the pole."

When asked who this Vlad character was, he would explain, "Nasty bugger just like you. He would go around sticking poles up people's backsides, just for the crack. Vlad the Impaler they called him."

"I don't go around impaling people," protested the individual.

"Oh no," said the older fireman, "well the next bloke to come down that sliding pole and gets that broom handle you have just left there up his arse, will no doubt want to disagree with you."

*

In order to transfer back to the London Fire Brigade, I had to vacate my Berkshire Fire Brigade house. I had then bought a small house in Pangbourne, and consequently had a very large mortgage. The Fire Brigade at that time gave a great deal of job satisfaction, but very little monetary satisfaction. So like many other firemen, I had two or three part time jobs, in order to pay the bills.

For around six months, I had been working as a truck driver for a firm of road hauliers in the Caledonian Road on Euston fire station's ground. During the course of the six months, I had driven all types of vehicles for the firm, flat bed box lorries, articulated vehicles etc.

At around this time, the government had decided to introduce heavy goods vehicle licences. To obtain one, an exemption certificate was required from one's employers, stating that you had driven that type of vehicle over a period of time. I would thus get an exemption certificate for class three ridged vehicles, from the fire service. If I played my cards right, I hoped to also get an exemption certificate for class one articulated vehicles, from my part-time employer.

The guvnor of the haulage firm's name was Gerald, and he ran a dodgy outfit, operating on the fringes of the law. He once telephoned me at Euston fire station, pleading with me to come to work for him the next day. When I asked why, he told me he had a load of copper worth twenty thousand pounds to pick up, and if he gave that sort of job to his own drivers, they would nick it.

When I first drove articulated vehicles for him, he merely gave me the key and the instructions, "When you want to go backwards, turn the wheel in the opposite direction to that in which you want to go."

I used to arrive at my destination, seek out a friendly driver of an articulated vehicle, and say, "Do us a favour mate, reverse this back in for me please."

For a time, I was working with a group of colonials, an Australian, a South African and a Rhodesian. They were working for the black economy, not having work permits. They were working as porters and we were delivering office furniture all over London.

The Rhodesian had been brought up on a farm and could reverse trailers with the greatest of skill. So I offered to swap jobs with him, he be the driver and I be a porter. The thought of driving a heavy vehicle through London's traffic appalled him. We settled for a compromise, I drove the lorry forwards, and he drove it backwards, i.e. he did all the reversing.

Working for the same firm, I once had to deliver a load of chocolates to a haulage depot in Kentish Town. I drove the lorry into the depot, and the porters unloaded it. As I was leaving, one of the porters said to me, "There's a box of chocolates in the back for you, driver."

"Thanks," I said and went on my way. When I arrived back at the Caledonian Road depot, I went to get my box of chocolates from the back of the lorry. I found not one box of chocolates, but a case of boxes of chocolates. I had obviously and unknowingly participated in a little fiddle.

At this time, I was travelling backwards and forwards to my part-time job by public transport. Wandering around London with a case of boxes of chocolates on one's shoulder could be a bit of an embarrassment, so I decided to unload some.

The girl who worked in the office at the haulage firm was a big lady, around twenty-five years of age. She was not fat, but solidly built; she was pleasant and efficient at her work, but not the Miss Universe type. I decided that I would give her one of my many boxes of chocolates as a present. With an exaggerated flourish, I presented her with one. She was so taken aback, "A box of chocolates for me?" she said. It was obvious none of the other drivers had given her any of their ill-gotten gains before. I went back outside and got another box of chocolates, saying, "Not one box of chocolates for the lady, but two boxes of chocolates." She was so overcome that I did not like to tell her that I had still got another ten boxes outside, and would have cheerfully given her half, just to get rid of them. This gallant gesture, had I actually made it, would then have saved me carrying them through London on my journey home, thus risking the attentions of Mr Plod and his, "Hello, Hello, what have we got here then?" The present of the chocolates made her day, and strangely enough, it made my day as well.

About two months after this incident, I decided to approach Gerald, the guvnor, and get him to sign my exemption certificate for driving group one articulated vehicles. He was in the office when I asked him. Gerald did not like to sign anything, lest it incriminate him, and he was busy thinking up reasons why he could not sign it. My chocolate girl swept him aside with one sweep of her arm. "Give that to me, Dave, I will sign and stamp it for you." Which she duly did.

Exchange is no robbery, two boxes of chocolates, one heavy goods group one vehicle licence.

*

This is the story of the fire at the end of which I mentally decided that I was now a fully qualified, experienced fireman, as good as most and better than some.

One of the disadvantages of serving at a divisional headquarters station, such as Paddington, was that occasionally firemen were required to do daytime or night-time watchroom duties. With the advent of teleprinter, mobilising these duties had been abolished at ordinary fire stations, so it was considered a considerable imposition that at divisional stations the firemen were occasionally required to keep a wakeful watch all night, whilst their luckier comrades, fire calls excepting, slept all night.

The problem was control room operators or rather the lack of them. They were usually retired firemen who came back to augment their pensions, doing the lighter job of control room operator. The wages paid for the job, coupled with the shift work and unsociable hours generally, meant that normal(!) people did not want the job.

When the control room was short staffed, the firemen at Paddington would have to cover the vacant shifts. This entailed relieving the control room operator for meals and taking his place in the watchroom from the hours of 11.00 pm till 7.00 am. If a large fire occurred in the division, or the pump escape at Paddington received a fire call, the control operator would come back into the watchroom to allow the fireman to ride to the fire.

It needed two firemen to carry out this relief. One would be in the watchroom from 11.00 pm to 3.00 am, the other from 3.00 am to 7.00 am.

On this occasion, it was a fireman named Chris Bull and myself that were doing the watchroom duties, we were both appliance drivers. Because the station was short of drivers, whilst we were actually on duty in the watchroom if a fire call was received, we would leave the watchroom and drive the pump escape, the control room operator taking our place in the watchroom.

It so happened that Chris Bull much preferred to drive the fire engines, whilst I preferred to ride in the back, thus get to fight the fires as opposed to being the pump operator. So it was agreed between us, that in the event of fire calls, Chris would drive the pump escape all night, and I would ride in the back.

Just after 3.00 am, Chris called me to the watchroom for my spell of duty. A scalding hot cup of tea readymade, as was the custom, then he retired to get what sleep he could.

There were three teleprinters in the watchroom, monitoring all calls that the other stations in the division were receiving. These were chattering away on and off throughout the night.

During the early part of my shift, the call bells and lights sounded twice at Paddington. One for the pump to a person shut in a lift and one for the turntable ladders to a fire call on a neighbouring station's ground.

During the last twenty minutes, I had been watching dawn break through the large picture windows in the watchroom. Outside the sun was shining, and it was a beautiful summer's morning. The Paddington station teleprinter chattered into life, the automatic lights came on, and the fire call bells started ringing.

I moved over to the printer to monitor the call as it came in, 'A21 Paddington's pump escape, pump and turntable ladders to a fire at the Leinster Towers Hotel, Leinster Terrace, Bayswater'. I switched on the appliance indicator lights to show which fire engines were going on the call, then went into the bunk room just off the watchroom to tell the control operator sleeping there that he would now have to relieve me in the watchroom, as I was going out on a fire call.

The officers in charge of the appliances were arriving in the watchroom to collect their ordering slips. The control room operator had arrived sleepy eyed to relieve me in the watchroom. I left the watchroom to jump up on the back of the pump escape, in the seat behind the driver. This seat was nearest to the watchroom, a seat left vacant for me as the dutyman, I was the last fireman on the machine.

As I slammed the appliance door behind me, the pump escape left the station bound for the address on the call slip.

Leinster Terrace was one of the many streets in the Bayswater area of London that led on down to Hyde Park. In its time, Leinster Terrace had been the height of elegance. Big six and seven-storey terraced houses with their elegant façades, which at one time would have housed a single family and their retinue of servants, had now been converted in the main part, into flats or hotels.

As the appliance pulled into Leinster Terrace, I was still drinking in the serenity of an early summer's morning in London. Just the odd early morning postman or milkman around the streets, most of the inhabitants still tucked up in bed. So different from what it would all be like in two hours' time. I gave no thought to the call we were attending; I had done it all a thousand times before.

The first indication that this call might be different came from the driver, Chris Bull, as he said, "Why are all those people looking out of their windows at this time of the morning?"

I did not pay any heed, there had been no indication of alarm in his voice as he said it, it had been just a casual remark. Then as we came to within 200 yards of the Leinster Towers Hotel, the driver spoke again, this time in a startled voice. "That's smoke pouring out from the ground floor. Jesus Christ, they are all shouting out for help!" My attention was now riveted to the proceedings.

This was to be something different. Around five or six of these large, terraced houses had been converted into one hotel, interconnecting doors made through the walls on each floor and the five or six houses being one whole unit. It seemed that at every other window was a group of people calling for help. From the ground floor, which would normally be the reception, dining area etc., of the hotel, thick smoke was punching out. My heart sank to my stomach, as perhaps a soldier when faced with overwhelming odds.

A single ladder rescue could take up to three, four or even five minutes, we would never get all this lot out in time.

I did not have time to dwell upon it, for as the pump escape came to a halt in front of the building, by almost a reflex action the crew, myself included, were off and around the back of the appliance removing the big 50ft wheeled escape. The escape ladder was turned in the road; its wheels crashed up onto the pavement and was positioned for the first rescue.

Because of the semi-basement and railings in front of the building, the ladder could get no nearer than fifteen to twenty feet to the building itself. This meant that the fifty-foot-long ladder would reach no higher than the third floor of the building. The angle of elevation on the ladder was lowered, using the carriage gear, then the ladder extended up to a third-floor window, from which a group of people were calling for help.

As the top of the ladder approached the window, the downward weight of the ladder due to the low angle of elevation was such that it was threatening to crash down into the basement. Six firemen where required to counterbalance the weight until it was safely lowered down onto the window opening.

As soon as the top of the ladder touched the building, and before the ladder could be secured with its wheel chocks, a fireman was speeding his way up the ladder to commence the first rescue. It had been my intention to be first on the ladder, but I had been waiting for the ladder to be secured before doing so, for a man moving on a ladder before it has been secured can cause the ladder to move back from the building and fall away, with disastrous results.

There were now two firemen up the top of the ladder, helping the people out of the windows, and one fireman securing the heel of the ladder. Under the circumstances, the great numbers of people awaiting rescue – I could safely leave the escape crew. The problem now was shortage of firemen, every other fireman was busily engaged in some task or other. I was on my own; whatever I did would be a solo effort. The only ladder that a fireman on his own can handle is the hook ladder.

I climbed to the top of the appliance to get a hook ladder. Whilst I was unfastening the hook ladder, I saw that two other firemen had the same idea, for they were already negotiating the parapet and balcony at the first-floor level. From there, they would gain access to the first-floor narrow balcony, which ran the whole length of the building. Hook ladder rescues are normally carried out by two firemen, and by lowering the rescued person down on a rescue line, hook ladders themselves being notoriously difficult things to climb, especially for unpractised members of the public.

When I went to the rescue line locker, it was empty. I assumed the two other firemen had already taken the rescue line. There was nothing left to do but press on. I might be able to persuade one or two of the people to climb down the hook ladder.

I pulled the hook out from the shroud of the ladder and pitched the ladder up to the stone parapet of the first-floor balcony. I then engaged the hook of the ladder over the stone parapet and climbed the ladder to the first floor. I now looked for someone to rescue. To my right, I could see the other hook ladder, suspended from a second-floor window, and a member of the public being helped down it. So I moved to my left and selected a window with two or three faces peering down from it. As I pitched the ladder upwards and then engaged the window with the hook of the ladder, the faces were beaming with delight, they were about to be rescued.

Whilst making my way along the balcony, I had been aware of the smashing of panes of glass and deep thumps, as objects hit the ground in the background. I had been assuming the worst, that people were jumping from the windows, which made the task even more urgent. I was halfway up the hook ladder to the second floor, when to my immediate right was an almighty crashing sound, showering broken glass all over me, followed by the same ominous deep thump. I lowered my head and closed my eyes to avoid the falling glass. When I opened my eyes again, there on the balcony below me I saw a suitcase. It had burst open spewing out its contents. To my relief, I realised that this was probably happening all along the face of the building. That it was suitcases falling, not people jumping, that was breaking the outward opening glass windows. This then raised a brief flash of anger in me. I was suspended from the face of the building attempting to rescue them. They were tossing out heavy suitcases with an apparent complete disregard for human life, the human life in particular being my own. It would have been rather ignominious to have it written on my gravestone 'Here lies Dave Wilson, killed by a falling suitcase' even if it had been a top-quality Samsonite.

I clambered through the window and into the room. There I was met by a man and a woman around fifty years of age, and a younger woman of around thirty years of age, who, just to complicate matters, spoke not a word of English. It then occurred to me that this language problem never arose in training school, everybody there spoke perfect English, something needed to be done about this problem in the future.

When I arrived in the room, and attempted by signs and gestures, to explain to them that they were expected to leave the room via the hook ladder, the first thing the man wanted to do, much to my surprise, was to throw his suitcase out of the window, which he duly did.

The windows to the room were centre hung casement windows, in that they pivoted at the centre and opened outwards at the bottom and inwards at the top. I placed a chair up against the window, which the younger lady climbed upon. I went outside the building again onto the top of the hook ladder.

The most dangerous point when working with hook ladders was actually getting onto the ladder. If the body weight were not kept well down below the hook, the ladder would tend to skid off to the side. So I was on the ladder ensuring that my weight would stop the ladder skidding off.

I assisted the lady through the window, and onto the top of the ladder, then helped her down the ladder onto the balcony below, telling her by signs to run clear of the still falling suitcases. It seemed an awful waste, having just been rescued at great personal risk to myself, to have her killed by one of those things.

I went back up the ladder again, back into the room. The other lady point blank refused to go down the ladder. I did manage to persuade the man, who having seen the girl demonstrate the method, went down the ladder quite easily and quickly. It crossed my mind that this gentleman was rather ungallant, for I was sure the lady he left behind was his wife.

I had intended at this point to go back down onto the balcony and ascend with the ladder to the next room along. But the lady who refused to go down the hook ladder complicated matters, I could hardly abandon her. I had no idea if the worst came to the worst, how I was going to rescue her, other than down the hook ladder.

I made my way to the door of the room, very slowly opened it, looked out and then peered into a long corridor. The corridor was thick with smoke, and there were little flames flickering all along it where the floors met the walls, suggesting a fierce fire on the floor below, but it was in my opinion passable.

I told my little lady as best I could by signs that I was going to get some more people to rescue, and that I would be back shortly. She did not appear too happy at my leaving her; indeed, if she had understood me at all I did not know.

I made my way along the smoky passageway, until I came to the next room. I opened the door – there were three people in the room and looks of utter relief came over their faces as they saw me standing there. I explained to them that I was taking them to the room next door, where there was a ladder. When they looked out into the passageway and saw the smoke and flames, they were not quite so keen to be rescued! They apparently preferred the safety of their own little room. Reluctantly, they came with me.

I then changed my plan. If I could gather as many people as possible from this floor in the one room before the passageway became impassable, it would then make it much simpler for any other ladder rescues, because the people would then be all in one place. They could then be rescued without moving the ladders up and down the face of the building.

Eventually, I wound up with around twelve people in the one room; it was surprising how many brought their suitcases with them! The younger and fitter ones I assisted down the hook ladder, and I think another three or four went out by this method.

Then all of a sudden, the door to our room opened, and there stood a sub officer from another fire station. Of all the people in the room, none was more pleased to see him than me. He had followed the firemen with a jet up the stairs, then gone ahead to search this floor. Which meant in effect, that all the remaining people in the room with me could be led down the stairs of the building to safety.

Later, I tried to work out how long this stage of the fire had taken; it seemed like only five minutes at the time. The sub officer who had appeared in the room came from Euston fire station. So assuming that Euston had been mobilised on the make pumps eight, ten minutes into the fire. Then, that it had taken them at least ten minutes to arrive, another five minutes for the sub officer to make his way up to the second floor with the branch crew, then a time period of thirty minutes would have been more accurate.

Having been rendered redundant, I went off in search of the Paddington crews. I found some of them up on the third floor, where a group of three or four of the junior members of the watch had a jet all to themselves and were doing sterling work.

They were though, a little bit puzzled by the behaviour of the fire. They were working along a long passageway, with rooms off to the left and the right. Here, as on the floor below, the flames were issuing from where the floorboards met the walls. They would extinguish this fire only to have it re-ignite minutes later. They were having the same problems with the rooms. They would open a door, find the room on fire, extinguish it quickly with the large jet, move on down the passage to the next room, only to be called back to the first room because it had re-ignited. I stayed with them and witnessed it myself; it really was most puzzling and frustrating, and something that I had not seen before. If I had not just come up from the second floor myself, I would have said that the fire was burning out of control underneath us.

I did not find out till after the fire was over, just how near to the truth I had been. The building had been so substantially altered, suspended ceilings in every corridor and room, new service ducts and lift shafts built in from the basement to the roof and not fully enclosed. There was in fact more of the building hidden from view than in sight. In a standard guest room or corridor, the ceilings would be about seven foot six inches in height. The old, original, hidden ceilings would have been eleven to twelve feet in height, so that between each visible ceiling and the floor above would be a hidden gap of between three and four feet. This was where the fire was raging, in the main unseen and spreading up and all over the building.

I stayed working with this group of youngsters for around ten minutes or so. Usually, a more senior fireman will commandeer the branch, and the younger firemen would be relegated to assist. But they were doing good work, and had coped well enough until I joined them, that I just assisted them, pulling the heavy hose when required. The smoke was pretty thick but quite bearable, and if heavy work made one choking and breathless, the air was pretty good down at floor level.

Later, when a group of firemen wearing breathing apparatus appeared, then said they had been ordered to relieve us on the jet, the youngsters were pretty upset and only reluctantly gave it up.

Redundant once again, I made my way down the stairs and out of the building. Most of the firefighting inside the building was now being carried out by breathing apparatus crews, so there would be no demand for my services. I had thought to clear my lungs and see what was happening outside the building.

Outside, there were fire engines all over the place. *It must be at least a fifteen pumper,* I thought to myself.

As I made my way along the front of the building looking for a familiar face, I saw to my surprise that people were still being rescued from the building by ladders. A thirty-five-foot extension ladder had been pitched to a first-floor window, over the basement area. The ladder was at a low level of elevation, and making her way down this ladder unassisted, was a woman. As I drew level with the ladder, I heard a sharp crack, and the ladder tilted to the left. One of the sides of the ladder had split, leaving the woman hanging grimly on and right over the basement area. There were already two firemen at the heel of the ladder, but to hold the damaged ladder and steady it was beyond their strength alone. The lady was terrified, gripping the ladder firmly with both arms, and would not move up or down the ladder.

I called to some policemen and ambulance men that were standing nearby and organised them underneath and on each side of the ladder, to support the weight. The lady still would not move, the only way to get her down would be to go up the ladder and get her.

Looking around the group of policemen and firemen, I was about the lightest one there in weight. I very gingerly made my way up the ladder, hoping that the defective side would not break any further. When I reached the woman, the ladder was very springy, and the lightest movement caused it to sway up and down. The lady had her arms wrapped around the ladder and was still refusing to move. I took hold of one of her feet and moved it to the rung below, then took the other foot and moved that to the rung below. In this manner, the lady, still with her arms wrapped around the ladder, inched her way down to safety. It was only once she had passed the most dangerous section of the ladder, then onto the section that was being supported directly by the helpers who were then immediately below her, that she relaxed and slowly made her own way down. It had really been quite a dangerous operation, and I could not think, nor did I find out, why the lady was being brought down the ladder when the firemen had gained access to that floor of the building.

Once more redundant, I decided to go and see what, if anything, was happening at the rear of the building. The rear of a building on fire can sometimes be a very exciting, or dangerous, place to be, depending on one's attitude. When firemen first arrive at a building on fire, their attentions will invariably be drawn to that which they see first, which will be any rescues etc., at the front of the building, and they will be busily involved in dealing with these. As soon as there is spare manpower, or crew available, they will be sent to check the rear of the building. At the back of the building, I found one person only, a very senior station officer from the Manchester Square fire station. I greeted him cheerfully. "Hello, Guv, you all on your own then?"

He replied, "Yes, I am officer in charge of the rear of the fire." Which I think was meant to be a caustic remark.

As I was talking to him, I became aware of someone shouting above my head. I looked up, and there on the fourth floor of the building was a lone head sticking out of a window, and shouting in a strong American accent, "I wanna ladder, I wanna ladder, someone get me a ladder," over and over again. At this stage in such a large and dangerous fire, I think firemen become a bit shell shocked and laid back.

I merely said to the station officer, "What's up with him then, guv?"

He casually replied, "I think he wants a ladder."

I then told the station officer that I was pretty sure that crews were working up on the fourth floor, and that I would go up and bring the man down the stairs. But he replied, "No, don't bother, I have sent that lazy sod John Smith," (a fireman on his watch at Manchester Square), "to get a hook ladder, let him do some work for a change."

John Smith was subsequently to receive a Queen's Commendation for bravery for rescuing that particular American gentleman by hook ladder – such is life!

I think it was quite likely that American gentleman, like a great many other people involved in fires, had slept through the first forty-five minutes or so of the fire. Perhaps a heavy sleeper, and a late night at the hotel bar. By the time he had realised the building was on fire, the fire was almost out.

My last memory of the fire itself was again an unusual one. I made my way to the top floor of the hotel, where the last of the fire was being extinguished. The fire was still burning quite well here, and a crew with a jet were hard at work. It was the crew on the jet that was unusual. It comprised of the divisional commander and two other senior officers. They were at it like kids in a sweet shop; it is not very often that divisional commanders and the like get the opportunity to work with a jet! They were making the most of it, their faces beaming with delight.

The top floor of a building on fire is usually the end of the battle, unless of course the fire has extended to the roof space. Then the tension comes off, the large jets of water will be knocked off, replaced with the smaller hose reel jets to save water damage. Those crews that have had a hard time of it, having fought their way up floor by floor, will now quite happily be relieved, now that the excitement is over, then make their way outside to the canteen van or for a smoke. The crews most recently arrived will be detailed to make a start in making up needed gear and hose.

I looked at my watch – it was a quarter past nine, we had been there for more than four hours. It does not seem a long time when you consider that the average working day is eight hours long. We had come on duty at six o'clock the previous evening, then four hours of constant nervous and hyperactivity, with the adrenaline flowing at maximum rate. This is all very well whilst it is actually happening, but when you stop, you soon feel very, very shattered.

At long last, the happy words from a control unit sub officer, "A21 Paddington's pump escape crew to go back to station."

The crew, anticipating this order, were all within earshot of the appliance. The escape ladder was re-stowed back on the machine, again needing six or seven firemen to recover it from its low angle of elevation against the building. Such hose as could readily be found was thrown roughly back into the lockers, and we were back off to the fire station.

At the end of Leinster Terrace was a small tobacconists, the appliance pulled over so that the smokers amongst us could replenish our tobacco supplies. It appears that at any large fire, only two out of ten smokers would have remembered to bring their cigarettes with them. So those two would have to supply the other eight with smokes for the duration of the fire. Today I was one of the two and had now run out of tobacco.

I went into the shop, which was crowded with customers. The man behind the counter ignored the rest of the customers and asked me what I wanted. "Half an ounce of cigarette tobacco please," I replied. He gave me the tobacco, and then refused my money.

I pressed him to take my money, but he said, "I was there from the very first moment you arrived" – meaning the fire. "Today I am not taking money from firemen, under any circumstances." I was a bit embarrassed about him not taking my money, but rather proud at that moment to be a fireman. Not many London shopkeepers give you something for nothing without a very good reason.

As we pulled back into the fire station, we were greeted by the day duty watch, who of course wanted to know all about the fire, how many had Paddington's fire crews rescued and the like. I think to a man, we were all too tired to go into any great detail of the fire. We told them briefly which equipment had been used, so that they could test it. The extension ladder which broke under the lady was one of ours. We told them what equipment was known to be still at the fire, then left them to sort it all out, retiring to the messroom for multiple cups of tea.

At around 10.30 am, I was ready to leave the fire station, but it was not the end of my day. I had recently taken on a rather large mortgage, and it had to be paid for. Despite today being a Sunday, I was due to go to my part-time job as a maintenance worker in a hotel in Earl's Court. So I made my way rather tiredly to the tube station to travel to work. One good thing about this part time job was that most of the maintenance workers were firemen. The hotel manager was a time served retired sub officer from the London Fire Brigade. He was also the father of one of the firemen I had attended training school with and still met socially.

When I turned up for work and was apologising for being late, he stopped me and expressed great surprise at my even being there. He had heard all about the big fire at Paddington on the news. I spent the first half an hour telling him all about the fire. He then gave me a room key, saying, "Here you are, Dave, this room is vacant. It's yours for the day, see you about one o'clock for a drink in the bar." What a great, understanding man! And I got paid my wages for the day.

The fire at Leinster Towers Hotel was one of the great fires of the times in the London Fire Brigade. The exact number of rescues carried out was never determined, but there were at least fifty and probably as many as seventy. All without loss of life or serious injury, which is really quite a remarkable feat.

This fire received a great deal of coverage in the national press, as a result of which, whilst I was washing my motor car one day outside my house in Pangbourne, a gentleman approached me and asked me if I was fireman Wilson of Paddington fire station. He was apparently a reporter from my local newspaper and he wished to interview me about the fire.

I invited him into my house, then being quite used to the ways of the press, me saying one thing and being quoted as saying something entirely different. I agreed to the interview on the proviso that he took written notes, which he did. When the interview appeared in the paper, it was fairly accurate, with one exception. The thing which apparently most frightened me at the fire, was the crashing of falling timbers! Either the reporter, or his editor, refused to believe that suitcases dropped from a great height can be lethal, and had substituted timbers for suitcases in the article.

*

It was time once again for the interviews for promotion to the rank of leading fireman. The interviews were held at Northern Command's headquarters at Wembley. This time I seemed to get an easy ride; the technical questions they asked me were relatively simple ones. Then they spent a long time asking me about the Kilbum High Road and Leinster Towers fires. I could not make my mind up whether they were genuinely interested as firemen, or this was all part of the interview.

About six weeks later, it was promulgated in Brigade orders, that fireman Wilson, of A21 Paddington was to be promoted to the rank of leading fireman. It had taken me almost ten years, but I got there in the end. It was a classic case of being in the right place at the right time. I was at a Divisional Headquarters station, and I was at the fire at Kilburn High Road, and of course lady luck helped a little bit.

The details came through of my new posting as a leading fireman, it was to be A23 Euston on the white watch. I knew Euston fire station well enough; I had stood by there many times on the red watch. I had never served on the white watch before, so I made enquiries about the white watch at Euston. It did not bode well. Apparently, they were a bunch of malcontents and misfits, also the divisional union rep was at the station, and tended to make life difficult.

Once again, I was to pack my bags and say my goodbyes.

Part of Leinster Towers showing multiple ladders including hook ladders 1964
(Photo courtesy: London Fire Brigade)

Chapter 12

Euston Fire Station – 1970ish

A23 Euston fire station was situated in the Euston Road, in the Kings Cross district of London. It was on the opposite corner of the road to Euston main line railway station. It had a large forecourt, with a large tree in the middle; the forecourt was enclosed with a low wall and railings. The building was quite a pleasant one, built I think in the 1920s, but its general appearance was spoilt, mainly by its red coloured, modern up and over appliance room doors.

I was once asked by a Berkshire fireman, who had just returned from a trip to London, had I ever served at Eveston (he pronounced it Eveston) fire station. I replied no, adding that I had never even heard of Eveston fire station. So he proceeded to tell me where it was, it was on the Euston Road, just past Euston railway station. So if you are passing by Eveston fire station, the 'v' in Eveston, carved in the stone above the station, is a roman script 'u', and it is of course, Euston fire station.

*

When I was at my first fire station, Camden Town, which then adjoined with Euston's fire ground, Euston was always considered a very busy fire station, which because of its surrounding commercial risks picked up some very big fires indeed. So from a firefighting point of view, I was not dissatisfied at being posted to Euston.

The station had a four-bay appliance room, and the appliances stationed there were pump escape, pump and turntable ladders. Which in turn meant the officer strength would be station officer, sub officer and two leading firemen, one of those, being myself. The station officer, Ted Kington, (we didn't call him Ted of course) had been at Euston for many years, I could remember him as being there myself from my Camden Town days.

When I reported for duty at Euston, I found there was no sub officer on the watch, he was on long term detachment at another fire station. The watch would be run by the station officer, and the two leading firemen.

When I had been on the watch for less than a week, I realised that the information about malcontents and misfits on the watch was totally wrong. The terrible divisional union rep turned out to be a very intelligent and humorous man by the name of Slag O'Conner and we became firm friends.

They in turn had been hearing rumours about me. A country fireman with his sub officer's ticket already, a promotion flyer, a divisional headquarters man, a bit of a bastard etc. Then when they found out I was really a cockney fireman, hailing from the London borough of Fulham, had been around a few fire stations in my travels, and that it had in fact taken me nine years to reach the rank of leading fireman, we seemed to hit it off fine.

Station Officer Kington had held the rank of station officer for a long time. He did not involve himself in the routine running of the fire station, this he delegated to the junior officers. Most day duties, he would be around the station ground, carrying out fire inspections and the like, leaving the station to run itself. He had a very disconcerting habit of appearing in the office, with his coat and hat on, then announcing, "Right, I'm off." He would then throw down the station keys on the table, say, "You're in charge." Then disappear off out of the station, leaving us without a clue as to where he was off to.

He was inclined to do the same for domestic upsets at his home. One night duty at around 9.00 pm, he was in conversation on the telephone with his wife at home. I was listening to the conversation, and it appeared that his pet dog had disappeared. Just like the character Radar in the television series 'MASH', I read his mind, and said, "I'll just go and check the number of riders on duty, guv," anticipating that he would want to go home. But by the time I got back to the office with the information that we had enough riders available, he had already got his hat and coat on and the keys were on the station desk.

This disappearing act could have caused problems, Brigade Control knew, or thought they knew, the name and rank of every officer in charge of every station in the Brigade. The divisional commander had the same information about stations in his division. He would telephone the station and ask to speak to Mr Kington, who according to his records was on duty at the station, only to be told he had just gone out to inspect a leaking fire hydrant Sir, or whatever plausible excuse we could come up with at short notice. We will get him to call you back as soon as he returns. But he, like the station officer, had been around for a long time. I think he knew of Mr Kington's little disappearing habits.

*

In 1965, the London County Council was disbanded, and a new authority, the Greater London Council, was formed, taking in parts of Middlesex, Essex, Surrey, in fact doubling in size the authority's administration area. The London Fire Brigade at the same time doubled its size in area and in numbers of appliances. Within this new Brigade, the 'A' division was a very insular and introverted division. It changed little on the formation of the Greater London Council, merely losing a few stations on the edge of the division.

The 'A' division considered itself the premier division in the Brigade and tended to look down its nose at the outer London divisions. Especially when their origins were with the former county brigades.

This feeling was prevalent amongst most of the former London County Council Divisions and the powers on high were in the process of breaking this down. They did so by encouraging the posting of officers and firemen across the divisional boundaries.

When I was posted to Euston, my background of stations, Camden Town, Chelsea, Soho, etc., marked me down as an 'A' division man, and therefore a good, reliable man. The other leading fireman on the watch had recently transferred to Euston from the 'G' division, and was an ex-Middlesex fireman, and therefore viewed with suspicion. He was in fact a good and capable leading fireman, but initially at his new station, Euston, he was a little out of his depth. Both with the type of fireman he had to manage, and the fire ground itself, where every building was at least four-storeys high and occupied by multiple occupiers.

*

I had been at Euston for around six weeks, when Station Officer Kington announced that he was off to Morton in Marsh for three months. Morton in Marsh was the fire service's college in Gloucestershire, and he would be attending a three-month course there in fire prevention procedures.

This in turn meant that in his absence one of the two leading firemen at Euston would be promoted to the rank of temporary sub officer for the three months. I quite naturally presumed it would be the other leading fireman, he having served longer in the rank, and been at Euston longer than me. But no, 'A' division deemed him not suitable, not used to inner city ways. Would not be able to cope with the incorrigible lot of rogues that the Euston firemen were supposed to be. So, Leading Fireman Wilson was now to become temporary Sub Officer Wilson, after only just six weeks of being Leading Fireman Wilson. Not only to be temporary Sub Officer Wilson, but officer in charge of Euston fire station, for three months.

*

Pentonville prison was in the Caledonian Road in north London and was on Islington fire station's fire ground. The Caledonian Road was the boundary between Euston and Islington fire stations.

One day, the telephone rang at Euston fire station; it was the officer in charge of Islington fire station. A familiarisation visit had been arranged to Pentonville prison, would Euston's pump like to attend as well? I accepted with thanks, for these visits served a useful purpose from a firefighting point of view, and as an added bonus were usually very interesting.

The visit was arranged for 6.30 pm on the first evening of the next tour of duty. The visit was scheduled to take around one hour, to be followed by a familiarisation visit to the prison officer's social club, to familiarise ourselves with the local brew on sale there.

At 6.30 pm on the day, we were waiting outside the big gates to Pentonville prison, Islington's pump arrived shortly after us, and we rang the bell on the door of the prison gates. A prison officer answered the bell and then opened the big arched gates to allow both fire engines to pass through. The big gates closed behind us, and then the inner set of gates opened to allow us to pass into the main body of the prison itself. A prison officer directed us onto the perimeter road and showed us where to park the two fire engines, alongside the big prison wall. We then set off, accompanied by two prison officers, to carry out the familiarisation visit.

Around half an hour or so had passed by when we were approached by a senior, or principal prison officer. He was quite friendly saying, "Hello, lads.

Enjoying your visit?" For around a minute or so, he engaged us in conversation. Then he said casually, "By the way, I was wondering, those ladders on the back of your fire engines, how long are they?" I thought to myself he was obviously a Fire Brigade buff. One of those people greatly interested in the Fire Brigade and its equipment, somewhat similar to train spotters. So I told him that they were Dewhurst extension ladders, made out of laminated wood, and 35 feet in length. He nodded his head slowly, as if understanding. Then he surprised me by changing the subject, saying, "How high do you think our prison walls are?"

I took a guess off of the top of my head and said, "Around thirty feet, I should think."

He replied quickly, "Absolutely spot on." Then directing his remarks at the two prison officers with us, said caustically, "What Prat allowed not one, but two thirty-five-foot ladders to be parked alongside the walls of the prison, which are only thirty feet high?" He had apparently been looking for us for at least ten minutes. He had in the meantime, stationed two prison officers with dogs to guard the ladders. As he left us, he was still muttering to himself, "Surprised we still have any bloody prisoners at all left in the nick. Two thirty-five-foot ladders, could have got the whole bloody lot out inside fifteen minutes." We moved the two fire engines back outside the prison gates before carrying on with the visit.

After the visit was over, we adjourned to the prison officer's social club. It was here I discovered that prisons must be a bit like fire stations, for words of our deeds had got around. We were greeted with the words, "Look out, lads, here comes the escape committee" and "Which one of you is Ronnie Biggs' mate?" Then, "I'm on night duties this Saturday, any chance of you lads getting me out for the night?" The beer tasted good, and it was very, very cheap, so we ignored them all.

*

It had been a quiet evening, not many fire calls. At around eleven o'clock in the evening, most of the duty watch at Euston fire station were gathered in the messroom. There was a lull in the conversation as boredom began to set in.

"I'm pissed off," said Slag O'Conner, "let's have a roach hunt."

Two or three of the other firemen said, "Good idea, we haven't had a roach hunt for ages."

I was puzzled by this, I had been around a few stations, but had never heard of roach hunting before. I said nothing though, for I knew from experience that if I were to ask the question, "What's a roach hunt?" somehow, I would become the victim of it, whatever it was.

I followed them out to a ground floor washroom that contained five hand basins. Two of the firemen returned carrying a length of hose reel tubing about fifteen-feet long. Most of the firemen were by now wearing their fire boots and waterproof leggings. I now knew that I had been wise to keep quiet about roach hunting – whatever it was, water was involved in it somehow. The hot tap on one of the washbasins was turned full on. Then when the water was running scalding hot, the hose reel tubing was jammed over it. I quietly withdrew from the room; being sprayed with cold water was a joke. Being sprayed with scalding hot water; I was not prepared to chance it.

From outside the room, I watched them, they were spraying the hot water all over the room. Over the ceiling, along the water and heating pipes and behind the wash basins. After a pause of a minute or so, all the firemen in the room began stamping and jumping up and down, like a bunch of mad dervishes. Shouting and screaming and at the same time saying, "Die you bastards, die you bastards."

The room was now filled with steam from the hot water being sprayed around. Any stranger happening upon this weird scene would think that he had stumbled upon some wild occult ceremony and exit pretty quick. Indeed, I almost de-camped myself, remembering the tales told when I was first posted – "That Euston white watch, they are a crazy bunch of bastards."

Finally, curiosity got the better of me, and I moved into the doorway to see exactly what they were up to. What I saw amazed me, the hot water when sprayed over the room had flushed out hundreds of cockroaches of all shapes and sizes. It was these cockroaches that they were vigorously stamping on and killing.

When all had calmed down and the frenzied stamping had finished, I expressed surprise at the huge number of cockroaches flushed out and killed. Slag O'Conner shook his head sadly saying, "No, nothing like the numbers we have killed at times," adding mournfully, "one of the other watches must have had a go at them recently."

*

199

Any fire engine that was stationed at Euston fire station, Euston being an inner, inner London station, would I think have a thousand-fold more chance of colliding with a lamp post or traffic lights, or other street furniture than colliding with a tree.

Three weeks previously, a driver on one of the other watches had lost control of the turntable ladders whilst going to a fire and had crashed them into one of the trees around Euston Square.

As we arrived for night duties, we were told the turntable ladders were off the run following accident damage. As soon as we came on duty, we were to pick up and put on the run a spare turntable ladder, which was at Finchley fire station. I was then invited to guess what the turntable ladders had been in collision with. I thought for a brief moment, then said, "Not another tree?"

"Absolutely correct." I was informed. "That tree." Pointing in the direction of the tree on the forecourt.

"Is the tree all right?" I asked.

"Not a mark on it," the man said.

"Thank God for that," I replied, "didn't much fancy having to pick up a spare tree from Finchley as well."

The accident was all deemed to be the fault of stand-by drivers and soft living. The stand-by driver had been used to power steering, and when he pulled out of the appliance room to go to a fire call, he hadn't managed to turn the steering wheel of this machine, which was not power assisted, quickly enough, and thus crashed into the tree.

That night on the white watch, we had only one turntable ladder driver on duty. It was usual when picking up spare appliances that were any distance away, to travel in one of the firemen's cars to avoid long, tedious journeys on public transport. The problem arose that the only private car that night belonged to the turntable ladder driver, so that if he used his car to collect the ladders, he would not then be able to drive both his car and the ladders back to Euston. I was a qualified ladder operator and driver, so I would travel to Finchley with the driver. I would then drive the ladders back and he would drive his own car back to Euston.

We collected the spare turntable ladders from Finchley fire station and made ready for our journey back to Euston. I was quite looking forward to the journey, it being some months since I last had a drive of the ladders. I did not know this part of London, so we agreed that the driver would lead the way in his car, and I would follow on behind with the ladders.

After twenty or so minutes of driving, the road direction signs told me that we were heading for Hampstead Heath. I was curious, I had heard so much about Hampstead Heath, but being born and raised in West London, had never actually seen it. When we arrived at the Heath, we were on a narrow country lane type road running around the edge of the Heath. Considering that Hampstead Heath is actually in London, I found it quite beautiful, like a green splash of country and woodland inside London.

The other driver in his car was now some two hundred yards in front of me, around a bend in the narrow road. I drove the ladders down a hill to negotiate the bend, which had an adverse camber. I applied the brakes to slow down; nothing seemed to happen. I felt sure the brakes had come on, but that the wheels had locked. The ladders carried on forward unchecked. I pumped the brakes two or three times but to no effect. I was now in the middle of the bend, and the road moved off to the right. Without much hope, I turned the steering wheel to the right, but the ladders carried on in a straight line. At the end of this straight line was a big tree. Initially, my speed had only been around thirty miles per hour, and I estimated it was now twenty miles per hour. The fire engine ran off the road, onto the wide grass verge, which thankfully gripped the road wheels and slowed me down. I was finally brought to a halt by the overhanging ladders at the front of the appliance striking a big branch on the tree.

Very little damage was inflicted on the fire engine. It would nevertheless have to be taken off the run for the ladders themselves to be examined by workshop staff. It would not be quite acceptable to have them extended 100 feet in the air, and then find they were damaged.

What was worrying me was the reaction to this back at the station. Yet a third accident involving the turntable ladders in two months, and all of them involving trees. The odds on this happening to a fire engine stationed at Euston must be astronomical, yet it had happened. This time, I blamed the accident on the tree itself. Wet leaves on the road were deemed to have caused the wheels to lock, and the resulting accident. Leaves are part of a tree are they not!

It was all rather ignominious, the banter went on for some weeks afterwards; a notice was immediately attached to the tree on the forecourt which read, "Beware of dangerous tree." They took to referring to me as 'Tree three Wilson'. Signs appeared saying "Logs for sale, contact Leading Fireman Wilson, A23

Euston." 'A' divisional headquarters got in on the act, an order telling me to stand by at another station read, 'Order your topiarist to standby at A22 Manchester Square for the watch'. The wags even took to calling the station Euston Forest.

*

During the period when I was temporary sub officer, and actually in charge of Euston fire station, we received a fire call at around 11.30 pm for the pump escape, pump and turntable ladders to proceed to a fire call on Kentish Town's fire ground. This was not unusual; it would normally indicate that Kentish Town's machines were out on another call.

The call was to a fire at the rear of the High Street at Kentish Town. The High Street was a long road of four-storey properties, all with shops at the ground floor level. Showing over the tops of, and to the rear of the properties, was a large ominous orange glow.

A member of the public was waving to us further down the road, and as we drew up to him, we could see a break in the row of buildings. As I walked down between the two buildings, I could see a sea of fire.

Hidden from view by the buildings was a large timber yard, about the size of a football pitch, well alight. Following close behind me was my driver, Curly Clifford, a big, amiable man, although somewhat overweight for a fireman. Curly had a habit whenever the officer in charge needed to send a message from the fire or incident of then appearing uncalled for beside him and holding a message pad and pencil. I turned around and said to him, "Send a make-up, Curly." Dictating, "From temporary Sub Officer Wilson at Kentish Town High Street, make pumps eight."

Curly looked at me quizzically and said, "Worth a good fifteen pumps, Dave."

"Yes, I know," I replied. "Make them eight. I will explain later."

The firefighting by the first crews was automatically performed; the whole of the timber yard was well alight. I just gave them general directions; concentrate on stopping the fire spreading to the surrounding buildings. Shortly, Curly Clifford came back to tell me the make pumps eight message had been sent. "Good, get your message pad out; I will give you the informative message to send."

I was now determined to show that I was a good and efficient fire officer, albeit a new one, that will be judged by the speed and correctness of messages or information sent back from the fire. The sort of message that would be sent back is as follows:

"From temporary Sub Officer Wilson, at Kentish Town, a timber yard and ancillary offices and workshops, covering an area of approximately one acre well alight. Danger of spread of fire to surrounding buildings." No sooner had I sent this message than a station officer arrived on the fire ground, he relieved me of my very short command of the fire and I then resumed general firefighting duties.

The timber yard was well alight, and only vast quantities of water would eventually put it out. Initially, the problem was the spread of fire to the surrounding properties. The timber yard was in the middle of a square of houses. All that separated the houses from the fire was their back gardens, on average about fifty feet long.

Flaming brands swirled over the houses, radiated heat was in some cases melting the plastic rain pipes and guttering. The wind was blowing the actual flames of the fire halfway along the gardens to the houses.

The fire was now a fifteen-pump fire, and as more and more firemen brought more and more jets of water to bear on it, the fire gradually came under control. The method of extinction with a big fire in the open was to keep adding the magic ingredient: water. There then eventually (hopefully) comes a time when the fire isn't roaring away quite so fiercely. From then on with a little luck, it's all downhill.

There had been one or two dangerous moments, the stacks of burning timber were up to twenty feet in height and weighed many tons. I had been working with Euston's crews, wielding a three-quarter inch jet between these huge stacks of timber. Then, without warning, a partially burnt, large stack just in front of us lurched sideways and crashed to the ground. It was like a two-storey house crashing down. Sparks and embers flew high in the air, and the stack rekindled itself in front of us. This stack had partially burnt away at the bottom, causing it to overbalance, which in turn, caused us to hurriedly examine the two large stacks either side of us for similar defects.

You gained a little knowledge at every fire you attended. I for one had not appreciated fully the dangers that burning stacks of timber posed.

Earlier on in the fire, fortunately before the firemen had got close in, from within the centre of the fire, had come a dull whoomph, followed by a huge, orange fireball. A large propane cylinder had burst in the heat, and its contents ignited. As if large, pretty, boiling, orange fireballs are not danger enough, the remains of the heavy metal cylinder were later found in the garden of one of the houses. It having passed midway between two crews of firemen to get there.

Approximately, three hours after we had arrived at the fire, we were on our way back to station. Somewhat wet, but happy – it had been an interesting fire. I went straight into the station watchroom, and over to the teleprinter, where all messages from the fire would be recorded. For me, it was a question of professional pride to see if they had substantially altered my original description of the premises that I had given on the first message during the course of the fire. I was very pleased to see the original description carried on throughout the many messages sent back from the fire, indicating that my initial hurried description of the unusual site – a large timber yard contained within a square of houses – had been good and accurate, thus deemed acceptable by the following senior officers.

Curly Clifford then came into the watchroom and I explained to him the reason I had only made pumps eight when I had known it warranted many more.

This is how it was explained to me by a wise old station officer in the past.

"The London Fire Brigade Headquarters at Lambeth is on the south bank of the River Thames. On the other bank of the river across Lambeth bridge is the 'A' division. It is possible, therefore, that senior officers from Headquarters can be in attendance at fires in 'A' division before the senior officers from 'A' division. Senior officers from Headquarters only start to move onto fires once they go above eight pumps. So by never making the initial make up more than eight pumps we then ensure that our own divisional commander gets to arrive at the fire before the Headquarters mob." He summed it up thus, "So, my lad, unless you've got a damned good reason, like Buckingham Palace going from end to end, never, never make pumps more than eight initially." Besides that, he said, "It makes the divisional commander look good if he can then make them fifteen. If the divisional commander's happy, everyone's happy."

Some years later, I had to explain this to a divisional officer who was querying why I had only made pumps eight at a fire, when it obviously warranted more. He was most impressed with the theory, but it was plainly obvious he had never served in the 'A' division.

*

It was whilst at Euston that I was introduced to the obscene telephone call. Repairs to firemen's leather fire boots and shoes were carried out by a contracting shoe repairer, or cobbler. He would drive around all the fire stations in a van, picking up the shoes that needed repair. In order to save time at the next station, he was to visit, and to ensure that fire boots etc., were ready for collection, he would ask the dutyman to telephone the next station he was to call at and warn them he was coming.

The duty man would then telephone this next station, using the Brigade's internal telephone system. When the telephone was answered with the standard salutation such as, "A22 Manchester Square," or such, the dutyman would speak in a low, derogatory voice into the mouthpiece saying the single, on the face of it obscene word, "Cobblers."

The reaction would very much depend on who answered the telephone. If it was an older or wiser fireman, or indeed even perhaps an officer, the reaction would simply be "Thanks very much, mate," and the telephone replaced. If it was answered by someone not accustomed to the devious ways and humour of firemen, or just someone who had never received this particular call before, the reply would usually be a startled, "I beg your pardon?" Then the allegedly obscene word would be repeated down the telephone line again. "Cobblers." This usually had the effect of the receiver of the call demanding to know who was speaking to him. He would be told, "It's A23 Euston, mate." This would invariably confuse him; obscene callers do not normally give identification. He would then say, "I am very sorry, I did not hear what you said, could you repeat it, please?"

"Cobblers," would sound out of the telephone earpiece once again, this time followed quietly, by the word, "coming." The receiver of the call was now absolutely sure that he was hearing correctly. Someone from Euston fire station was shouting "Cobblers," down the telephone at him.

The caller from Euston would now take the initiative, "Did you get that message all right, mate?" The receiver, if he had any spirit in him at all, would then reply, "Yes, and cobblers to you too, mate."

This conversation could have been carried to any lengths, but the outcome was always the same. When the receiver of the call was informed that this was not an obscene telephone call but that the message was, "The cobbler is coming, the shoe repair man is on his way to your station next," he would then suffer acute embarrassment, having himself shouted obscene words down the telephone.

This little gag could have interesting complications in the not-too-distant future when we had female firepersons on the stations and answering the telephone.

*

One single short ring of the fire bells echoed throughout the station. This was the signal that a senior officer was in attendance on the station.

I would put on my undress jacket and hat and make my way to the appliance room to meet him. I was still in the rank of temporary sub officer and in charge of the station. So this would undoubtedly be a 'just popped in to see how you are doing' visit.

In the appliance room was Divisional Officer Colenut, second in command of the division. I was partly right in my assumption, he was apparently just passing by and thought he would pop in and see if the station had subsided anymore. He may have been trying to catch me out, for to subside means to sink lower.

I knew that some people did not have a very high opinion of Euston. I nevertheless did not think that a senior officer of that rank would actually voice that opinion. But I was ahead of him. In the far back corner of the appliance room, set into the wall with cement, was a butterfly shaped piece of glass.

Some eighteen months previously, a large building, some twenty or more stories in height, had been constructed on the site next door to the fire station. Soon after its completion, a large crack appeared in the appliance room wall. The weight of the building next door was affecting the foundations of the fire station. The butterfly shaped piece of glass had been cemented across the crack, so that the slightest movement would break the piece of glass and indicate that the subsidence was continuing. The piece of glass was still in place and not broken. Something which he could just as easily have found out by making a simple telephone call.

"Whilst I'm here then," he said, "I might as well watch a few drills." This man was a divisional officer! Why didn't he just walk in and say, "I would like to see the men at drill." Instead of as with all senior officers, going through the performance of 'I was just passing by so I thought…'

The appliances were taken out into the drill yard. I knew full well he had not come to see the men at drill, but rather to watch me conduct the drill. The men were lined up in their crews, and I detailed them for a standard drill. Slip and pitch the escape to the third floor of the tower, hook ladder to the fourth, jet to work on the fourth floor of the tower.

Now an unforeseen problem arose. The firemen on the station all had nicknames, which were commonly used by all on the station, including myself. Biff Baker, Curly Clifford, Speedy Close, Ginger, Lurch, Slag O'Conner. How they came by these nicknames, and what they meant, in most cases I hadn't got a clue.

For a new temporary sub officer to shout out these endearing nicknames in front of a divisional officer was just not on. "Get a move on, Slag; Speedy go slow; Lurch back up Biff on the branch." Not the sort of words of command that would impress a divisional officer.

I would have to use their formal titles. "Get a move on, fireman O' Conner; fireman Close go slow." Now came the problem, for then as now, I couldn't remember Lurch's real surname. It was the same with some of the other firemen, I just could not remember their surnames, only their nicknames.

Even when I did get the surnames right, it still caused problems. The shouted command, "Fireman Clifford stop," had no effect on the man whatsoever. Although his name was Clifford, nobody ever called him that, everyone called him Curly. Eventually, when the command was repeated, "Fireman Clifford stop," he turned around, and then pointed his finger at himself questioningly, as if to say, do you mean me?

Sod it, I thought, and gave up trying, reverting back to my normal style. Then I issued the words of command, "Lurch, Biff up back on the branch," whereas I should have said, "Lurch, back up Biff on the branch."

Despite the above, the Euston firemen were very good at their job, and the drill went smoothly, pleasing the divisional officer. He had a smile on his face. I think he had spotted the temporary sub officer's dilemma with the names. Not only had I coped with it, but I think also amused him somewhat.

After the drill was over, the divisional officer engaged me in an informal conversation in a quiet corner of the appliance room.

"How are you liking Euston?"

"Fine, sir. I get on well with everybody at the station."

"What do you think of Mr Kington?"

This was a loaded question, for I knew that Station Officer Kington was regarded as a wily old bird at Divisional Headquarters. The question was no problem to answer, because I actually admired Mr Kington, with his beautiful laidback approach to life and the job.

"Do you miss Paddington?"

"Not really, sir, this is a new adventure to me here."

"How would you feel about going back to Paddington?" So this was what the visit was all about! They wanted me back at Paddington.

"I am very sorry, sir," I replied. "But I really could not volunteer to go back to Paddington. I have built up a great rapport and loyalty, with Mr Kington and the white watch at Euston. I feel it would be disloyal of me, now, to volunteer to go back to Paddington so soon."

I had said all the wrong things, the fact that I could get on well with Mr Kington, and his incorrigible Euston rogues, made me even more desirable back at the flagship, as Paddington was known.

I could see by his expression that he was a bit annoyed, he had wasted two hours of his time coming to see me.

I continued, "But if on the other hand, I were to be posted back to Paddington, I would not complain too loudly."

A month after this visit, Station Officer Kington informed me that I was being posted back to the white watch, Paddington. I was very sad to leave them, but I knew in my heart the sooner I got the rank I wanted, that of station officer, and the flagship was the place to be at to attain that, the sooner I could once again put down roots.

I had only been at Euston for around six months, but they had been a very happy six months. The white watch made me welcome and I enjoyed their company and their jokes, and indeed, I can still remember most of their nicknames, if not their surnames.

Station Officer Kington unknowingly paid me a great compliment. I overheard him complaining bitterly in the office, "Just as soon as we get a decent leading fireman on the watch, they post the bugger away."

Chapter 13

A21 Paddington White Watch

I was back at Paddington again, this really was a career move, for I much preferred the smaller, two or three appliance stations. On the smaller stations, the firemen tend to get on, or move on, that is move on to other fire stations. At a large station like Paddington, if firemen cannot get on together, they will tend to form separate groups, rather than one big happy watch. The white watch at Paddington was like this. My first impression was three or four subgroups that did not necessary get on well with each other.

The senior officers of the division were determined that Paddington, as a Divisional Headquarters station, would be a happy and popular station. My posting to the watch completed a radical change of the officers on the watch; when I arrived, they were as follows: the station officer, Knocker White, a very good choice, for he was a friendly outgoing man. He was an ex-semi-professional footballer and loved all sports. His father had been a fireman before him, and Knocker loved to go to fires.

The sub officer, Des Platten; Des was the only officer to remain on the watch after the changes. He was a long serving experienced sub officer, and superb on the fire ground. He was rather quiet natured, but once you got to know him, a friend for life. Yet another man to whom the Brigade was more than just a job, for he had a brother serving as a station officer.

The other leading fireman was Niel Wallington. Paddington to Niel was like myself I think, a career move. He also wanted the excitement of the busier inner London stations. His career had begun I believe, in the small Croydon Fire Brigade, which subsequently amalgamated to form the Greater London Fire Brigade. Niel was very outgoing, and very energetic. So much so, that when I got to know him better, I would tell him, "For Christ's sake, Niel, slow down, I get breathless just watching you."

One of my better memories of white watch Paddington was of a very good and happy office staff. Perhaps it could be said of us that we had formed our own subgroup.

*

I was taking escape ladder drills with two crews in Paddington's large and spacious drill yard. The escape ladder was the large fifty-foot ladder that was manoeuvred around on large five-foot diameter wooden wheels. Now this ladder, before it could be put to work and extended at fires, first had to be put in position. This often entailed pushing it along pavements, winding in and out of parked cars, and even under low archways to enter mews properties and the like. Whenever possible, I liked to simulate fire conditions in my drills.

We had almost finished the drill period, and there was twenty minutes left before stand-easy at eleven o'clock. I said to the two crews, "One last quick drill each and then we will knock off for stand easy." Their faces dropped, they thought we would finish drills there and then.

I detailed the drill for the first crew. Slip the escape ladder from the appliance once around the drill tower. Enter the appliance room by the pump bay and leave by the escape bay, then place the escape ladder back on the appliance. The purpose of the drill was to practice manoeuvring the ladder, as required on the fire ground, in, around and under obstacles. The drill commenced when I gave the order, "Get to work."

The crew jumped down from the appliance and ran to the back of the machine. For some strange reason, their demeanour had changed, for they were now all happy and smiling. I was soon to find out why. They removed the escape ladder from the back of the appliance, then to my surprise, put down the wheel chocks on the ladder where it stood. Then, minus the ladder, ran once around the drill tower. They ran into the appliance room through the pump bay, then out through the escape bay. They then ran back to the appliance, removed the wheel chocks, placed the escape ladder back onto the appliance. Then with huge grins on their faces, fell in at the rear of the appliance, in the drill complete position.

I could see the funny side of it; they had done exactly as I had told them, no more, no less. They were no doubt, expecting me to make them do the drill again. They had merely been testing my sense of humour. I had a smile on my face, it had been funny, all I needed to do was come out of it with dignity. In my best

Sergeant Major's voice, I said to the crew, "I suppose you thought that was funny?" I paused to let them think about it. I then said, "Well, it was funny, fall out." Thus taking them all completely by surprise, for they fully expected to have to do it all again. It was the old show business motto, always leave them laughing, and they will think they have enjoyed themselves.

It was now the next crew's turn, they had big grins on their faces, they too had enjoyed the joke. This time, the drill detail was precise. Slip the escape ladder, take the escape ladder once around the drill tower. Lower the escape ladder in the carriage, then take the escape ladder into the appliance room, exiting through the pump bay, and so on until the detail was complete. To my complete surprise, when I finished the drill detail, the smiles had gone off their faces, and they were actually complaining. Complaining that the previous crew had not had to push the ladder around the tower etc. My Sergeant Major's voice came back again, and I snarled at them, "Do it," and they did it. This had been one of the very rare occasions that I had ever found the London firemen to be surly and lacking in humour.

During the time I was stationed at Paddington and Euston fire stations, I travelled back and forth from duty on British Rail trains. Travelling forth was pretty straight forward but travelling back sometimes had its problems. The trouble was that I still liked to go for a drink with the lads after the first day duty. No matter how determined I was for it not to happen, I always found myself running to Paddington railway station in order to catch the last train home.

As most regular commuters know, British Rail have perfected the art of always having the heating in their trains either too hot, or too cold. Too cold in the mornings on the way to work so that you shiver. The last trains at night are invariably too hot. This, coupled with a few drinks, guarantees a nice doze on the way home. It also guarantees a nice doze all the way past the station you wish to alight at. I've been everywhere! Didcot Junction twice. The first time after a wait of some hours, I was fortunate enough to get a train back. The second time there were no trains and the price of a taxi home amounted to a day's wages. So I walked back to Pangbourne – it was only seventeen miles. A delightful little walk, right across the lonely Berkshire downs in the small hours of the morning. Owls hooting and all the noises of the night. If I had been sober, I would have wet myself. Of course, I didn't walk all the seventeen miles home, a milkman on his way to work at around five o'clock in the morning kindly gave me a lift for the last mile on his milk float.

I've been to Goring, and I've been to Cholsey, but these are scarcely worth mentioning, being merely the next two stations down the line. Goring was interesting; the lights were still on in a public house, so I went in through the only open door to try to make a telephone call. I found myself in the middle of a late-night drinking session. They let me use the telephone, and even gave me a pint of beer, very nice people they were. This may have had something to do with the fact that at that time, firemen wore similar blue shirts and ties as policemen.

I've been to Oxford, city of the dreaming spires, but it was one o'clock in the morning and it was shut. Once again, I could not afford the taxi fare home, and it was too far to walk. I hired a taxi to take me out to the ring road, at the point where I would be most likely to hitch a lift in the direction of Reading. The very first lorry that came along stopped.

The driver wanted to know if I had any cigarettes.

"I roll my own cigarettes," I said. "I could roll you some if you like."

"Jump in," he replied. I rolled him five or ten cigarettes and we began talking. He could see that I was a fireman because most unusually I was wearing my uniform. He wanted to know what I was doing in uniform at this time of the morning.

"I've been up to London to have drinkies with the Lord Mayor," I told him. He didn't of course believe me so I told him the story.

The Lord Mayor of Westminster had invited a selection of people that worked in the borough – firemen, nurses, postmen and the like – to a reception at Westminster City Hall. A station officer, sub officer and leading fireman (myself), plus two senior officers were attending on behalf of the Fire Brigade.

The reception was a rather a swish affair, held in the penthouse suite at the town hall. Smartly dressed waitresses, dishing out unlimited supplies of red and white wine, a finger buffet, consisting of lots of fiddly things skewered on pointed sticks to eat.

Being a beer drinker myself, I was not terribly impressed. I would have been far happier with a pint of beer, and a nice, big, thick cheese and onion sandwich.

During the course of the evening, I could not help but notice that the very senior and venerable station officer, with whom I was standing, would, every time the waitress came along with her trays of wine, take one glass of wine for himself, which he then gave to me to hold. He would take a further two glasses of wine from the tray and take them across the room to where the two senior fire officers were in conversation. He would present the two full glasses of wine to them. This duty being carried out entirely unasked for by the senior officers.

I had observed this servile service throughout the evening. I considered it totally out of character of this senior station officer, who was certainly not renowned for his deference to senior officers. After about one and a half hours had passed, and I had supped around eight glasses of wine, thus becoming quite bold, I decided to comment on it saying, "Here, guvnor, it's come to my notice that you are a bit of a snivelling bastard, aren't, you?"

Fortunately, I had judged my moment well, for he also was quite mellow. He nevertheless raised his eyebrows and said slowly and meaningfully, "Really, young Wilson, why in your opinion, is that then?"

I replied, "Well, guv, I've noticed that every time you have a glass of wine, you take an extra two glasses then act as butler to those two over there." Indicating with a nod of my head the senior officers.

He smiled a slow, gentle smile before saying, "Young Wilson, some words of wisdom…" He went on to tell me, "When out drinking with persons of higher rank, or station, always without fail, make sure that they get pissed first, before oneself gets pissed. That way, one's own little indiscretions will be seen in an entirely different alcoholic light by one's seniors." He went on to add, "If you care to look at those two gentlemen across the room, you will observe that they are quite mellow already, it is therefore quite safe for us to continue drinking."

These were words of great wisdom, which I never forgot. I wasn't always able to carry them out as effectively as he had done, but I never forgot them.

Later, after the function had finished, when I cheekily (if somewhat alcoholically), cadged a lift back to Paddington fire station in the senior officer's staff car, I found the venerable station officer's ploy had worked. For I found myself, then a lowly, humble, leading fireman ensconced quite happily, if somewhat cramped, in the back seat of the staff car, between two very affable, very senior fire officers. Then in reply to my statement, "Damn good piss up, wasn't it?" Found them nodding their heads happily in agreement.

The lorry driver who had been quite happy listening to my stories, and smoking my cigarettes, went right out of his way and dropped me off at the top of my road in Pangbourne.

Why is it that when you get home in the early hours of the morning, you have not got your door key? Then when you throw stones at the bedroom window to wake the wife, why is it that the next-door neighbour's wife invariably hears them long before your own does?

*

By far the most exciting of these late-night trips I have ever made, was to Old Oak Common railway sidings. This time, I had not fallen asleep on the train, but had left the pub late as usual. I had dashed onto Paddington railway station, just as my train was leaving its usual platform. I just managed to clamber on board it by the skin of my teeth. As soon as I shut the door behind me and entered the carriage, I knew I had goofed again. I was the only person in the carriage, and the train was now going too fast for me to jump off.

I made my way down the carriages and every one of them was empty, where was the train going to, I wondered?

In one carriage, I at last came across the guard, with his back to me and reading a newspaper. When I spoke to him, it clearly startled him.

"What are you doing here?" he said.

So I told him, "Well, I thought I was going to Pangbourne."

"Well, you're not," he snapped back, "you are going to Old Oak Common sidings, this train has finished work for the day."

Different! I thought to myself. *I've never been there before, sounds quite exciting.* "Will I be able to get a train back again?" I asked him.

"No, not till the morning," he replied with an air of finality.

Seeing my downfallen face he relented, then said, "I might be able to get you back to Paddington tonight, come with me."

He made his way over to a carriage door and let down the window, then looked out. "You're in luck," he said. "There's one coming now." He then waved and shouted out of the window something that sounded like one for Paddington. He then opened the carriage door and said to me, "There you are, off you go."

"Off I go where?" I asked.

"Get on that train there," he said, "it's slowing down for you." He then pointed to a train two tracks away and going in the direction of Paddington.

Looking back on it, all I can say is that I must have been drunk; I certainly wouldn't have done it sober. Upon reflection, the guard must have been drunk also, to have let me even attempt it. The problem was not jumping off the first train, that was easy and the most that could have happened was a broken bone or two. It was getting up onto the second train that was a worry. When a train is on its rails, and you are standing on the track alongside it, the floor of the carriage is about four and a half feet up in the air. This alone can be difficult enough to negotiate. Then trying to climb up onto a moving platform four feet up in the air, remembering that when climbing up onto this moving platform bloody great three-foot-diameter iron train wheels are waiting for the slightest slip to mince your legs to pulp. Changing trains in midstream is not for the fainthearted, nor is it for sober people.

*

We were attending a social evening at Paddington fire station for wives and families of firemen stationed there. This was one of the few occasions when my wife travelled with me to London for a Brigade social event. The evening had been a very jolly evening, and I had enjoyed myself, meeting all the family and friends of my workmates. I was very slightly tipsy. I saw that my wife was in conversation with the divisional officer at the far side of the room and I went over to join them. As I arrived, I could hear that my wife was complaining to the divisional officer about her husband.

"Lives, eats and sleeps Fire Brigade," she was saying. "Look at him he's hardly said a word to me all night, talking to all his mates about fires."

Women! Wonderful, enigmatic creatures are they not! If I had said to my wife, "Look, I've got a promotion interview coming up, see if you could say a few nice words in the divisional officer's ear for me," she would not have had a clue as to how to go about it. Now without even knowing it, that was exactly what she had just done!

I had been enjoying myself so much I had completely forgotten the time. It was eleven twenty-five and our last train for home left Paddington station at eleven thirty. The divisional commander overhearing me tell my wife this, offered to take us to the station in his staff car, which I gratefully accepted. His driver was summoned and we got into the staff car with three minutes to get to the station. There was a line of cars waiting at red traffic lights, the driver switched on the blue flashing beacon, and around them, we went. The car drove into Paddington station and onto the very platform where the train was waiting. We just had time to say our thanks, then stepped onto the train, and it pulled out of the station, leaving the rest of the passengers to wonder who were these very important people the train had apparently waited for?

The divisional officer's driver who drove us to Paddington station was a character in his own right. He was reputed to be the fastest staff car driver in the Brigade; he certainly was the fastest in 'A' division. The divisional commander was reported to have said that no matter how big or dangerous the fire was, that he would be attending, "It was always an anti-climax, after the hair-raising drive to get there." The driver's name was Peter, but he was usually called 'Harpic'. He was an older and quiet natured fireman, and solitary by nature.

I once asked him how he acquired his nickname, 'Harpic', but he merely muttered, "Clean around the bend," and simply wandered off. I then asked one of the other staff drivers, who told me that he was named after the famous brand of toilet cleaner, 'Harpic', who's advertising slogan was, 'Cleans around the bend' (of the toilet).

He then went on to say, "Although you might think that Harpic is a bit crazy, or around the bend, he is in fact the only man in the London Fire Brigade who can prove he is sane. He has got a certificate from a psychiatrist, stating that he is sane." The Brigade at some time in the past was trying to discharge Harpic on psychosis grounds. He then went to his own specialist and obtained the certificate stating he was sane. He then apparently thought that since he was proved to be sane, he could now safely to go around acting like he wasn't.

*

The time was now approaching for the written examination for promotion to the rank of station officer. Having passed the sub officer's examination, I was qualified to take this exam. The examination was quite a comprehensive one, taking over two full days to complete.

Des Platten, the sub officer, and Niel Wallington the other leading fireman on the watch, were also both taking the examination that year. The Institute of Fire Engineers, examination at graduate level, also qualified the holder for promotion to the rank of station officer.

Some months earlier, Niel Wallington had told me that he was sending off for the entry forms for this examination. He asked me, "Would you like one also?"

I thanked him and replied, "Yes." Both Niel and Des played a major part in my later success.

On the closing date for applications to take the Institute of Fire Engineers examination, Niel asked if I had sent off the entry form that he had obtained for me. I said, "Dammit, Niel. I filled it in but forgot to post if off." He gave me such a telling off, that he Niel had taken the trouble to get the form for me, adding that I couldn't then be bothered to send it off.

Just to pacify him, I telephoned my wife, told her where the form was, got her to write out a cheque, and then to post it straight away, reasoning that the Institute of Fire Engineers was unlikely to turn down a cheque for twelve pounds then a considerable sum of money, and part of the reason why I had not returned the examination entrance form in the first place.

The fire authorities' examination for station officer rank came and went, and I failed it. Niel's persistence had got me another bite at the cherry, through the Institute of Fire Engineers exam. This also was a two-day examination and conducted in depth.

These yearly examinations were like Brigade reunions, you met old friends from previous stations. Some aspiring station officers had met and made good friends simply by attending the examinations year after year.

On the second day of the examination, I had lunch with Niel and Des Platten, and we made our way back to the examination building early. I had intended to renew acquaintances with some old friends I had seen in the exam room.

The next exam on the afternoon agenda was 'Fire Service Law'. Everyone but everyone was reading up their notes, there was no one at all to speak to. Niel was reading his notes, and Des had a pile of small notebooks he was working his way through. I had not got a single note with me, I was bored, so I asked Des to lend me one of his notebooks.

Des was an unusual man, in that the writing in his notebooks was entirely legible, even to me. The book of notes he gave me by chance, I found very interesting. It referred to the legislation governing Saturday morning cinema performances for children. I had been to dozens of these Saturday morning inspections of cinemas, and I did not know half the things that were in this notebook. The law apparently specifies the number and minimum ages of attendants, per one hundred children, in the cinema. The minimum ages of children to be admitted, no children to be allowed on the balconies etc. Pages and pages of things that I did not know, despite attending so many inspections.

The examination started, seated at my desk the invigilator gave the instruction to turn our papers over and begin. I glanced quickly through the questions to be answered, and then could not believe my eyes. There were six questions of which I had to answer four. Two of them I had actually read up in Des' notebooks during the lunch hour. One of them was about the regulations governing Saturday morning cinemas, which I had found so interesting and absorbed almost completely.

I subsequently passed the examination and was now qualified for the interview for promotion to the rank of station officer. Thank you, Niel; thank you, Des. I'm sorry Des, you read the wrong notebook, for you failed that particular exam.

Niel Wallington also passed this examination, and subsequently went on to become chief officer of a large county Fire Brigade. This did not surprise me, for Niel was a gentleman.

Some years later when we were both station officers, I met Niel on a course at the fire services college in Morton in Marsh.

Wednesday afternoon at that time was designated for rest and recreation. I would normally go to the college library and get some good books on the fire service. Then I would spend Wednesday afternoon lying on my bed reading them.

One Wednesday, Niel asked me to go on a visit to bird-land with him. "Sounds interesting," I said to him. "What is it, dolly bird-land, scantily dressed ladies, and all that?"

"No," replied Niel. "Dickie bird-land."

"What, with feathers on?" I said. "You mean give up my Wednesday afternoon to go and look at dickie birds, in cages, you must be joking."

"I don't see why not," said Niel indignantly. "I always come out drinking with you of a night-time." I said Niel was different! What kind of a man is it that looks upon it as an imposition to go socialising around the pubs in Morton of an evening?

I relented and agreed to go with him to bird-land, but worse was to come. Had we hurried we could have got a quick drink in the village pub before going into bird-land. Not Niel, he wanted to have a cream tea, in a fancy tearoom, buttered scones, fresh cream, pots of tea, pretty little cups, the full works. If some of my other London firemen mates had seen me in that pretty tearoom, I could have lost every single bit of my street credibility.

Then to add insult to injury, he volunteered me for a five-aside football game the following Wednesday afternoon. I hated it for the first five minutes, then got quite carried away with the game, making up for my lack of skill by attacking anything that looked remotely like a football, furiously. By half time, the other players had taken to calling me Norman.

"My name is Dave," I told them.

"We know that," they said, but nevertheless carried on calling me Norman. That evening, Niel explained to me my style of football was like a famous football player called Norman Hunter's style of playing. I was flattered, he then went on to explain the man's nickname was, "Norman bite your ankles Hunter."

Ridiculous! I didn't bite anybody's ankles. I then took to thinking that compared with coarse volleyball, as played on some fire stations I had served at five-a-side football was a softy's game.

I said Niel was a scholar and a gentleman, he must have been, because hairy arsed firemen don't go miles out of their way to look at dickie birds in cages. Hairy arsed firemen don't have posh cream teas when the pubs are still open. Hairy arsed firemen play coarse volleyball and try to mutilate each other over the top of the net. Niel was not therefore a hairy arsed fireman. I was not surprised at all when he made the rank of chief officer in later years.

*

Whilst at Paddington, I attended a fire call to a restaurant in the Saint John's Wood district. When we arrived at the address, there was no one at all to meet us. The restaurant was on a corner of the street and was an expensive Indian style restaurant. All the plate glass windows had fallen out and lay in pieces on the pavement outside the premises. Initially, we had no idea as to why the Fire Brigade had been called.

Going inside the restaurant, we could see that the lightweight plastic fittings, such as lamp shades etc., had melted. There was some evidence of heat damage to the inside of the restaurant, but no initial sign as to what had caused it. Another unusual point was that somebody had been using a butane gas blowlamp to remove plastic floor tiles. The dissembled blowlamp and gas cartridge were lying on the floor. There was something very unusual about the heat damage, and the broken shop windows that we could not immediately understand.

Shortly afterwards, a police constable came into the shop, and what he then told us solved the mystery. The owner of the shop had been using the gas blowlamp to burn off the plastic floor tiles, when the gas cartridge ran out. The shop owner had just purchased the blowlamp especially to burn off the floor tiles and had never before changed the gas cartridge. The owner of the shop was an Indian, and spoke English well enough, but he apparently did not read English well. He failed to read the instructions on the gas cartridge.

Changing the gas cartridge entailed unscrewing the blowlamp from the cartridge holder, placing in a fresh cartridge, then screwing back the blowlamp onto the cartridge. As the blowlamp was screwed back on, it pierced and then sealed the new cartridge. The Indian gentleman had simply tried to force the new cartridge onto the blowlamp. Whilst doing so, he had pierced the top of the new cartridge, but not sealed it. The gas cartridge was roughly the same size as a standard tin of baked beans. The gas that escaped from just that small cartridge had ignited, blown out all the shop windows and caused all the heat damage to the shop. The shop owner had subsequently died of the burns he received.

*

Brigade Routine Orders were published, and under the heading, 'Promotions and Transfers' was the following entry: 'Leading Fireman D Wilson, A21 Paddington, promoted to the rank of sub officer, transferred to 'A' divisional headquarters, day duties'. Thus, I was now to be a Monday to Friday, five day a week, nine to six, staff wallah. Although I might not class this as an adventure, it would certainly be a new experience.

The posting did not entail much personal disruption; just remove the contents of my locker on the second floor, only to replace them in a locker in the ground floor divisional headquarters.

The five-day week routine took a bit of getting used to. After the second day at work, my biological clock kept telling me I could have a lie in this morning, as I was due to go onto night duties.

In the staff office, I was to take over the duties of a temporary Sub Officer Kennedy who would be reduced back to his own rank of leading fireman and return to his own station. I had known Tom Kennedy since my A3 Camden Town days; he had then been stationed at the next fire station, Kentish Town. I was rather sad that I was displacing Tom, but he was very philosophical about it, saying, "Hurry up and get promoted station officer, and I can then have my job back."

Tom Kennedy was one of life's practical jokers (demonstrated by the filing system I inherited from him). Tom, I think, worked on the theory that if nobody but him could find anything in the filing system, that therefore made him irreplaceable. His main duties I subsequently found out, for they became my duties, were general dogsbody and tea boy. With a bright character like his, that alone should have made him irreplaceable.

It was his practical jokes that he was famous for. Early on in his career, when he was still a relatively junior fireman at Kentish Town fire station, he had been told by his station officer to replace a button missing from the double row of buttons on the front of his fire tunic. He appeared on parade several days later with the button still missing from his tunic.

His station officer, who at that time was a bit of a tartar, began to admonish him. Then, whilst he was doing so, from out of the front of Tom's tunic popped a silver button, dangling on a piece of black thread, which for a while gently swung to and fro, then slowly made its way up the front of his tunic to finally rest neatly and exactly in the place of the missing button. All the time, this was happening Tom's eyes were fixed firmly and unsmiling to the front. But his right hand down by his side was pulling gently and slowly on the other end of the piece of thread. I think Tom was a man who was under achieving. If his mind was not taken up with something worthwhile and absorbing, he would soon find something to occupy it.

The divisional officer had decided that the outside of the divisional headquarters was dull and drab. That it needed brightening up with some flowers, shrubs and small trees in pots. The station officer in charge of the staff office delegated to Tom the job of liaising with the GLC Parks Department. Tom was to select the various trees and shrubs and then get them delivered.

Around two weeks later, the telephone on the staff station officer's desk rang. The call was for Tom Kennedy. The station officer called him over to take the telephone call. Tom picked up the receiver and began to talk in a loud voice so that all the staff office could hear, "GLC Parks Department! Good I've been waiting to hear from you." He then carried on a conversation with the telephone handset. "They are that big, are they?" Pause. "Well, I suppose we could get a crane, what size do you think we'll need?" He then said in an aside to the staff station officer, "The trees you ordered are being delivered."

By now, all conversation in the staff office had stopped. They had all heard the word trees, and they had all heard the word crane. They had put two and two together and it added up to bloody great big trees. Tom carried on his conversation, "Thirty tons! As big as that, how much will it cost? Good grief," said Tom, "three hundred pounds, just one moment I will have to speak to my station officer. We are going to have to hire a crane to unload the trees, guvnor," he said. "It will cost about three hundred pounds."

The station officer was getting agitated; this was getting out of hand. Initially, just a few bulbs and shrubs had been intended; now it seemed like he was being asked to take delivery of a forest. Tom spoke again into the telephone. "Sorry you will have to cancel the order; the guvnor says we cannot possibly afford three hundred pounds." Pause! "What, you have already taken delivery, so we will have to take them." Tom indicated to the station officer what the Parks Department had just apparently said that the trees would have to be delivered.

Tom again continued his conversation, "What do we want to close the road for?" Pause. "I see, to enable the crane to unload the trees." Tom was thinking out loud the logistics of this. Saying, "We could contact the local police, but then it would also mean placing an advert in the local paper to warn the public."

The station officer, finally losing all patience, snatched the telephone away from Tom. Shouting loudly and angrily into the mouthpiece, "I didn't want bloody trees in the first place, so you can damn well send them back where they came from, I will refuse to sign for them. As for hiring a crane and then stopping up the road, you must be crazy. It would be quicker to grow the bloody trees than go through all that paperwork." The station officer ranted and he raved, but the man at the other end said nothing!

Tom Kennedy, with a huge grin on his face, was replacing the telephone handset on his own desk. There was no man at the other end of the telephone line; Tom had been talking to himself for the past five minutes. In fact, Tom had even dialled the station officer's extension, and then asked to speak to himself.

*

After I had been in my new job for only four weeks, I had to attend a previously arranged course of two weeks' duration at the fire service's college, Morton in Marsh, which is in Gloucestershire. Tom Kennedy got his old job back and proceeded to complain that I had mucked up his infallible filing system.

Whilst I was attending the course, I received a summons to return and attend a station officer's promotion interview, to be held at Brigade headquarters, Lambeth, London. By passing the station officer's examination, I was automatically included in the interview lists. I had only been a proper sub officer for one month, and now they were dragging me all the way back from Gloucestershire to London for an interview that would be a mere formality.

Although I was a bit cross at travelling all this way for a mere formality, I was thus very relaxed and the interview went well.

The chairman of the interview board was a very senior officer, who had been at the honour and awards enquiry I had attended months earlier and, I think, liked me. The whole interview was smiles and happiness, nothing like the interviews I had suffered previously. It was only as an afterthought that they remembered to ask me a technical question. The question was on the subject of foam making branches and equipment, which any recruit could have answered. But I was so laid back that I got the answer wrong. I did not care, it had been a nice, pleasant interview. *See you all next year*, I thought to myself as I left.

Around three weeks later at 'A' divisional headquarters, the station officer called me into his office, and enquired did I know a good tailor. I was puzzled. "Why should I know a good tailor?" I replied.

"Because you are going to need one," he said. "The jungle drums say you are being made up to station officer."

At first, I refused to believe him, promotion from sub officer to station officer, after only two months in the rank, was almost unknown. He went on to say that I must appear surprised when the divisional commander officially informed me of my promotion, then I realised it must be true.

The next day, the divisional commander summoned me to his office, and I appeared duly surprised when he informed me of my promotion. I told him I had not expected promotion for at least two years. He then said, "Yes, that's about right, I think someone has been pulling strings for you." My mind was busy thinking which senior officer would pull strings on my behalf, and I could think of none. Then with a smile on his face, and I think jokingly, he said, "I reckon it was that Tom Kennedy. He would do just about anything to get his cushy little job back off you."

Isn't life strange? Nearly ten years struggling to get promotion to the rank of leading fireman, then inside the space of one year and one month, promotion from the rank of fireman to that of station officer. A few interesting and lucky fires on the way, but I was still the same man that spent ten years struggling. Robbie Burns had the answer when he said, "Wei the power the giftie gie us to see ourselves as others see us." Would the power that God gives us, to see ourselves as others see us.

The station officer's rank was the one that I had always wanted. When I was on duty, I would be in overall command of the fire station. Senior officers would only occasionally visit to ensure that all was well and running efficiently. I would be in command of all fires and incidents on the station's ground. Senior officers would attend only on four pump fires, persons involved, and above. In my mind, I had formed a picture of the kind of station officer I wished to be. It had been formed over the previous ten years, taking the good points, discarding the bad points, of every station officer that I had met, or served under. The time had now come to put my ideas into effect. I would acquire my new skills, practising on the officers and men of D25 Chiswick red watch, which was to be my new posting.

I was very sad to be leaving the 'A' division, the only London division I had ever known, up till then. I left the division a very confident, bold, practical fire officer. I may face new administrative and man management problems in the future, but the fire ground held no fears for me, I had some of the best firemen and officers in the world as my tutors, and I had learnt my trade.

Chapter 14

D25 Chiswick Fire Station – 1970

D25 Chiswick fire station lay just out of sight of the Chiswick High Road in west London. It stood on a large triangular piece of land at the junction of Heathfield Terrace and Wellesy Road. The station was built around the late 1950s and was of modern construction. It comprised a two storey, frame-built building, with a flat roof, looking rather like a square box. It had two appliance bays, with a very large drill yard, all surrounded by a handsome brick wall.

The station was built by the now defunct Middlesex Fire Brigade and was of a design way ahead of its time. Middlesex Fire Brigade built a large number of new fire stations around this period in time, and they were all built to a standard design, so that it was possible for a fireman to walk out of one Middlesex fire station and into another and know the exact layout of the new station. Stores, offices, messrooms, bunkrooms etc., would all be in a standard place in the stations.

Compared to an ex-London County Council station, for a small two-appliance station it had a vast drill yard. The drill ground was triangular and covered an area of around a quarter of an acre.

Although Chiswick was a busy London borough, the fire station to my eyes, had a rural aspect to it. All along the front of the station, stretching the length of the wall surrounding the drill yard and station was a delightful grass lawn and flowerbeds, some fifteen to twenty feet in depth. Set into the lawn and flowerbeds were small trees and rose bushes. These lawns and gardens were maintained by the local borough council to a high standard.

Stretching down the back of the fire station was a plot of land about fifteen feet by sixty feet in length. This plot of land was divided into three and used as vegetable plots for the three watches on the station. Usually, the mess manager tended these plots, the monies for seed coming from the watch mess funds. The resulting produce ending up on the watch's mess table.

Overhanging this boundary wall and planted in the garden of the next-door private house, was a beautiful pear tree, which in its fruiting season could be induced to shed a large percentage of its harvest on the fire station side of the wall, usually in the dark of the night.

The station's fire ground was comprised mainly of middle- and upper-class residential properties, interspersed with small factory and commercial areas. There were also large areas of parks, greens and public recreation land, with the River Thames running down the station's western boundary. The above mix did not give a very high rate of fire calls, and in general, Chiswick was considered a quiet station operationally.

My new watch on the station was basically a very good watch. A very experienced senior sub officer, who had been in charge of the watch for some six months prior to my arrival, a good and capable leading fireman, who was as the saying goes, 'in the frame' for a chief officer's commendation for brave conduct at a fire – which usually, but not always, indicates good firemanship qualities. The remainder of the watch were a good blend of old and younger firemen.

The watch was not in total harmony though. For my predecessor on the watch, Station Officer Henry Stretton, a station officer very much of the old school and around fifty years of age, had been a bit lax. I was later to find out that he spent a great deal of his duty time inspecting the Fuller's brewery, which was on Chiswick's fire ground. He would arrive for night duty with a case of Worthington Green Shield (a very strong bottled beer), in the boot of his car. He was also apparently a very good window cleaner and had a very lucrative window-cleaning round. I somehow got the impression that Henry Stretton used Chiswick fire station as a place to rest and recuperate after his busy off duty days. He did apparently have plenty of character, and I am sure had I met him I would have liked him.

So now, instead of Henry Stretton as the station officer, the watch had a younger man. Not only a younger station officer, but an 'A' division man. Not only an 'A' division man, but an ex-A' divisional headquarters man. In any organisation in life, people are usually very wary of headquarters, or head office men. The firemen at Chiswick were in for a bit of a surprise if they thought that their new station officer was a headquarters type fire officer.

The quiet life, on a quiet fire station, may suit some older firemen, but not the younger ones, or indeed myself, so I decided to liven it up. It was the station drill period, and the crews were rigging in their fire gear. When they were ready, I ordered both appliances taken out to the front of the fire station and parked in the road there. The two big appliance room doors were shut behind them, I then sent a fireman to shut the rear entrance doors to the drill yard.

I then lined up the two crews in the appliance room and gave them the drill detail as follows. Slip and pitch the thirty-five-foot extension ladder to the second floor of the drill tower. Get a jet to work there, provide a covering jet to work on the ground floor. Hook ladder to work from the head of the extension ladder to the third floor, get a jet to work there.

This is a fairly standard drill and should cause no problems to efficient crews, and is in fact, pretty routine stuff. I was getting quizzical looks from the firemen. What they didn't yet know, was that I was about to lock them and all their equipment, outside the fire station and drill yard.

The station and yard were surrounded by a six-foot high brick wall. I was smiling contentedly to myself as I thought, I bet the buggers haven't done this drill before.

After detailing the drill as above, I then broke the news that they would be locked out of the fire station. That they now had one minute to discuss the problem before I gave the order, "Get to work." After the initial shock and surprise, they went into a huddle to discuss the problem. A fireman came over to me to check that the back drill yard gates were locked, and could they force the locks?

In reply, I answered, yes, they were locked, and no, they could not force them. The fireman then came back to ask could they use the fire hydrant in the station yard? The perverse side of my nature was enjoying itself. I replied tersely to the fireman, "All equipment, hose and water comes over the fire station wall." Then just as an afterthought told them that they were to observe all signs saying 'Keep off the grass'.

I then gave the order, "Get to work," and they sprang into action. I could see by their manner that they were determined not to let this new sprog station officer beat them.

The fifty-foot wheeled escape was slipped from the appliance and bridged across the grass lawns, then lowered down onto the brick wall. Two six-foot scaling ladders joined together provided access down to the drill yard from the top of the wall. The two drivers were busy connecting into the fire hydrant at the junction of Wellesy Road. The thirty-five-foot extension ladder was manhandled up the escape ladder then lowered into the drill yard, as was all the other equipment required. Lines of hose snaked from the hydrant to the pump, then up the ladder and over the wall, the pump's engine roared as it pumped water.

All around us a large crowd had gathered, the public were getting a free show. I thought to myself; had I but known, I could have sold tickets. A lady came up to me and enquired, "Is the fire station on fire?"

"No, madam, we are practising, just in case it ever does catch fire," I replied.

Finally, when the drill was finished and I gave the order. "Knock off and make up." I was rather disappointed. Our public might at least have given us a clap or a cheer. We had just entertained them for twenty minutes, but instead they just drifted quietly away. This I think is the British way of life. Let's all leave now, in case the man comes around with the hat, looking for money.

After the drill was over and all the gear made up and put away, the firemen were in a cheerful mood – they had actually enjoyed the drill. The drill was different, and a challenge to them, and was completed successfully. They then ask me if they had carried out the drill in the way I had wanted them to. Instead, I told them that in this kind of drill there was no set solution. If they carried out fully the tasks I set them, the manner in which they did it was entirely up to them. Part of the exercise was in the crews thinking out problems and solving them, not in just carrying out standard drill book drills.

Chiswick was in some ways an ideal station for newly promoted officers. Its lower level of operational activity, which could at times be frustrating, gave time for new administration and management skills to be assimilated. I had time to think up new drills and exercises, time to arrange visits to all the fire risks on the station's ground. Then having made all the prior arrangements that these visits and drills entailed, to be then able to carry them out without the interruption of fire calls.

*

My opposite number, the station officer on the blue watch at Chiswick fire station, was one Paddy Wright. I had known Paddy from my Camden Town days, where he was the station officer on the blue watch there. Paddy was a big man with a quiet nature and spoke with a delightful soft Irish brogue. He had been famous at Camden Town and was renowned at Chiswick for his appetite. Paddy would eat vast quantities of anything. Food that would normally be considered inedible, and thrown away, Paddy would eat with relish.

When coming on duty, Paddy would investigate the contents of the fridge. Then finding a sweet, comprising of something with custard that had been abandoned days earlier, that which was now brown and curling up at the edges, he would sample it, and then say, "It's rhubarb, I love rhubarb," and then shovel it into his mouth. The 'I love rhubarb' statement was just a cover. It didn't matter what it was he found in the fridge, he always loved it.

The messes at Chiswick purchased their meat supplies at wholesale prices from a butcher that delivered to the station. The mess managers would also take orders from the firemen for meat etc., for the firemen's use at home. The mess managers would then parcel up the individual orders and place them in the fridge, from whence the firemen would collect their parcels after paying for them.

One morning on the blue watch, Paddy Wright's watch, whilst they were drinking tea after roll call, the whole of the watch was seated around the mess table. Paddy was seated in his normal position at the end of the table. The mess manager stood up and speaking loudly and forcibly said, "Last night, some bastard paid for a one-pound pack of bacon and has taken away a two-pound pack of bacon. If that person does not return the two-pound pack of bacon, that will be the end of cheap meat supplies for the watch." The watch listened in stunned silence. To steal from one's watch mates was an unthinkable crime; it must have been done in error.

For a full minute, nobody said anything. Paddy Wright, who had a habit of drumming his fingers on the table, was now doing so furiously. He cleared his throat, as the watch station officer he was going to make a statement. No doubt to back up the mess manager's anger at pilfering from messmates. Instead, "I was wondering," he said very thoughtfully, in his soft Irish brogue, "what would happen, if the person that took the two-pound pack of bacon…" All the watch were now listening intently; Paddy had been the number one suspect all the time. Paddy repeated, "What would happen, if the person who had taken the bacon, had already eaten it?" He paused nervously to say, "And could not therefore bring it back." Bloody amazing! Paddy lived on his own, he had gone home last night, cooked, then sat down and had eaten, two pounds in weight of best back bacon, at one sitting – bloody amazing!

It was agreed the matter would be settled if Paddy paid for the extra pound of bacon he had taken. After Paddy had left the room, the mess manager was now displaying a two-pound piece of bacon, shaking his head and saying, "That's how much the man ate, at one meal, I don't believe it!"

Paddy once confided to me in his soft manner, with a note of wonderment in his voice, "Did you know that the lady who lives in my house feeds her pet poodle on freshly cooked chicken breasts? It's true, Dave – I've seen them with my own eyes," he told me. I had a sneaking feeling that on that occasion at least, the lady's poodle never got to actually eat the chicken breasts.

*

Chiswick, being a quieter fire station, got a bigger share of reliefs at fires. Reliefs at fires were not popular, for it was only when all the real firefighting was done and all that remained was the boring work of making up gear and damping down the smouldering remains, that reliefs at a fire were called for.

Pumps would be ordered onto the fires to relieve the original firefighting crews. They would stay for periods of around three or four hours, before being then relieved themselves, or the fire being fully extinguished.

At around three o'clock in the morning, the bells went down, and Chiswick's pump, station officer in charge, was ordered as a relief to a barn fire at Feltham Borstal, Feltham, Middlesex. I was cross, I didn't like reliefs, and I didn't like barn fires. I thought I had seen the last of barn fires when I left the Berkshire Fire Brigade. Now back in the London Fire Brigade, they had just got me out of bed at three o'clock in the morning to go and play wet nurse to a heap of smouldering straw.

When we arrived at Feltham Borstal, I was met by a leading fireman in charge of the pump already there. He showed me the fire, which was not a barn, but just a large stack of smouldering straw. He then went on to tell me that he had requested a station officer on this relief because he thought the relief could be closed down. He then went on to tell me that as a mere leading fireman, he didn't feel qualified to do so. I agreed with him, then told him acidly that he was displaying all the qualifications of a good senior officer, which he strangely enough took as a compliment.

I left the firemen to connect Chiswick's machine into the hose lines and went to take stock of the situation. Although the call was to Feltham Borstal, the premises was in fact the borstal farm, used no doubt to give the boys an occupation during their stay. There were some large fields growing potatoes, and a large number of buildings with pigs at all stages of growth in them.

It was just coming up to daylight, and I was amusing myself digging up buckets of potatoes and feeding them to the small pigs. One fireman was left in full command of the fire, and the rest of us were following agricultural pursuits, i.e. feeding the pigs.

As daylight came fully upon us, I saw leaning over the top of a wall what at first appeared to be a hippopotamus. It was a huge animal. The wall was about five feet high, and the beast was resting its elbows on the wall and looking at us. The animal was standing on its hind legs and appeared to be around eight feet tall. Its huge head was around two and a half feet across at the eyes. It was a pig! The biggest pig I had ever seen, and I had seen a few, working at Reading market in my Berkshire days. A beast this size could be a frightening thing, but this one appeared to be a happy, friendly pig. His happiness could be perhaps due to his occupation, for he was a boar, and it was his duty to serve some dozens of sows on the farm.

Such a big friendly pig had to be given a potato, and I dug up a big potato and gave it to him. His huge jaws made short work of that potato, so I resolved to find a really big one and see how he coped with that. Soon all the firemen were busy digging in the potato field, looking for that really big potato. The one the pig would not be able to manage, but we never did find one that beat him. No matter how big the potato, the pig ate it, with a big smile on his face and the juices running down his jaws. The size and power of his jaws was awesome. I made a mental note not to get my head too close to them, lest he think he had a really big potato to chew on. This digging of potatoes was in fact much harder work than damping down the stack of straw, but was much more rewarding and interesting, especially for city firemen.

The fireman delegated to be in charge of the smouldering stack came over to me, saying, "We are wasting our time, guv, the fire is all out now." I went back to the stack with him to check, and then sent a message to fire control closing the job down. It was six o'clock in the morning by the time we had made up the gear and got back to Chiswick fire station; it should be breakfast time. After a delightful morning in the country, and having fed and watered all the livestock, we would be more than ready for that breakfast, even though one of the main ingredients happened to be slices cut off a pig's belly bacon!

*

In the 1960s, the laws preventing the brewing of beer in private homes was repealed in Great Britain. I then took up the hobby of home brewing and wine making. Around the mess table at Chiswick fire station, I was recounting the time I had taken a sample of my beer into Reading fire station for the firemen there to taste. At that time, I was new to home brewing, and had got the sugar content wrong, so that when I proudly opened my bottle of home brewed beer for the firemen to taste, it frothed and gassed, and gassed and frothed, for half an hour or more. Then the entire contents frothed out through the neck of the bottle, leaving nothing to be tasted. This did not of course stop the wags, who tasted the froth with a spoon and declared it horrible stuff, nobody to it at all.

After telling this tale, the Chiswick firemen were now interested in home brewing. They asked would I be prepared to instruct them on home brewing. Of course, I replied. If they obtained the ingredients, would I be prepared to demonstrate a brew on the fire station was the next question, again I replied yes. Thus from innocent beginnings was started the D25 Chiswick Red Watch Brewing Society.

At the peak of its production, the society was brewing twenty-two gallons of beer a week. That is one hundred and seventy-six pints of strong beer, most of this being for home consumption by the firemen, but it had the attraction of being brewed whilst on duty in their stand down time. Then again using GLC equipment, heating and power, to produce the beer.

The production of beer involved two main processes, the brewing and fermenting, and the bottling, usually done on separate nights. The leading fireman was the head brewer and the mess manager was in charge of bottling. On brewing nights, the station would be a hive of activity, rotas being made out for various duties and imposed by the firemen themselves.

On brew nights, the activity took place in the station kitchen, as the ingredients were mixed and heated, the whole station permeating with the smell of the mash. The resulting liquor was then poured into two eleven-gallon plastic dustbins, (Fire Brigade issue) then left to ferment in the warmest place in the fire station, which was the ground floor boiler room.

On bottling nights, the activity took place in a ground floor washroom. Dozens of two-pint beer bottles had to be washed and then filled by siphoning the beer from the dustbins. When filled the bottles had to be transferred to the cellar. This was the room where a big fuel oil tank to feed the boilers was kept. The station rang with the sound of cheery voices, and the clink of glass, as the bottles were washed and filled.

The firemen made their own rules regarding the consumption of the beer, although I tended to watch this closely. On night duties, each fully paid-up member of the brewing society was issued with one bottle of beer free of charge. He then had the right to purchase for sixpence, a second bottle of beer. That was his quota, and when he had drunk it, no more beer was allowed from society supplies. Stand-by firemen at the station would be sold their first bottle of beer for sixpence. They would then be observed, (remember this was a strong beer), if they were deemed to be becoming under the influence, no more beer would be sold to them. Or alternatively, they might be allowed to share a two-pint bottle with another fireman.

Initially, the subject of brewing dominated station conversation, new words crept into the firemen's vocabulary, Goldings and Fuggles, both varieties of hops. Mash, wort, liquor, specific gravity, all of these words used in the brewing trade. To 'glug' or not to 'glug', did a particular fireman glug when he poured beer. When pouring home brewed beer from the bottle, particular care must be taken not to disturb the yeast deposit at the bottom of the bottle. If the yeast deposit is disturbed, it will result in a cloudy, yeasty tasting beer. It must be done gently and smoothly, in one long slow pour, requiring a very steady hand. If the beer slopped back and forth whilst pouring, this was known as a 'glug'. A 'glug' would disturb the yeast deposit at the bottom of the bottle. The word 'glug' then entered the watch vocabulary as a threat word – "Glug his beer for him," or, "If you don't shut up, I'll glug you." Or a classic, heard at a particularly smoky fire, "This bloody smoke is thicker than glugged beer."

With this big interest in brewing on the watch, it was decided to arrange a visit to Fuller's Brewery, which was on Chiswick's fire ground. The visit was to be arranged under section 1(1)d of the 1947 fire services act. This section of the fire services act enabled firemen to visit premises on the fire station's ground to gain information to assist them in any future fires involving the building or premises. It also enabled firemen who were interested in the art of brewing to see how the professionals did it, and to do so in the Fire Brigade's time.

Fuller's Brewery was a small (by today's standards) traditional brewery, and I think still in the ownership of a single family. We were able to follow the process of brewing through every stage. The head brewer who was conducting our tour I think was amazed at the questions asked. Normally, firemen will only be interested in what the beer tastes like, but this group wanted to know everything about its production. Words like, original and specific gravities, head retention, the fining down or clearing of beer, this was long before the Campaign for Real Ale made these words fashionable.

Not a single question was asked about firefighting requirements, except perhaps, when the subject of water supplies was mentioned. But even this was in relation to beer making. The brewery drew its water supplies to make the beer from its own well. This the firemen noted, and I had visions of them digging away in the middle of the watch vegetable patch, searching for their own water supply.

The visit came to an end with a visit to the tasting room, with liberal tastings of Fuller's beers. It was now five o'clock in the afternoon, we had been at the brewery for two and a half hours. We had been so absorbed in the visit that we were now overdue back at the station. I thanked the head brewer for the interesting visit and said that we really had to go now. He looked very surprised and said, "But I have put on a barrel of our best beer, especially for you firemen. If it isn't all drunk, it will only spoil over the weekend." What a dilemma, we certainly couldn't drink a whole barrel, and we were due to go off duty at six o'clock.

One of the firemen asked, "Could we take some with us?"

"Certainly," said the head brewer.

As I walked back to the appliance accompanied by the head brewer, I saw that the firemen had opened a locker on the machine and removed the chimney buckets. The firemen were now busily swilling out the buckets, using water from the appliance tank, through an open delivery on the machine. The chimney buckets were two-gallon, galvanized iron buckets, and were used in the Brigade for just about every purpose imaginable. For carrying soot and rubbish at chimney fires, decanting sewage and filthy water at flooded premises, at road traffic accidents, or suicides under trains, even brains and odd bits of people went into them. The firemen were now giving them a quick swill out with cold water, then were intending to fill them up with free beer to drink back at the station!

*

It was a particularly fine summer's day. I was standing on the station forecourt with one of the senior firemen on the watch.

I was admiring the gardens and shrubs at the front of the station when I saw a flash of green below the rose bushes. It was a small bird with green and yellow or gold markings and looking closer, I then saw that there were in fact two of them. I commented to the fireman with me, "Look at those two birds, they must have escaped from an aviary."

Ted, for that was the fireman's name, laughed. "No," he said, "they are Goldfinches; they are feeding on the dandelion seeds."

"What, Goldfinches flying free in the middle of London?" I asked him.

"Yes," he replied. "They are quite common around this part of Chiswick."

Amazing! From my previous fire stations, the only birds I had ever seen had been scruffy, brown sparrows that cheeped and grey, asthmatic pigeons that coughed. Now in a single morning, on a beautiful day, in the middle of London, two Goldfinches were in the fire station garden.

*

It was around three thirty in the morning when the bells rang and the lights came on at Chiswick fire station. The teleprinter was busy chattering out its message, 'Boat on fire, the Hollows, off Brentford High Road, D25 Chiswick's ground, D25 pump escape and pump to attend'.

I knew well enough where Brentford High Road was, but I had never heard of the Hollows before. Fortunately, the driver of the pump escape knew of it, and we would follow him there.

When we arrived at Brentford High Road, the two appliances stopped at a point where it was mainly commercial buildings. There was no sign of any water, let alone a boat, or boat on fire. The firemen dashed off down a small passageway between two buildings, so I followed on behind. After about twenty-five yards, the passageway emerged out to the River Thames, this I was told, was the Hollows. Just a small path alongside the Thames and serving as a permanent mooring point for boats.

Lying alongside the river wall was a large, old fashioned type sailing boat, about sixty feet long and twenty feet wide; looking rather like the famous Thames sailing barges, which at first, I thought it was. In the centre of its main deck, over where the main hold would be situated, was a raised cabin roof with side windows fitted. The windows and doors were closed, but from every crevice, smoke was percolating, indicating a fire down below. The firemen were laying out a line of large delivery hose from the pump twenty-five yards away in the Brentford High Street. Three breathing apparatus wearers arrived at the boat, still buckling and adjusting their sets. I told them to wait for the hose line to be charged before attempting an entry into the boat.

Author on left in old style Station Officer's uniform 1971 at Chiswick fire station
(Photo courtesy: London Fire Brigade)

The owner of a neighbouring boat had told me that the boat on fire had been converted below decks as a houseboat. It was not a Thames sailing barge, but instead had the delightful type name of 'West Country Sailing Ketch', which conjured up visions of sailing the blue seas off Devon and Cornwall, under full sail. Now she was moored in the murky waters of the River Thames, at Chiswick, London and on fire.

The fire hose bucked and kicked as the water came through it. At last, it was fully charged, with a small half-inch nozzle fitted at my request. Fighting ship fires is rather like fighting basement fires, with one or two other hazards thrown in. The firemen have to descend down into the vessel through the heat zone to fight the fire.

The best time to judge heat levels is when the hold is first opened, and like opening an oven door the heat surges free.

The three BA firemen were ready with the jet, and I was going to open the doors to the boat's accommodation. As I opened the door, the heat and smoke rushed out and enveloped us. Initially, the heat was so severe that the three firemen who were standing upright, backed away from it. I was kneeling down on one knee, and so a lot of the heat passed over my head, and I held my position. The heat then died away slightly as I had hoped for, indicating that the initial pent-up gases and heat had escaped. The heat now coming up from below was from the burning fire itself and was of an acceptable level. If the three BA firemen got down onto the lower deck quickly, and stayed there, keeping the jet working on spray to cool it down, the fire would be confined to the accommodation area only.

The ability to make a snap decision like this can only be acquired by attending and then entering many basement fires and experiencing heat levels. As when cooking, food in an oven at a high heat setting, when the oven door is first opened, a terrific surge of heat comes out, then dies away. The same principal operates with a basement fire, when the door is first opened, the heat will be at its severest. If the fire does not then come up the stairs and chase you away and if the basement is not too large and complicated, you have a reasonable chance of extinguishing the fire.

The three BA firemen had gone down below and I could hear the jet working. There was only one sure way to find out if the fire was under control, and that was to go and look at it. So with a quick dash, I descended the stairs and got down on my tummy on the deck.

The fire had been confined to fittings and furnishings. The big jet of water was really excessive now, and I was anxious about water damage. I told the BA firemen to sit with, and nurse, the remaining fire, whilst I got a smaller hose reel tubing down to them.

Back on deck, I was now relaxed. I gave instructions for the hose reel to be taken below, and I now thought about messages from fires.

As I have said before, the London Fire Brigade was and is very particular about its messages from fires. It of course had special messages regarding boat fires. Now came the most difficult part of the whole proceedings, trying to remember exactly what those messages were! 'The fire is under control but not fully extinguished, and all around me is activity'. After much thought, I finally dispatched the following message. 'Stop for the West Country Trading Ketch GLORIA, a vessel of approximately one hundred tons, lying at the Hollows, Brentford High Road. Ship's accommodation area on lower deck damaged by fire, one jet, three BA sets in use'. This was the one and only time in my whole career that I had to use that kind of message. I thought I did extremely well and was quite pleased with myself. You don't come across many West Country Trading Ketches in the middle of London.

Dawn had just broken; the BA firemen had come up from below. Two other firemen were now cutting away and damping down below. I was seated on the ship's rail, talking to the leading firemen, and thinking how beautiful and quiet the River Thames was at first light. The people who lived on this boat had an ideal location to live in the summertime.

I noticed that tied to the rail, I was sitting on was a piece of string, the other end of which disappeared down into the River Thames. Out of curiosity, I pulled on the piece of string, and to my surprise out of the murky water appeared a quart-sized bottle of beer. It was obviously immersed in the river to cool by the owner of the boat. A quick search revealed yet another quart bottle of beer suspended from another piece of string. Shared between all the firemen still at the fire, the two bottles of beer amounted to around half a pint each, but it was one of the most enjoyable half pints of beer I have ever tasted. Later, when the owner eventually returned to his boat, I confessed to having drunk his beer, but he quite cheerfully said, "You were welcome to it, lads."

*

It was around eleven o'clock in the morning on our first day duty at Chiswick fire station. One short ring sounded on the fire bells, the signal that a senior officer had arrived on the station.

Divisional Officer Smith came into the station office and greeted me. After an exchange of pleasantries, he came to the business he had called in for. "You have put in for a posting back to the 'A' division then, old Wilson."

"Yes, sir," I replied.

"Don't you like it here then?" he asked me.

"Yes, sir," I again replied. "It is just that I much prefer the busier stations."

I had thought that perhaps he had come to try to get me to change my mind and stay at Chiswick. He then took me completely by surprise by saying, "How would you like a transfer to D23 Hammersmith Wilson?" Adding, "That is in the general direction of the 'A' division, and it is a very busy station."

I did some very quick thinking. D23 Hammersmith was an old London County Council fire station and bounded onto the borough of Fulham where I was born. It was a very busy fire station, with an interesting and varied fire ground. To offer such a station to a relatively junior station officer was a compliment. I decided then and there, yes, I would accept the posting.

Leaving Chiswick fire station, and the red watch firemen, was sad for me. I had spent a happy time at Chiswick and made some very good friends, but the station just was not busy enough for me. If I was going to travel some fifty miles into work each day, I needed to feel at the end of each day it had been worthwhile. That could only happen at a busy firefighting station. I also needed to find a station that I could settle down in, and become permanent, rather than keep moving from station to station. I felt that Hammersmith fire station might just possibly be the one.

I had one big regret about leaving Chiswick; I never did get to fire the Shermully rocket gun! The Shermully rocket gun was one of the leftovers of the old Middlesex Fire Brigade. All stations that bordered with the River Thames were issued with them; they were intended to be used to fire a line to boats on the river. The gun fired a rocket, which carried a light line with it, which would then be used to haul a heavier line out to the boat. Chiswick still carried this equipment, and it fascinated me. I had arranged several times to go to nearby Dukes Meadows to fire it, only to be thwarted for various reasons. Now that I was leaving Chiswick, the chance would be gone forever.

Chapter 15
D23 Hammersmith Fire Station – 1971

At the time, I did not know it, but with my arrival at D23 Hammersmith fire station, I had now stopped my wanderings around the fire stations of London.

As I wearily made the dozen trips up the four flights of stairs, up to the station officer's room on the second floor of the fire station, carrying all my accumulated gear and uniform to stow in my locker there, I did not know that over the next sixteen years, I would make this journey thousands of times, at all hours of the day and night. That in the years to come, on countless occasions, after busy and exhausting long nights, these same four flights of stairs would be the last hurdle to cross before I could relax in the privacy of the station officer's room and await the next call.

How strange it is, that I should particularly remember the stairs of a fire station. When the duty began, day or night, I would stride up the stairs two at a time. But at five o'clock in the morning, on the second night duty, after our fourteenth fire call, I would then go up at a slow, weary pace, knowing full well that before the hour was up, I would need to do it all over again.

Hammersmith fire station was in the Shepherd's Bush Road, not twenty-five yards away from Hammersmith Broadway. It was an older type London County Council fire station, built in 1914. It was a brick built, five-storey high building, with three appliance bays, still retaining its original inward opening, handsome timber appliance room doors. It had very little forecourt to speak of; the appliances turned out directly onto the Shepherds Bush Road. At the time of my transfer, only the ground, first and part of the second floor were used by the station personnel. The remainder of the accommodation being let to tenants who were serving firemen and their families. Both firemen and tenants used the common staircase to gain access to the upper floors. Balconies provided access at each floor level to the tenant's flats, at the rear of the station.

On the ground floor of the fire station was the three-bay appliance room, the station office cum watchroom and general-purpose storerooms. On the first floor was the kitchen and messroom, locker room and billiard room. These last two rooms also served as a dormitory with trestle beds being set up at night-time. Taking up only one half of the second floor, was a television room cum lecture room, then a station officer's office and bunkroom, the leading fireman and sub officer also being provided with a room each on this floor.

The station fire ground was large, varied and interesting, comprising roughly one-third commercial premises and two thirds residential. The residential properties ranged from millionaire's mansions to pauper's hovels, from swish, upmarket penthouses and flats to cardboard box dwellers and derelict dossers. In between was represented the whole stratum of society, bed sit properties, council houses and flats and owner-occupied houses.

The commercial properties included an oil refinery, a sugar-producing factory, a large food factory, two huge warehouse complexes, a vast valve and electrical component factory. All of these buildings were old five and six-storey brick-built complexes of the highest fire risk, set in the midst of residential property.

The fire ground extended from the BBC centre at Wood Lane in the west, to Barnes on the other side of the River Thames in the south. From the borough of Kensington, in the north, to Chiswick in the west. The fire ground had possibly one of the longest direct frontages to the River Thames in the whole of the London Fire Brigade. For the fire ground carried on over the River Thames, taking in the borough of Barnes, thus including both banks of the River Thames. Also on the fire ground were four major hospitals, six tube stations, two open-air street markets and the huge Olympia Exhibition Hall. Then a vast council estate, comprised of blocks of flats, which alone could provide ten percent of all calls received at the station.

Sometimes when all the activity, noise, bustle and fire calls generated by the above became too much, I would book out on the pump, and go and inspect the Barn Elms reservoirs across the River Thames in Barnes. Inside this bend in the River Thames was an area of around 500 acres of playing fields, public garden allotments, four vast water reservoirs, an oasis of green and water, not open to the general public. But our fire engine and uniforms gave us access.

On some days, it seemed we had the 500 acres all to ourselves, yet we were barely half a mile away from the fire station. Visually, it was possible to get the peace and serenity of the open countryside, but forever in the background was the noise of the busy city. Then from above, came the almost constant noise of the aircraft on the approach path to Heathrow Airport, which in all the city's bustle, I had never before even noticed.

Although Hammersmith was a three-appliance bay station, it only ever housed a pump escape and a pump. At this time in the early 1970s, the station received an average of 3,500 fire calls a year, which breaks down to ten in twenty-four hours. Ten in twenty-four hours does not seem too much of a workload, but with even the quickest of calls – a false alarm – taking a half hour of station time, with the going to and then returning from the address, then completing paperwork, the simplest of genuine fire calls will often take at least an hour of station time, doing the same. This would mean the twenty-four hours is slowly being used up, without the thousand other activities in a fire station's day. Then in the very rare event that no fire calls should be received in a twenty-four-hour period, that meant the average was ten behind, and we could possibly receive twenty fire calls the next day.

*

Here at Hammersmith, my being an ex- 'A' division man was an advantage, for in the LCC days the station was in the 'A' division itself. In the past, I had stood by at Hammersmith fire station whilst serving at Brompton. D23 Hammersmith was on the outermost fringe of the 'D' division, which comprised mostly ex Middlesex Fire Brigade stations.

Hammersmith was perhaps considered by them to be almost like an unruly adopted child. It was by far the busiest station in the 'D' division, and it was recognised that the standards of firemanship were high. On the downside, it still retained a lot of quaint old LCC ways which it refused to cease. From a senior officer's point of view, if the station in general behaved itself, and caused no problems, it was best left well alone. Nothing but trouble could come from unnecessarily stirring this can of worms was, I think, their opinion.

This could have been an anxious time for my new watch, the new guvnor had arrived – what would he be like? I was aware of them watching me closely as I struggled to carry my gear up the stairs to the station officer's room, but initially no one offered to help. Eventually, the leading fireman, Eddie Thirkettle, came over to assist with carrying my gear. We had met before. Eddie Thirkettle replaced me on the blue watch at Camden Town all those years ago and we had met socially over the years.

My transfer paperwork, including my personal card, had been left lying already opened on the station desk. I know the ways of firemen; it would have been already looked at. My previous postings and stations noted, my Brigade qualifications would have been noted. Motor driver, turntable ladder operator, emergency tender rider, they would be building up a picture of my past experience. Then lastly, in the honours and awards section of my personal card were two entries, this was most unusual in the London Fire Brigade. They would be watching me closely on the fire ground. Of that, there was no doubt. They would want to know did I earn those entries, or did I just talk my way into them?

I also was taking stock of my new watch. I had by now had a quick look through their personal cards. Most of the firemen had been at the station since their postings as recruits. Those that had not were some of the senior firemen who had arranged postings to this station and were here by choice.

Arthur Halsey, the senior fireman, on the watch, had been at this station for twenty-two years. He was a big, jovial man, and was the watch mess manager. He was currently on light duties suffering from a knee injury, and so spent all of his time in the mess. He was very popular with all the watch members, and although he was in his late forties, still had boundless energy. Most importantly, the quality and quantity of food in the watch mess provided by him was excellent.

My first duty on the station was a night duty. During the course of the supper meal that very first night, a very important subject for the firemen was broached. During the meal, Arthur Halsey enquired of me in an offhand, non-committal manner, "Do you like a drink, Guvnor?" As soon as he uttered the words, I knew instantly what the worry was. They all obviously did like a drink and would now like to know what the new guvnor's feelings on the subject were.

My reply was deliberately non-committal. "I like all things in moderation, Arthur." Whereupon Arthur immediately came back at me, with a big smile on his face, saying, "Ah good, so you do like a drink, we had heard that you did, will it be all right if we bring the bar out later on?"

I had heard about Hammersmith's bar. It belonged only to the white watch and was an ingenious device that was wheeled around the first floor of the station. They had acquired it from the Olympia Exhibition Hall. It comprised of a portable bar on wheels, it was oval shaped and decorated with wine and spirit bottle labels. It carried one eleven-gallon barrel of beer, with ancillary pump and gas cylinder fittings, and it had storage shelves for glasses etc. It was quite smart and practical, being purpose built as a bar for use in the Olympia Exhibition Hall. When not in use, or the watch was off duty, it was kept locked in a storeroom off the billiard room.

I made a ruling that the bar could appear only after nine o'clock at night. Although this did not stop Arthur having one or two pints whilst he cooked the meal, for he would simply go to the store cupboard and draw them off.

Some months later, Arthur did try it on though, for I was working in the station office on the ground floor, at around 7.45 pm, when I heard a deep rumble sounding through the ceiling overhead. I knew instantly what it was, Arthur was wheeling the bar and heavy barrel down to the mess. I waited for the rumbling sound to cease, which meant that Arthur had reached the messroom with the bar. I then buzzed the messroom telephone extension. Arthur answered with his bright and cheerful usual reply of, "Messdeck."

I simply said into the handset, "Take it back, Arthur."

Equally as bright and cheerful, he replied, "Right away, guv," and the rumble passed back over my head in the opposite direction.

*

Bill McGraw, or Mac as he was commonly called, was around the same age as myself. He had originally started his career at Hornsey fire station in north London, having joined the Brigade a few months before me. He had then travelled around various London fire stations, before settling down at Hammersmith. He was around five feet ten inches in height, and of a slim build, with prematurely greying hair. His father, and I believe his grandfather, had been London firemen before him, and it showed. The Fire Brigade was I think in his blood, for given our similar ages and fire service experience, both on the fire ground and in actually fighting fires, I considered Mac my equal in every way. Mac had never considered promotion in the Brigade, for his own reasons, but he certainly had the ability. He would instead enter other projects with great zeal and enthusiasm. He was a qualified London taxi driver, with a green badge, which meant he could play for hire all over London. To obtain the knowledge to qualify for this green badge entailed fourteen months to two years travelling around London on a bicycle or moped, in all weathers, with examinations every six weeks or so.

Mac decided he would like to play a musical instrument, so he bought a clarinet, then joined the Fire Brigade band to learn how to play it. It was here he gained the nickname 'bad news, McGraw', for he would often be missing from the station, having to attend band rehearsals, or playing at band engagements. Failing that, he would be taking leave given in lieu of some off duty band commitment. Despite these other absences from the station, I don't think he ever missed a fire of any significance.

He would arrive at the fire station at around eleven o'clock at night for duty, having been on a band rehearsal since six o'clock. He would arrive in the mess invariably clutching some sort of exotic take away meal to eat. Prior to his arrival, we would have had a relatively quiet night. As soon as he had eaten, the meal down would go the bells. A working fire of some description would be the inevitable result. "You're bloody bad news, McGraw, do you know that?" is how he got his nickname. He took up photography; he brought his cameras in to show us. He had every camera, every lens and every gimmick available in his posh state of the art camera bag. He then took up fishing. I went fishing with him in between night duties at the Barn Elms reservoirs.

The reservoirs on the other side of the river from Hammersmith had been stocked with trout. Mac fancied trying to catch some trout, so the trip was arranged. It cost us five pounds for a half a day's fishing. The local water authority who owned the reservoirs required reams of paperwork to be filled in before being allowed onto the water.

Finally, we sat down at the waterside and started to fish. Whilst we fished, a man was making his way around the reservoir, talking to the fishermen. When he arrived at our side, he introduced himself as the fishing bailiff, and could he please see our fishing permits. We showed him all the paperwork the man at the gate had given us. No that was not what he wanted, he wanted to see our river authority fishing permit. I told the bailiff, "If it's not amongst that lot" – indicating the paperwork I had just given him – "then I haven't got one."

Mac was all smiles. Delving into his inside jacket pocket, he produced a wallet. He held the wallet up with one hand, and released a fastening, the bottom half of the wallet fell down, about two feet. This revealed a clear plastic sleeve, containing dozens of credit card style fishing permits. It seemed that Mac had permission to fish just about every bit of water and down every manhole in London.

Displaying his wallet, Mac said proudly to the bailiff, "There you are, mate, help yourself, it will be in there somewhere."

The bailiff worked his way through all the cards in the wallet, then announced, "No, you have not got the right permit either."

Mac's pride was wounded. "What do you mean I have not got the right permit? I've got every permit there is. I can fish anywhere in London. If there is a permit I haven't got, you tell me about it and I will get it." Mac was a totally dedicated fisherman, you could easily tell that by the number of fishing permits he had obtained.

The bailiff subsequently reported us to the Thames water authority, who had sold us the tickets to fish the water, their own water, in the first place. We later received notices of intending prosecution. When I explained by letter that the only piece of paperwork we were not required to produce before being allowed to fish their own water was this particular permit, issued by themselves, the prosecution was withdrawn, and they even gave us an apology.

Mac liked to be first in many things, and he was certainly the first on the watch in the early 1970s to buy a home freezer.

We had patiently listened to him as he explained how for an outlay of only pence in electricity vast savings could be made in the bulk purchase, and then freezing of goods. He then went on to inform us that he had ordered a whole lamb from his butcher at a great saving, which he would then freeze down.

Some weeks later, he had made no mention of this whole lamb he had purchased, which was unusual, so I asked him about it. His face took on a despondent look, and he shook his head, saying, "No, guv, I got seen off, the butcher was a crook."

I could see that he didn't want to talk about it, but I pressed him, and he told me the tale. "When the meat came all jointed up and in packs, before I put them in the freezer, I counted them. I counted the legs and there was only two instead of four, the thieving butcher had nicked two of the legs."

When I asked him how many shoulders of lamb he had received, he said that was all right. "I got two of those okay!"

Mac was a happier man after I gently told him that the shoulders of lamb were in fact its front legs. So therefore, the butcher was not a crook but an honest man. Mac had indeed received his total of four legs, albeit that two of them were called shoulders.

*

Mac had just arrived on the station at around 11.30 pm to begin his night shift with the watch. The watch had already been on duty since six o'clock that evening. Up until then, Mac had been at band practice at Brigade Headquarters, Lambeth.

On his arrival, he would first find me to report himself on duty and enquire which machine he was to ride. Then he would get himself booked on duty in the station log by the dutyman. Finally, he'd place his fire gear on the machine, and add his own name to the appliance nominal roll board. Then he would return to the messroom, clutching his little carrier bag of goodies.

This could be quite an event for the rest of the watch, who would have eaten their supper at 8.00 pm some three and a half hours before, and by now would be feeling quite peckish. *I wonder what Mac's got for his supper tonight?* would be the common thought.

On special nights, Mac would unveil a banquet from his paper carrier bag. Removing from his takeaway bag silver foil cartons of all shapes and sizes, he would place them lovingly on the long mess table at the end nearest the door where he always sat, fetch a plate and knife and fork from the kitchen, then sit down at the table and begin the ceremony of the opening of the cartons.

The eyes of all those gathered in the messroom would be upon those little square silver boxes as he removed the lids. As the lids came off the cartons one by one, the contents would steam. The scent of the food would waft around the messroom. A dozen pairs of nostrils would be quivering to find out what Mac had for his supper that night. Someone enviously enquired, "What have we got tonight, Mac, Indian or Chinese?"

"Chinese," Mac would casually reply. Then with his fork in his hand, occasionally dipping food into the sauces in the containers before placing it into his mouth, he would describe in great detail the delicacies held in each container. God, he was insufferable!

"These are Pacific king prawns deep fried in a delicious batter, and they are wonderful if you dip them in the chef's special sauce." He would then work his way through and describe the whole of the meal with mouth drooling descriptions. To the rest of the watch, it was bloody unbearable, and Mac knew it.

"Hope we get a shout before you can get it all down you," grumbled one envious fireman. Others, unable to bear it any longer, would simply stalk off out of the messroom. This was known on the watch as having a severe case of the gastronomics, there was only one known cure for it.

Very often, Mac's banquets would result in the entire watch getting severe attacks of gastronomics. The junior fireman would be sent for to effect the cure. The junior fireman, armed with a pencil and pad, would take orders from the firemen for take away – take away meals from the kebab house two doors along from the fire station, in the Shepherds Bush Road.

"You cost us a bloody fortune, McGraw," grumbled one fireman, as he gave the junior fireman the money to pay for his double hamburger with cheese and green salad, and the portion of chips he had just ordered.

On one of Mac's banquet nights, the 'bad news McGraw' jinx struck, only this time, it struck Mac himself. For he was only halfway through his exotic meal when the bells went down. His watch mates were ribbing him. "The jinx got you tonight then, Mac, you didn't have time to finish your supper for a change."

The green and red indicator lights on the appliance room ceiling were indicating that both appliances were going to attend the call. So that was it, Mac's hopes of a one appliance only call, and therefore returning to the mess to finish his supper, were dashed. All Mac could hope for now was a quick mickey, or false alarm call, in order to return to his meal before it was irretrievably spoiled.

The call was a fire call to Hargreaves House on the White City Estate. A very large council estate, comprised of a large number of blocks of flats. We knew our way to the White City Estate like the backs of our hands, so numerous were the calls to it. A quick reference to a special map in the appliance room told us where Hargreaves House was situated on the estate.

The two fire engines left the fire station together. It took the machines around three or four minutes to reach the estate, traffic being light at this time of night.

The White City Estate had started life in a very grand manner; it had been built as an adjunct to the nearby White City Stadium. The estate had been built to house the athletes, who had participated in the Olympic Games events that had been held at the stadium. Then after the Olympic Games were over, the estate was given over for municipal housing. At the time of its building, the estate was the latest in community housing projects, but over a period of time the estate degenerated. Perhaps it was too large for a real community to develop, or perhaps a thousand other reasons. It was not a popular place to live and had more than its fair share of social problems.

As we approached Hargreaves House, the first indications of a working fire were people in the middle of the road waving their arms at us. In this district, people tended to ignore fire engines, unless they were simple minded, drunk or their own house or flat was on fire. Or as in this case, the fire had reached proportions that could not be ignored, so that around a dozen people waving their arms to attract our attention indicated something out of the ordinary.

The two machines pulled to a halt in front of Hargreaves House. The building comprised of a block of flats, around three hundred feet long, by fifty feet deep. It was five-storeys high, and unusually had a pitched and tiled roof along its entire length. It was served by a single central staircase, and open communal balconies, with the doors to the flats leading off the balconies.

As was our habit and routine, the two fire engines stopped at the centre of the block of flats where the central staircase was situated. From here, there was no sign of a fire, but the people were pointing upwards and towards the far end of the block. I could now see smoke swirling from the end of the building on the upper floor. Then I was pulled to the end of the building by a member of the public. I could now see the fire, it was a very angry fire, and was issuing from a window on the top floor at the side and end of the building.

As I made my way back to the central staircase, the crews had already gone up ahead of me, taking with them a line to haul up hose. The two drivers on the ground floor were working hard, one was flaking out hose ready to haul aloft, the other was setting into a street fire hydrant. Already I realised that this fire would most probably be classified as a four-pump fire, but before sending the message, I would take a closer look at it.

Making my way up the staircase to the top floor, I was aware of a sense of urgency. Unusually, people on seeing me striding up the stairs, stood aside with their backs to the walls to let me pass. I was not counting the floors as I passed them, for this fire was on the very top floor of the building. When the stairs stopped, I would have arrived.

When I reached the top floor, there was a small knot of people gathered around the head of the stairs, and they pointed along the balcony to the direction I must take.

As I walked along the balcony towards the end flat, I saw two firemen outside the door of the flat. They were peering over the balcony. They had a line in their hands and were waiting for the hose to be attached to haul it aloft. There were occasional eddies of smoke coming out from the open door to the flat behind them.

As I reached the halfway point along the balcony, there was a lady standing in the open doorway to a fiat, and she moved to speak to me. Before she could do so, I was suddenly aware of a figure hurrying along the balcony towards me. It was Bill McGraw, Mac and in his arms, he was carrying an inert bundle.

The bundle was a small child, and there was a sense of extreme urgency about him, so that he hardly wanted to stop as I spoke to him. "Are there any more in there, Mac?"

"Yes, guvnor, another three I think."

"Where did you find that one?" I asked, meaning the child he was carrying.

In short, hurried, staccato bursts of fireman's language he told me, "Front door, short passage, turn right, back room, in there." Mac hurried away carrying his tragic burden.

I now hurried along the short, final length of balcony. The two firemen there were still waiting to haul hose aloft, and I issued crisp commands to them. "There are kids involved, get the driver to make pumps four, persons reported. I am going into the flat to look for them, and for Christ's sake hurry up and get that jet working."

I entered the door to the flat and made my way forward down the short passage. I had been in these flats many times before. I knew from experience that the doors to my right and left were the kitchen and the bathroom. The passageway reached a T-junction and then went to the right and the left. To my left, there was a fierce fire raging in a room at the end of the short passageway. The tongues of flame were reaching along the ceiling then down towards me. Because the fire had vented out of the window at the side of the building, the smoke was not too dense, but it was a swirling and moving smoke. I turned right at the T-junction in the passage; the only light in the darkened flat came from the fire itself. Tongues of flame leapt across the ceiling above my head to light my way. Crouching down to avoid them, I made my way forward. After just a few paces, I came to a door which was partially open, hopefully this would be the back room that Mac had described. I then entered the darkened smoke-filled room and started to feel my way. On my left, my hand found a settee, so this was a lounge or living room. I pushed the door to the room open and found the right-hand wall; here I would begin my search. I was only halfway along this right-hand wall when something obstructed my feet. It felt soft and giving. I knelt down to check what it was, and already I had found one of the missing children. I scooped up the child in my arms and then crashed blindly out of the fiat, hurrying along the balcony with it in my arms.

My intention was to get it to the ambulance and resuscitation equipment down below in the street, as quickly as possible. At the head of the staircase were two policemen, who moved back to let me pass, but instead I deposited the child into their startled arms. I said curtly to them, "Get it down to the ambulance, there are still more children involved."

I dashed back along the balcony, pausing only to shout to the firemen now struggling to haul the hose aloft. "For Christ's sake, get some more bloody firemen up here, there are still more kids involved." Then as I moved away to re-enter the flat, one of the two firemen attempted to come with me, but I stopped him. It was far more important at this stage to get some water onto the fire, for it could still spread to the rest of the flat.

I quickly made my way back along the passage into the rear living room, shutting the door behind me to hold back the fire, and again began my search. I started again where I left off, halfway down the right-hand wall. This search was not the fine detailed search they teach in the training schools. This was a crude, crashing search, no respect for unseen furniture or fittings, which were pushed roughly aside with sweeps of my hands and feet. Unseen ornaments and precious objects crashed to the floor with the sound of splintering glass, as I blundered into them.

Unusually, I was able to do this search standing upright, considering the severity of the fire at the other end of the flat. Also, that I was not wearing breathing apparatus. The heat and smoke levels in this room were just bearable. Always at the back of my mind though, was the fire raging out in the hallway. I was relying very much on those two firemen getting that jet of water to work without encountering major problems.

I had now almost completed my first search of the room. I could feel beneath my hands the settee, which I felt to my left when I first entered the room. This told me that I was now approaching the doorway to the room. I did a quick search with my hands along the length of the settee and found nothing. Moving back to the end of the settee, I pulled it roughly away from the wall, then inserted my boot into the gap between the settee and the wall. I stretched my leg out, searching with my boot for something soft and yielding, and I found it.

Pulling the settee back and clear of the wall, I went behind it. This time, feeling with my hands, I discovered that the something soft and yielding was another child.

I gathered the child up into my arms; it was limp and unconscious. Very carefully, I opened the door to the room, fearing that by now it might be impassable through the fire. I was mightily relieved to hear the crashing sound of a jet of water at work.

Making my way out of the flat, I had now to squeeze past the two firemen, who were working the jet of water on the fire in the rear room. I left the flat and went out onto the balcony carrying the child in my arms. Bill McGraw was returning in a hurry along the balcony, followed by other firemen, some of them wearing breathing apparatus.

I deposited the child I was carrying into Bill's arms, telling the breathing apparatus wearers that there was possibly one child unaccounted for still in the flat. I directed them to the room where the other three children had been found, telling them I had conducted only a crude search of the room.

How long all this had taken, I could only guess, but I would think around five or six minutes. It was not usual; although of course not unknown, for station officers to be so involved in rescues at fires. During the five or six minutes I was involved, no one had been in overall command of the fire. At the back of my mind had been another particular little worry. This was why I was anxious to look at the fire before I made pumps four, and before becoming involved in the rescues.

The handsome tiled pitched roof to these flats, which stretched the entire length of the block, had what is called a common void. That is, the roof space stretched the entire length of the block of flats, without a firebreak. I had gained this knowledge from previous fires on the estate. If the fire should break out through the ceiling of the top floor flat, it would then involve the entire length of the roof space and be worth a good six to eight pumps.

Back down on the ground floor, I looked very carefully at the tiled roof. Smoke appeared to be percolating out from amongst the roof tiles. I then decided to take no chances and treat the fire as if it had spread to the roof space.

First, I called over the driver of the pump and told him to make pumps six. He raised his eyebrows in query, and I explained to him that I thought the fire might have spread to the roof void. I then beckoned over the turntable ladder crew and instructed them to pitch the ladders to the middle of the roof, then to set up as a water tower, to cover the roof in case of spread of fire. I instructed them that they were on no account to get to work and direct water at the roof without my express permission. For I intended to make an entry into the void and send in BA firemen to fight any fire there from the inside.

The large and powerful jets of water from turntable ladders, and firemen, do not mix well. The jets tend to knock the firemen from their lofty perches, or at the very least, dislodge heavy tiles or debris down onto their heads. The turntable ladders had been positioned and set up as a long stop.

Fires in roofs can be very difficult fires to fight, for roof voids are large open spaces with very difficult access. The roof coverings of slates or tiles are designed to deflect water and prevent it from entering the roof space. So very often, the only way to extinguish them is to make an entry into the roof space, either through the tiles or slates, or through the ceiling or trapdoor below. Again, I knew from experience that the trapdoor entry into this roof void was at the head of the staircase enclosure.

I called across to the sub officer from North Kensington fire station, whom I knew well, then very quickly told him what I wanted done to prevent spread of fire in the roof void. He was to get a breathing apparatus crew into the roof void, via the trapdoor at the head of the staircase, taking with them a large jet, and with the jet prevent any fire gaining hold and spreading in and along the void. I also told him about the turntable ladder standing by ready for use, but that it was not to be used without my permission and withdrawing the breathing apparatus crew first.

Having made pumps six; I was now required to send an informative message to control by radio, giving the fire situation. I detached one of the appliance drivers from his job, and dictated a message, indicating the reason for the make pumps six was that the fire had spread to the common roof void, then instructed the driver to send it.

Having done that, I thought I had now better see what the fire situation was in the top floor flat, and if they had yet found the fourth child.

Making my way up the stairs, I found that hose was already in place for the entry into the roof void. On the top landing, two firemen wearing breathing apparatus were preparing to go up the ladder and into the void.

Entering the flat at the end of the balcony, I found all was in darkness, and the fiat was wreathed in a grey murk, which was a combination of steam and smoke. The only light came from the occasional flash of a fireman's hand lamp.

In the back room where the main fire was were four firemen, two of them still holding the large jet which occasionally they turned on very briefly. I was then greeted by Eddie Thirkettle, Hammersmith's leading fireman, who had assumed command there.

"Hello, guv, everything is under control, I have sent down for a hose reel tubing, to keep the water damage down. We are just waiting for it to arrive to finish off." As he said this, he indicated with his hands the small pockets of fire still smouldering and burning. He then carried on to say, "We have found number four, it's a small baby," meaning of course the fourth child.

"Good," I replied. "Where was it?"

"Over there," he said, pointing to the charcoaled remains of a still gently smouldering bed.

"Okay, Eddie," I replied, then quite unnecessarily said to him, "don't disturb anything till I can take a proper look." For I knew that if that was where they found the child, that was where it would still be, given the severity of the fire in the room, just a charred, blackened lump would remain.

I flashed my hand lamp over the ceiling of the room, and in several places, the plaster had spalled completely away. Now I knew for sure the fire would have spread through these holes, and still be burning in the roof void above, and I had to give all my attention to it. Eddie was unaware of the fire in the void above. I explained the problem and told him to keep the number of firemen in the room down to a minimum – to keep them as much as possible in the doorway opening of the room. Then, at the slightest sign of debris coming through the ceiling, to get out of the flat, lest the roof crash down upon him.

At the head of the stairs, there was a Brigade ladder leading up to the open trapdoor into the roof void. Visible on the top of the ladder was a pair of legs, clad in fire boots and leggings. The top half of the body was out of sight in the trapdoor opening.

I went up the ladder and tapped the legs. The top half of North Kensington's sub officer appeared, his eyes and nose streaming from the effects of smoke. "How is it going?" I asked him.

"Not too good, guv," he replied, "it's going like a bomb in there, and the two BA men can't make any progress because of the smoke and heat."

The situation was now quite dangerous; the fire could flash along the whole length of the roof of the building, which was 300 feet long, unless something was done quickly. I think that mentally I had known or feared that it might come to this and had thus made my plans. I ordered the sub officer to withdraw the BA men to the trapdoor opening. They're to keep the jet of water going in an attempt to keep the void cooler. Then I went to tell Eddie Thirkettle and his crew at the other end of the building to stay where they were and not to move, for I was going to ventilate the roof using the turntable ladders.

On the ground floor, the turntable ladder crew were lounging around bored, not expecting to be used. They were most surprised when I approached them and said they were going to get to work, for no fire was visible. They were I think, even more surprised when I told them what their job would be. To use their large diameter nozzled, high powered monitor to strip away part of the roof covering of tiles and ventilate the fire and hot gases.

Whilst the turntable ladder crew were preparing to get to work, I was arranging with the police to get spectators, both at the front and rear of the building, well clear. Roof tiles falling from a height of one hundred feet can be deadly missiles, and I did not want any more casualties.

I had briefed the fireman at the head of the turntable ladder before he went up the ladder, and this was the plan. Whilst the pressure in his monitor was being worked up to one hundred and fifty pounds per square inch, he was to direct the water jet over the top of the building. When the water pressure to the monitor was right, I would then tell him over the telephone intercom. He was then to direct the jet midway onto the roof, at its highest point just below the ridge in an attempt to use the high-pressure water jet to strip off the tiles and roof covering. As soon as he had made a hole around six feet square, he was to direct his monitor back over the top of the roof and observe the results.

The fire pump was screaming in protest at providing one-hundred-and-fifty-pound pressure up to the one and one quarter inch nozzle of the monitor. Over the intercom, I told the fireman at the head of the turntable ladders, "Right, hit it now." He then dropped the stream of water onto the roof just below the ridge.

The solid jet of water was hitting the roof at right angles, and immediately the heavy roof tiles flew in every direction. In less than a minute, it had made a hole six feet square. I called over the intercom to the fireman at the head of the ladder to direct the jet over the top of the roof again, so we could see the results. Smoke and hot gasses were belching out of the hole in the roof, hopefully ventilating the roof void. Telling the turntable ladder crew to knock off the water and stand by in case they were needed again, I left them to make my way back up to the top floor.

Here all was now going well, with the roof void ventilated of the hot gases and smoke, the breathing apparatus crew were making good progress. They had already extinguished the main body of the fire and were already calling down for a hose reel to make their job easier. I climbed the ladder into the roof void for a quick look; all was well. I could see neither the fire nor the BA crew, who had disappeared into the grey murk. Standing upright, there was very little heat remaining, and when I called along the void to the crew, they replied confidently that they had got the fire. I was feeling quite pleased with myself, I had anticipated the spread to the roof void, and averted the loss of the whole roof of the building.

I was more than just a little pleased with myself. For I had never known this unorthodox ventilation technique to be used on an occupied building before. In the past, we had often used the method to strip off the roofs of derelict buildings and the like. This was the first time I had seen it used to stop a real live fire. It had worked well, and I was mightily relieved. For it could have been a career buster, had someone got injured in the process.

At last, I could relax a little, and decided to go and get first details of the child's body still in the flat, before the debris was disturbed.

On the way to the flat, I met Bill Mcgraw, who told me something that reversed my self-satisfied mood. The three children that Mac and myself had rescued from the flat were all dead on arrival at hospital. At first, I could not believe it, "Not all three, Mac, surely?" I said.

He just nodded his head, and said sadly, "That is what the police have just told me, all three, dead on arrival."

These words 'dead on arrival' are terrible words to a fireman's ears. They always seem to cancel out all of our efforts, make null and void all the risks taken in the rescue. In the fire service, the pay isn't that great, but the job satisfaction can be. There is no job satisfaction to be had in carrying dead bodies out of fires.

Although I carried two of the children out, I haven't a clue what they looked like. Even whether they were boys or girls, it was all done so quickly. I had been so busy since, I hadn't been able to spare them a thought. At the back of my mind though, I believed that I personally had saved two young lives, and that is very, very satisfying, but now apparently, I had not.

A good fire that went well, including three rescues, is now a very bad fire. A total of four young lives had been lost, that can only be a bad fire. It does not help any that I now had to examine the charred body of a small child in the back bedroom where the fire started. It was a routine that I had done many times before, but it never got easier, especially with small children. I had to record details for the coroner's report; position of body in relation to room and debris; the clothing the child was wearing and any other details, no matter how minor, which may help the coroner. This entails very close contact with the pathetic remains of the child. Then there were the other three children who were removed in our futile rescues. Bill McGraw and I would now have to try to remember as well as we could exactly where we found their bodies in the darkened smoke-filled living room of the flat. At the best of times, I disliked paperwork, and this most certainly was not the best of times.

An attempt must be made to determine the cause of the fire, the back bedroom where the fire started was totally gutted. The plaster had spalled off the walls and ceiling in the fierce heat and covered the contents of the room in a layer of rubble. After much deliberation and examination, it was possible only to say that the fire started in or around one of the beds in the room. Then, given that the dead child in the room was too young to have been playing with matches or the like, then no evidence being found of electrical causes etc., the finger of guilt began to point at its dead brother and sisters.

The picture we began to build up, which may have been right or may have been wrong, was as follows. The children were left unattended in the flat. One of the older children was playing with naked lights in the bedroom, i.e. matches, or whatever, and set light to the bedding. The older children retreated from the fire to the living room of the flat. The smoke and fire gases then asphyxiated all four children before the fire was discovered. The heat of the fire then broke the window of the rear bedroom. This ventilated, and fed the fire with oxygen, which increased the fire's intensity so that it was then discovered. The ventilating of the fire and inrush of oxygen also swept away most of the dense, thick, choking smoke and fumes, which had asphyxiated the children. The four children were dead before the Fire Brigade received even its first call to the fire.

This fire was a six-pump fire, down below in the control unit was a divisional officer grade III.

This gentleman was nominally in charge of the fire. He was issuing a steady stream of messages back to fire control, as officer in charge of the fire. He had of yet, to come up the stairs and even enter the flat, where the fire had occurred. This was not necessarily a bad thing, as he would no doubt only hinder operations and get in the way. The firemen called him 'Fluff', he kept his fire helmet in a special linen bag to stop it getting scratched and dirty. He had immaculate uniforms, and even immaculate fire gear, which he habitually brushed with his fingers, flicking away imaginary or otherwise pieces of fluff, hence his nickname. This man was the senior officer in charge of this fire!

I was doing my rounds to complete the final details of damage caused by the fire to enter into the fire report. A little lady who lived in the flat next door to the one where the fire occurred, had been directed to me, she apparently had fire damage in her flat. I accompanied her back into her flat, and I was amazed by what I found.

This estate housed a vast cross section of humanity. Some of the flats that I had entered in the past, had been absolutely filthy, stinking hovels. This lady's flat was the complete opposite, it was – or had been – an immaculate palace. The lady was, I think, of Hispanic origin, and everything in the flat was immaculate. Delightful showcases and ornaments, all around the living room, beautiful artistic pictures on the wall, a very house-proud lady.

When the turntable ladder had been using its monitor to make a break in the roof to ventilate the fire, some of the roof tiles had crashed down through the lady's ceiling, taking the plaster ceiling with them. Some of the water from the firefighting jet in the roof void had also found its way through the fallen ceiling. The lady's proud living room looked a sorry state.

I was trying to be of assistance to her, explaining that even if she had insurance problems, the Brigade may be liable, mainly because the damage had been incurred in our trying to prevent the spread of fire. She then surprised me, saying in her delightful Spanish accent, "It doesn't matter, fireman, perhaps now I can get out of this place," meaning the estate. "I have been trying for years to transfer away from this place, perhaps now this has happened, they will move me."

I never did find out, but I hope very much that lady got her transfer. At least then, one good thing would have resulted from that fire.

As we pulled back into the appliance room at Hammersmith and I gathered up my pile of notes to make my way to the station office to begin around three hours of paperwork, I met Bill McGraw on the way and could not resist telling him, "McGraw, you are bloody bad news, do you know that?"

"Yes, guv," he replied, "you would have thought that at least one of the little buggers would have lived, wouldn't you?"

Epilogue

This book covers a period of around the first ten or eleven years of my career in the fire service. At the time, I first started writing, I had thought my story warranted only one book. Alas, when the manuscript tally reached some 360 plus pages, I found I was only one third of the way through my story, and had to stop somewhere, hence, To Ride a Red Engine.

I went on to spend the next sixteen years serving as a station officer at Hammersmith fire station, itself one of the busiest two appliance stations in London. During which time I experienced many more adventures, excitement and indeed humorous incidents, enough for one more book at least.

The cause of my retirement from the fire service is a story in its own right! After twenty-seven years' service during which, I had rescued people down every conceivable fire service ladder. Rescued people from high structures, and under and over bridges across the River Thames. Survived encounters with flashover's/backdraughts, scalding oil and collapse of building, all with only the odd bruise, burn, or even stitch or two. Played nursemaid to many decomposing acetylene and propane cylinders, akin to unexploded bombs. Not even to mention thousands of extremely rugged games of coarse volleyball; all survived relatively unscathed. When the end came, it was rather ignominious; I FELL OUT OF A FIRE ENGINE! No, it wasn't travelling down the road at fifty miles an hour attending a fire call at the time; instead it was parked up safely in the appliance room at Hammersmith fire station returning from a fire call.

The cab of a fire engine is a mere four feet from the ground. If one trips and dives headfirst from that lowly height, then collides with a solid object on the way down, i.e. an appliance battery charger, the outcome can be pretty damaging to human flesh. Such an accident ended my fire service career three years short of fully timed served. I hasten to add it was not the accident injuries in itself that ended my time, but the treatment of them revealed to the brigade's doctors long-standing back and neck problems no doubt in part a legacy of the Terry O'Neil carrying down days (Chapter 3). Unfortunately, for me, the London Fire Brigade was to use a modern phrase, downsizing at the time and so it came about, that I got my cards, medically discharged. It can be quite a shock to be one day a very busy active fire officer, commuting regularly to London then seemingly the next, unemployed.

It took around a year or more to recover back to almost full health, then I embarked on my second career, that of agricultural smallholder. With my commutation monies, I purchased a parcel of land near my home in Pangbourne, Berkshire. Beef cattle was the thing to be into before the days of BSE or mad cow disease scourged the land. Unfortunately, my divergence into farming coincided with two glorious summers, in which the sun shone all day, and it never rained at all. BOTH of these magic ingredients sun and rain are required to make the grass grow. So there I was with a field full of hungry beasts, and only three strands of wire separating them from better greener pastures. Once again, I dreaded the early morning shout. Only this time, it took the form of a ring on the doorbell of my house, and "Mr Wilson, do you know your cattle are out again!" After years of fire station banter and comradeship, I discovered that out in the middle of that idyllic countryside, THERE WAS NO ONE TO TALK TO. So I decided to cut my losses. I still have my fields, but now nothing but a small flock of geese and some geriatric chickens. Then literally hundreds of free-range rabbits' gamble on my now emerald-green pastures.

Suffering a minor cash flow crisis, I decided to empty out one of my building society accounts, an account which held around one hundred pounds only. To my surprise, the computer credited my account with further hundreds of pounds, unknown of interest from wealthier days "Thank you, Computer!" On the premiss of what you didn't know you had, you don't miss, I decided to squander this money on the purchase of an Amstrad 9256 word processor. Thus, Dave Wilson the fire officer, cum window cleaner, cum lorry driver, cum just about every other trade you could think of, became Dave Wilson the writer. Upon reflection perhaps the style 'writer' or 'author' sounds a little too grand for an ex 'airy arsed fireman, I think teller of stories sounds best.

I have done the rounds of most would be aspiring authors, the manuscript for this book has winged its way backwards and foreword to some of the most prestigious publishing houses in the land. Unfortunately, it appears that unless you have qualified as a serial killer, (SAS or otherwise) fornicated with the high and mighty, perhaps even plundered the odd pension fund or two, or on a more artistic theme, displayed ones mammary's at Twickenham rugby ground, then you are not even considered for publication, by these exalted establishments.

So it came about that I approached a minor publishing house, on a small trading estate in my home village of Pangbourne. "From now on, I must be careful what I say, for publishers, have the power to turn black into white! If there are any glaring white gaps in my writing from now on, he will have done just that!" I deposited some sample chapters of the manuscript with the publisher named Tim, a gentleman dressed in voluminous brown corduroy trousers and adorned with an ever so slightly eccentric haircut, and a pair of spectacles perched on the middle of his nose. So that he gave the appearance of a professor of some sort of an Ology, rather than a publisher of books. He promised to read the chapters within the week, three weeks later he was still fobbing me off. I gave him an ultimatum, read the bloody thing or I will come and pick the manuscript in three days' time. He must have read them that same night, for the next day over the telephone, I was informed that I was to be a published author.

So if you have enjoyed reading this book and would like to read future publications by the author on the same subject, tell all your friends about it. Do not whatever you do lend them your copy. Make 'em buy their own! I need to get the sales up to impress Tim the publisher to then publish further volumes. If you did not enjoy the book, I can only suggest that you must have an inordinate amount of time on your hands to squander, or that you are a glutton for punishment. For what are you doing; still reading it, through some hundreds and more pages to the bitter end!

Pyromanically and Cheerfully Yours,
Dave Wilson.